Extremes

EXTREMES

Contradictions

in Contemporary Japan

G M Thomas

Kaichan
Europe

Copyright © Graham M Thomas 2004
First published in 2004 by Kaichan Europe
43 Little Heath
Greenwich
London SE7 8EB

Distributed by Gazelle Book Services Limited
Hightown, White Cross Mills, South Rd, Lancaster, England LA1 4XS

British Library Cataloguing in Publication Data
A catalogue record for this book is available from the British Library

ISBN 0-9546789-0-7

Typeset by Amolibros, Milverton, Somerset
This book production has been managed by Amolibros
Printed and bound by T J International Ltd, Padstow, Cornwall, UK

'A thousand books have been written about Japan; but among these, the really precious volumes will be found to number scarcely a score. The fact is due to the immense difficulty of perceiving and comprehending what underlies the surface of Japanese life.'

Lafcadio Hearn, 1904.

Acknowledgements

Extract from 'From Sea to Sea' by Rudyard Kipling is reproduced here with the permission of A P Watt Ltd on behalf of the National Trust for Places of Historic Interest or Natural Beauty.

Contents

Preface

On my lap, I held a worn and faintly corroded tin. Printed on its lid was a portrait of a young woman, clutching a posy of white daisies, wearing a red off-the-shoulder satin blouse with mutton sleeves. Her face was turned to one side but her eyes stared straight at me, a teasing half-smile curved around her mouth, with lips tinted as deep red as her blouse.

Marguerita read the portrait's title, emphasizing her sultry looks – at odds with the tin's prosaic contents: an assortment of biscuits manufactured by Burtons of Blackpool. Called the Gold Medal Collection, the biscuits had fancy names like Rich Fruit, Milk Delicious, Chocolate Harmony, Rich Shrewsbury, Floral Shortbread and Kiddy Kream. Bought at Christmas sometime shortly after the Second World War, the biscuits were laid out for visitors and, when all were eaten, the tin reused for storage.

In this moment of anticipation, I realised I might instead find disappointment. Some years ago I had moved to Tokyo via Singapore and Hong Kong, married, set up an advertising agency for Saatchi & Saatchi, and opened a contemporary art gallery. Now I was sitting in the garden of my parents' Oxford home, and I wanted to be reminded of the images and daydreams that had set me on this path. Inside the tin, I expected to find a collection of items that, in my childhood, had both kindled my passion in all things Japanese and given the impetus to travel the world, but I wouldn't have been surprised to find they'd been long discarded.

On a day like this, I could picture a garrulous John Betjeman writing a poem, seated on a Lloyd Loom chair, nipping at one of the Gold Medal biscuits whilst sipping tea with milk and two sugars – a poem that would evoke memories of a missed England for a distant traveller or a putty-eyed sentimental ex-pat. Where the sky wasn't flicked with wisps of smudged cloud, it shone bright blue and shimmered with heat. Wasps crawled along the sticky rim of a teacup. The roses' fat blooms were heavy enough to bend their stems. Shrubs lined up like soldiers around the squared-up lawn, and, as the breeze nudged them, there was a faint rustle of leaves.

A job was never done until finished perfectly. That's what Dad believed. Surrounding me on this burnt summer's day was the result of his efforts: a suburban garden packed with a palette of discordant colour and texture but without a blade of grass untrimmed, a weed intruding or a shrub untrained. Even in the heat, no leaf wilted.

Thin ridges of sweat broke out on my arm. 'Anything to drink?' I shouted to Mum – a shadow in the kitchen. She offered a can of beer, a schooner of sherry or a glass of orange squash. I chose the beer, took a sip and opened the tin.

I had to pull hard to remove the lid, using my fingertips to prise away along the lip. It hadn't been opened for years. Once the tin smelt sweet; the inside now smelt sour.

I tipped out the tightly packed contents and shuffled through them: loose photographs, faded carbon copies of notes typed on tissue-thin paper, envelopes that had yellowed and lost their crispness, souvenir postcards, bank notes, torn cuttings from newspapers and a collection of paraphernalia from a wartime's service in the Royal Navy. It was thirty years or so since I had looked inside the tin but, more or less, it seemed, the contents were as I remembered. My expectations rose. I started to read one of the typed notes:

H.M.S Urania

27th March

Sale of Kit

The kit of the late signalman Walker will be sold by auction this evening at 1630 by the After Tubes. Ships Company may purchase articles of clothing by making remittance from the ledger. Articles as long as they are passed back to the Centre may be resold if the purchaser subsequently does not require the article.

I smiled. I had always smiled when reading this note. Even as a kid I realised this was the antithesis of the clean and heroic picture of war presented in the movies I watched and the comics I read. In these, the dead hero's possessions were never sold by auction with, as I had imagined, fractious bidding for the coveted items. Where was the deference to Walker's memory? This was subversive. And what made Signalman Walker's kit so desirable? Did he own a souvenir jacket or baseball hat – gifts from an American comrade whom he served alongside – that no one else had? An unusual battle memento perhaps, filched from a captured enemy sailor? Which items of clothing were most popular? Did he hoard a collection of saucy cards and pin-up shots (items that couldn't be despatched home to a mother or wife)? Maybe nothing was set aside for his family. His cigarette case, lighter, playing cards, whistle and watch were all auctioned. Back in Blighty, the bereaved family would be none the wiser.

This note and the rest of the tin's contents belonged to Uncle Roy – Dad's older brother. Every item related to Japan, where his ship – a Royal Navy destroyer – had been stationed at the end of the Second World War. Roy had been billeted initially in Kobe and then Tokyo. These were the precious mementos of his stay, precious not for their monetary value but for the memories they held and because of all the places he'd visited, Japan had been the country most loved and enjoyed.

I must have been five or six when I first looked at them but I had never tired of any, particularly not the photographs: black and white scenes of waterfalls taller than any found in England; views of giant cedar trees, rocky coastlines, and of snow-capped Mount Fuji framed by the ubiquitous branches of cherry trees. Others included hand-tinted photographs of temple interiors whose walls and ceilings were carved with gold-leafed decoration more ornate and rich than I had ever seen in Oxford when growing up. Leafing through them now, in some I could see little had changed. Even the snow's outline, draped like a French tablecloth over the summit of Mount Fuji, was familiar.

But there were also scenes of war's devastation. Tokyo razed to the ground: a cityscape of blackened rubble and cinder, bar the occasional and singular building left standing. One that had resisted the bombs and fires; along with unscathed rows of telegraph or electricity poles, still with unbroken cables running between them, and the only means by which the original layout of streets could be identified.

Roy kept photographs of Hiroshima: of him and his shipmates wearing heavy great coats, shoulders stooped, picking their way through the deserted and flattened city centre. In some views, no building remained intact, and the ground was a level silent plain until it reached distant mountains. Here no telegraph pole stood upright, only trees, denuded of leaves, their bare branches twisted in agony, flung out in desperation towards the sky.

When a scamp of a boy, these scenes of devastation fuelled my lust for playground war games until, as I grew older, the fangs of puberty bit deep. Then I spent more time closely studying another subject: the photographs of *geisha*. Each one has become an adolescent treasure. Was I surprised that, over the intervening years, none of their beauty had diminished? No, I wasn't. They wore the most opulent *kimono*; their hair piled high and decorated with a lavish array of ornaments. They posed in groups or singly, each with a smooth and symmetrical oval face, smiling as if they held not a care in the world and the war had never happened, every one of them stunningly attractive. But there was one girl in particular with whom I had always been struck: younger, her *kimono* even more ornate than the others and, now I knew about these things, I identified her as a *maiko*, an apprenticed girl. To my relief her photograph was still here.

If anyone could be described as a butterfly it was she, and I could imagine her image lifting from the photograph and floating away. But, more than her unworldly attractiveness, a more intriguing facet had always caught my imagination. Unlike the others, she didn't smile meekly. Within her almost translucent face, she had a detached look, an air of defiance as she glanced to one side, deliberately – but with great subtlety – ignoring the camera lens. Sometimes I slipped her photograph into an inner pocket, keeping it until my next visit when I would silently return it, hoping that Roy hadn't noticed. Alone in my bedroom, I would stare at her, mouthing silent questions, waiting to see whether she would turn and look at me. What made you so detached? What haunts you? Was it something that had happened during the war? Where are you now? At times I wanted to be her brother, to be the only person who cared for her.

When Roy allowed me to first peek at the tin's contents, I didn't appreciate their significance and meaning – although I sensed this was a special privilege – but slowly I realised that for Roy, those years had been the best of his life and these mementos were more than just a randomly amassed record of a visit. Whenever I visited his home, I asked to be allowed to delve into the tin's treats. We sat side by side swapping photographs, and a time came when

I could tell by the hint of dampness in his eye that he wished he were still there. Slipping from the present, he was back among the laughing gang of sailors, arms draped over each other's shoulders, seated on deck around a table drinking beer out of thick quart bottles. He remembered how one day they were walking through the most unimaginable remnants of horror and then the next laughing with the equally unimaginable exquisiteness of the *geisha*. Roy was one of those for whom the war had been a divide. He never fully adjusted to post-war life, delaying marriage until his forties and he saw himself, as I later found out, at odds with those who hadn't fought or suffered.

Roy's funeral had taken place before I could return to England. His wife had died before him, they had no children, and my parents took possession of the tin. Now it was mine to keep, to become my own box of memories: of Roy, of childhood, and the genesis of my starry-eyed, romantic dreams of Japan, and the day when I could travel the world as a sailor adventurer.

Far from being a disappointment, the tin's contents had brought much alive and, when I returned the photographs to the tin, I kept one back, slipping the portrait of the *maiko* girl into my wallet. She would remind me that my journey had come full circle.

Another tantalising glimpse of Japan had popped up in 1967 when I first watched the James Bond film, *You Only Live Twice*. To describe me as a Bond fanatic would be an understatement. On the streets of Oxford, I was – if only to my own eyes – Sean Connery incarnate. From the Temple Cowley public library, I borrowed, read, borrowed again and reread all the original books. One Christmas I had found in Santa's sack, the Aston Martin toy car with a working ejector seat, a model of the car Bond drove in *Goldfinger*. I kept annuals, scrapbooks full of newspaper cuttings and without fail I sat in the audience as soon as the films arrived in Oxford.

You Only Live Twice had been shot extensively in Japan. Of the many sequences, all too predictably, the scene of Bond being bathed, rubbed and pampered in a hot tub by a group of giggling girls became one of those inerasable and defining memories. I fell in schoolboy love with the two lead actresses, Akiko Wakabayashi, and Mie Hama – whose costume for most of the film, was a scanty white bikini. Only thirteen years old, they and the *maiko* became my first secret loves. A seed was sown and spilt.

But I had to wait a few more years before I met a Japanese in person, face to face and then not a beautiful girl but two earnest schoolboys.

Returning from a trip to Morocco in the late hot summer of 1974, I discovered these two teenage boys – both studying English at an Oxford language school – were boarding at my parents' house. My parents hadn't known what month, week or day I'd planned to come back from Morocco, I'd not bothered to forewarn them and my journey had lasted several months. From Paddington Station I made a cheery phone call to say I would be home by six p.m. My mother answered. Instead of bubbling with delight, she sounded flustered. 'Your Dad is in Birmingham,' she told me, 'and we have two Japanese boys staying and one is using your bedroom. Can you sleep in the spare bed? And can you make your own way back from the station?' This wasn't the open arm and flag waving welcome I had imagined but what could I do? Okay, I said with more than a tinge of sulkiness in my voice and caught the train to Oxford.

Today my recollection of the boys' names is a blank. Their English was poor, our conversations were sparse and tortuous but over the next two weeks I took them most evenings to my favourite pub – the Chequers off The High. My parents were delighted and surprised by my uncomplaining selflessness, unaware that behind this altruistic behaviour lay a selfish motive: my plan was that one night the boys would bring their fellow female students. And then the real fun would start.

Every morning I drove the boys to a language school on the Banbury Road. A chore, yes, but allowing me to drool on a wonderful vision of the Japanese girls who were also being dropped off. Each was as exotic as Akiko or Mie. Hanging out of the car window, a cigarette smouldering, I daydreamed of the sunken bathing tub – although where I could find such a thing in Oxford, I wasn't sure.

But realising my dreams was to prove difficult.

Unless on an official chaperoned evening's entertainment, the boys explained (although not quite using those words), the girls had to stay in. I tried persuading the boys to encourage the girls to flout the rules. They need to experience life, I pointed out. I'll look after them, I promised. At least tell them what pub to come to and how to get there – giving the boys easily followed, diagrammatic instructions they could hand to any of the girls. They agreed to pass them on. Every night I waited, willing these wonderful girls to walk into the Chequers, passing the time by teaching the boys to play darts in lieu of conversation (a game they never mastered).

My school friends – who had also enjoyed what is now known as a gap year but which we called 'a year off' – were returning from their own travels prior to going up to university: Richard Smith and Jon Banks from Florence, Jonnie Archer and Martin Corral from Australia among others. Motivated by my vivid, sometimes lurid descriptions of the girls, they helped enthusiastically. Did they really believe my nonsense that Japanese girls had triangular vaginas, they smelt differently and that I could confirm this from experience? I think they did because that's what I believed. We introduced the two boys to the curiosities of English beer from Morrells our local brewery, and to make them feel at home – or so we thought – the experience of Oriental food at the Golden Palace Restaurant. How were we to know that Japanese and Chinese food was different, and that furthermore the Chinese food we ate was a nasty coagulated bastardisation of the real thing?

Before returning to Japan, the boys presented my parents with a gift: a top-of-the-range integrated Sony cassette deck and radio – both fathers worked for Sony I learnt – which thirty years later still sounded perfect. This was our only gift for in the end the girls remained a tissue fantasy. Their vision never materialised in the upstairs bar of the Chequers and I had to wait until 1995 before I met a Japanese girl and took her out.

In those intervening years, I had fought to go beyond the modest ambitions expected of me: ambitions that barely stretched beyond getting away from the banality of life in a 1930s'-built suburb, working fewer hours with longer holidays and earning more money than my father. Mine were bigger than that, and I had escaped: London, Paris, Frankfurt, Hong Kong, Singapore were all places I had lived, putting as much distance as I could from where I had started. Yet for some reason I had forgotten about my childhood fascination, and the Japanese became the irritating, camera-wielding tourists who spilled out of coaches, clogged the pavements and sullied the romance of visiting any major attraction.

Until I visited Japan for the first time in 1993.

Then I immediately and unquestionably realised that I had to live there. It struck me like a metal tray hitting my head.

On this first flight to Tokyo, I had re-read a book by Lafcadio Hearn titled *Japan – An Interpretation*.

Born in 1850, he was of mixed Greek and Anglo-Irish parentage and had settled in Japan in 1890. He married a Japanese girl, took Japanese citizenship and adopted the name Koizumi Yakumo.

I had come across him by chance when visiting Dublin a few years earlier. Browsing through the shelves of a second-hand bookshop, I had found a 1905 edition of the book — the cover faded, the spine cracked. A series of minor coincidences then connected: whilst walking through Dublin I had seen a plaque bearing his name in Leeson Street, and then a poster announcing that a lecture on his life was to be given at Trinity College. And now in this bookshop I found a book he had written. It was cheap, had a pretty illustration of a temple maid as a frontispiece and so I bought it, along with an eighteenth-century book on the agriculture of Gloucestershire.

During the late nineteenth century, Hearn had written many books and magazine articles on Japan. It is said that he was, and remains, one of the best interpreters of the Japanese soul, grasping the essence of the people and the illusive Japanese character. But he himself wrote, 'After having discovered that I cannot understand the Japanese at all, I feel better qualified to attempt this essay.'

Hearn's reputation as a Japanologist is rock solid, both in the English-speaking world and in Japan (a nation that has long savoured the notion that its character is impenetrable to the outside world). But as I discovered subsequently, he was also capable of writing nonsense. For example, he claimed it was impossible for non-Japanese to learn the language fluently but this just isn't the case and was nothing but an excuse for his own poor abilities. He used a number of questionable observations to underline his assertion that the Japanese lived in a strange world, diametrically opposed to the West, and they were fundamentally distinct from those that lived in, as he called it, the Occident. For example, he noted that the Japanese slip the eye of the needle over the point of the thread rather than putting the thread through the eye of the needle. No Japanese girl I have ever asked does this and as one said, '…neither did my mother nor the mother of my mother.' He wrote of 'foodstuffs of unimaginable derivation', 'strange masks and toys that commemorate legends of gods or demons' as if this was a characteristic uniquely Japanese. He seemed obsessed with there being some genetic explanation that rendered the Japanese uniquely able to be Japanese, with the Occidental being denied Japanese skills by dint of birth.

Flawed as he was, I found in his writings a beguiling account of the Japanese way of life, one that seemingly had altered little for over a thousand years. But he wasn't alone in bringing alive the medieval nineteenth-century Japanese world: Basil Hall Chamberlain, Percival Lowell and Isabella Bird, for example, had equally captured the Japanese life, and were as insightful in their understandings.

Their books and writings I bought when, eventually in 1997, I took the decision to live in Japan. Using these as a guide, I set out to discover how much of what they observed still remained. Not so much the physical such as buildings but how much of the old Japanese character and traditions could be found. After all, the Japanese like to think they are but an unbroken continuum from when the race was founded by the Sea Goddess, Ameretsu, in 660BC.

Already by the eighteenth century, Japan had one of the most urbanised societies in the modern world. Edo-Tokyo was the world's biggest city; Kyoto and Osaka had populations exceeding half a million but many of the nineteenth-century Japanologists shared a common concern: that Japan, by embracing the West and modernising, would lose her character and all that was best. Rudyard Kipling, writing in 1889, already argued that Japan had sold her soul by seeking recognition from the West, selling 'her birthright for the privilege of being cheated on equal terms by her neighbours'. He foresaw a time when Japan would be burdened by heavy debt, with everyone wearing Western clothes, the land despoiled by American soap factories, and the defilement of Tokyo streets by Western-style buildings.

> 'There are many American missionaries in Japan,' he wrote, 'and some of them construct churches and chapels for whose ugliness no creed could compensate. They further instil into the Japanese mind wicked ideas of "progress" and that it is well to go ahead of your neighbour, to improve your situation, and generally to thresh yourself to pieces in the battle of existence.'

Ten years later, Hearn wrote of the misery that industrialisation was bringing to Japan. He predicted her old charm – the politeness, moral values, simplicities of life, and the grace of manners – would rapidly disappear. Along with Kipling, he saw that money-power, driven by Western capitalism, would take over and that the essence of Japan's culture would be lost forever. In turn, this would be a grave loss for the world.

And, to this day, comments by teachers, politicians, the media and opinion leaders continue to bemoan the fact that Japanese culture is being diluted by the West, and overrun by the wicked forces of American globalisation. Of course, Japan is not alone in worrying about its identity being usurped by the foreign, that what the West offers isn't necessarily better as it panders to the squalid lowest common-denominator of taste.

Like Hearn, I had married a Japanese girl. My dream come true – thus proving that riches come to those that wait. So, I enjoyed a letter that the English philosopher Herbert Spencer wrote to senior Japanese statesmen in 1892. He too was advising the Japanese to be conservative in their dealings with the West, and to keep the English and Americans 'at arms' length.' As part of his counsel, he touched on the subject of whether Japanese and foreigners should marry.

'It should be positively forbidden,' he said. 'There is abundant proof, alike furnished by the intermarriage of human races and by the interbreeding of animals, that when the varieties mingle, the result is inevitably a bad one in the long run…I happen to be staying in the country with a gentleman who has much experience respecting the interbreeding of cattle; when, say of the different varieties of sheep, there is interbreeding of those which are widely unlike, the result, especially in the second generation, is a bad one – there arise an incalculable mixture of traits, and what maybe called a chaotic constitution.'

I ignored his advice but occasionally wondered whether it contained a kernel of truth.

My interest in seeking Japan's past was matched equally by wanting to understand what Japan tells us of our future. A plethora of commentators have argued that Japan creates – or at least presents a picture of – the world that the West will eventually become. The artist Takashi Murakami has said, 'Japan doesn't have high culture, only sub-culture. That's why Japan is the future. We don't have any religion, we just need the big power of entertainment.'

But when people talk about Japan, I quickly discover they really mean Tokyo. For I saw a schism between Tokyo, the world's biggest mega-metropolis – a window through which we might foresee the world's urban future – and the values, traditions and culture of an older more rural Japan. Tokyo is the world that represents Japan to the outsider.

Japan isn't Tokyo and yet Tokyo is Japan: a parasite in its own country. Like a parasite, it grows inextricably whilst draining the rest of Japan of its lifeblood, sucking in thirty-one million inhabitants – in particular the young – leaving behind cities, towns and villages that, if it weren't for massive government subsidy, teeter on the verge of extinction. Tokyo has created a world far removed from the rest of Japan, one that has created the many paradoxes and contradictions that riddle the nation and which have unbalanced the relationship between change and continuity.

Above all else, I found in Tokyo a city that has lost perspective: physically, morally, emotionally and culturally. Physically its urban sprawl spreads uncontrollably – and like a huge bloodstain – across and beyond the Edo plain. Within its boundaries the old is relentlessly torn down, and replaced by the new with a passionate disregard for the past. As late as the 1930s, the Englishman John Morris could still write that Tokyo was a pretty town with none of the 'rows of sordid little houses or semi-detached villas that so disfigure our own towns'.

For Tokyo's people and government, whilst the physical past is irrelevant there is no attempt to define a sustainable future. Of only importance is what's new today: an increasingly alienated and displaced society fuelled by voracious consumption, and a culture driven by a vast entertainment industry, devoid of Japan's traditional values.

Tokyo's relationship with the rest of Japan is complex, ambiguous and conflicting. Tokyo alone has been responsible for re-defining Japan – allowing it to find new meaning – following the humiliating defeat at the end of the Second World War; a meaning defined by the miracle that transformed the nation into the world's second richest economy.

And it is this wealth that has supported, subsidised and allowed the traditions of Japan to live on elsewhere.

Despite this largesse, to many of Japan's inhabitants Tokyo is an uncontrollable monster, an urbanised Godzilla. It has polarised and unravelled society across Japan, and has created a new society within its boundaries that verges on the morally and spiritually bankrupt, a society that Kipling might well say has lost its soul.

In the writings that follow, I have sought out Japan's spirit and traditions, using as a reference, the experiences of nineteenth- and twentieth-century Japanologists. I have travelled to places that have rarely if ever been evoked in English language writings and added a wealth of personal experience.

I have no axe to grind. I have wandered through Japan with no grand design or mapped-out path. Neither did I follow the journeys of Hearn, Lovell, Chamberlain, Kipling or Bird. I have not written a far-reaching scholarly analysis of what constitutes modern Japan.

In unravelling the puzzle of the contradictions all too apparent across Japan, I challenge conventional wisdoms, and through my own experiences attempt to bring a freshness and vitality to my descriptions of contemporary life.

At times, I have been surprised by what still exists: to discover that what I thought were modern manifestations in fact were seen many years ago — such as the habit of people spending hours in a newsagent reading a magazine from the rack but not actually buying it (John Morris was bemused by this in 1938) or that the confusing method of giving a house an address has befuddled visitors, taxi drivers and citizens alike for decades if not centuries.

What I found at the core of the nation was a people who, whilst sharing much in common, live life torn by contradictory modes of behaviour.

The Japanese define their relations with society based on *tatemae* (their outer obligation to society) and *honne* (their inner private aspirations).

Tatemae is less about what mustn't be done but more about what must be done. To their colleagues, community and the world at large they present their *tatemae* or surface truth — a sanitised persona that unquestionably conforms to social expectations and standards. More often, the *honne* (the real truth) is concealed, revealed only occasionally. And this I believes applies not only to people but to all aspects of Japan — as much as possible is sanitised for everyday consumption: a way of life that Japan both presents to the world and to itself. The real world is deeply hidden, only to be seen rarely by the Japanese and if possible not at all by the foreigner.

And as a consequence, I have often wondered whether the Japanese have forgotten their inner self or have become so confused and befuddled that they no longer know who or what they truly are.

Chapter One

Death and Marriage

'Almost everything in Japanese society derives directly or indirectly from the ancestor cult; and that in all matters the dead, rather than the living, have been the rulers of the nation and the shapers of its destinies.' *Lafcadio Hearn.*

Stood in a small cemetery, on an isolated headland buff surrounded by winsome pine trees, I listened to the murmured chant of a Shinto priest. The distant wail of sea birds – drifting over the waves – sounded like displaced ghosts calling those loved ones who still lived and had been left behind. The ashes of one of Satoko's aged aunts were being interred in the Okada family plot – on the island speck of Hiroshima.

A small group that from a distance would look like a smudge of ink circled the grave: sisters, daughters, cousins and husbands, all dressed in elegant solid black, the women wearing pearls – a symbol of tears in Japan – and each clutching a black handbag. The priest too was dressed in a plain black outer robe embellished with a gold collar wrapped around his neck. Some weeks ago, the aunt had been cremated. The tradition is to leave a gap before the ashes are interred.

At lunchtime, we had gathered in a fleet of three cars at the Marugame Ferry Terminal, and taken the short trip to the island, the ashes carried by Satoko's mother in a white urn, placed in a white box wrapped with a simple white cloth. For someone who didn't know, she might have been carrying a cake.

Marugame is a small city lying on the northern coastline of the island of Shikoku – the smallest, remotest and least visited of Japan's four main islands. It was here that my wife, Satoko Okada, had been born and where her parents, sister and many of her relatives still lived. Hiroshima, (sharing a name but nothing else with the famous city) laying a few miles offshore, was the Okada's ancestral home.

The ferry had the shape of a squashed sea slug and was one of a dwindling fleet plying between the small islands of Japan's Inland Sea. Over recent years, the few industries on these islands had been in dramatic decline. In some instances, extinction had been reached. Young people had escaped – with no intention of returning – to the big cities, leaving behind the old to die off. Our ferry would stop at three islands on its round trip, and the total number of passengers was less than fifty. Our three cars joined three light vans belonging to island traders returning from their weekly trip to Marugame to buy basic household goods.

The ferry was years old but still looked as if it had been built yesterday. Its red and white paint was bright and unstained; along its bows, there was hardly a streak of rust. The decks were scrubbed, the brass fittings shone with polish, every rope and chain was perfectly coiled and stowed.

On the bridge, the captain sat upright, arms folded, his eyes scanning left, right and forward. Stood alongside him, a mate in blue overalls watched the radar screen and chewed on a toothpick. Ahead lay a long, grey-green hump, looking like the back of a sleeping whale, which marked our destination.

The priest had been late for the ceremony – drinking, someone said – and this matched the mood: neither sombre nor sad but light-hearted and more like a picnic outing. Whilst we waited, the granite monument was scrubbed with water, and two bunches of white lilies placed on the grave. This mood was further lightened when it was found that the urn seemed initially too big for the space within the marble monument. Another urn had been previously interred and trying to fit both in the small niche proved a squeeze, provoking much giggling. Then it was discovered that no one had brought incense sticks. Luckily, a discarded pack was found in the cemetery shed. More giggling. But the atmosphere hushed when the priest's solemn chant began, filling the air with the rhymes of death. One by one the mourners knelt in front of the tomb, placed an incense stick in a jar and said a silent prayer. Satoko urged me to do the same and I obliged.

This was a Shinto ceremony. The aunt's spirit hadn't died but had become *kami* – a god. In Shinto, all the dead join the ranks of the *kami* and this underlines the belief in ancestor worship. The *kami* hold divine powers upon which depend the fortunes of the living but they in turn also need the living world for happiness, nourishment and shelter; bonds that should not be broken without expecting the direst consequences unite both the living and the spiritual worlds.

When the chanting finished, the ceremony was brought to a close. The priest walked off. Brows were mopped. For the happy mourners, it was time to have tea at the family's ancestral home – where the aunt had lived before dying – a house in a village that lay below this headland, squashed between the mountains and the sea. I looked down and counted the rooftops of thirty or so houses. Satoko pointed to the roof of her ancestral home.

Before we left, Satoko and I stood on the bare gravel plot, reserved for her parents and any other present-day Okada family that might wish to be interred there – including Satoko, her sister and, maybe, me. As the island was the ancestral home of the Okada, they maintained the custom for the family to return when dead and buried on their land. I kicked a pebble.

'What do you think?' Satoko asked. 'Do you want to be buried here?'

'I've never thought of where I want to be buried.' Would I feel an outsider here, I wondered? I looked over the sea towards distant islands, a beautiful view now.

'Do what you want to do.'

'Would I appreciate the view once I'm dead?' I asked.

'We'll have to find out. Whatever you want to do, I will certainly be buried here,' she continued.

'Are you saying we'll be separated in death?' I said.

'Not if you come here. Where else can you go?'

'England.'

'And who will look after you? You'll be forgotten.'

'So will I be here.'

'Forgotten in life maybe, but someone will always look after the spirits. If you like we can split your ashes. Some here and some in England. But I want all of me to be buried here. Please remember that if I die before you. And remember I'll be here all the time.'

For a moment, we stood in thought. Not an unpleasant pause – standing on my future grave if I so chose – but one of sober reflection that lacked any sense of morbidity.

Arriving at the old house, I felt as if I were entering the bedroom of Miss

Haversham. The aunt had been the last person to live here but Satoko referred to the house as her grandmother's – the aunt's sister – as she had owned it. The house was 300 years old, more pavilion than house, and built around a sandy courtyard planted with thick evergreen shrubs: a main family residence, smaller storerooms and a large warehouse, the outer walls faced with blackened wood. The main house was raised above ground level to allow air to circulate, keeping the house cool in the hot summer – as it was now – and avoiding dampness in the rainy season.

Inside it was dark until the screens were opened and light surged in, flooding even the furthest nook and crevice. Unlike Western houses, once the house is opened up there is no dividing line between the inside and nature outside. When warm, the outer *amado* doors and the inner *shoji* screens can be completely removed so that the garden and rooms become one.

Now, the timber joists and ceiling planks were warped with age and browned with smoke, reminding me of the limbs of mummies. On the sliding screens separating each room, the light tumbled across painted decorations of flowers and animals now faded to a watermark. The floor was uneven and everywhere stood or hung artefacts of a lost era and past lives.

Over many years, despite the unstoppable march of death, no belongings had been removed, including the pair of tiny reed sandals placed outside the room where the aunt had sewed *kimono*s – waiting for her feet that would never slip inside them again – and so small they might have been the shoes of a child.

Calendars dating from the mid-eighties hung on the walls. Every day was ticked off. Clocks could be found in each room.

Three framed and faded photographs of the old Emperor and his family hung from a wall, alongside sepia portraits of two brothers who had died in the Pacific during the Second World War and whose bodies had never been returned to these shores.

Two wooden gilded shrines contained the ashes of relatives. They sat under a shelf where rested twenty or more wooden tablets recording the names of the dead. Set in front of each were small cuttings of white paper called *hitogata* (mankind shapes), which represented the members of the household and were displayed as protection against sickness and misfortune.

In the nineteenth century, Sir Ernest Satow translated the words of Hirata – at the time one of Shinto's foremost scholars. He declared that all virtues derived from the worship of ancestors:

> 'It is the duty of a subject to be diligent in worshipping his ancestors, whose minister he should consider himself to be. The custom from adoption arose from the natural desire of having someone to perform sacrifices; and this desire ought not to be rendered of any avail by neglect. Devotion to the memory of ancestors is the mainstay of all virtue. No one who discharges his duty to them will ever be disrespectful to the gods or to his living parents. Such a man also will be faithful to his prince, loyal to his friends, and kind and gentle to his wife and children. For the essence of this devotion is indeed filial piety.'

In turn, Satoko's family believed that their ancestors far from being dead, remained among them acting as unseen guardians of the home and well-being of the family. Here, the spirits could gather in one place, sharing the joy and comfort of their ancient home.

Whilst Satoko's parents lived in Marugame, they were now obliged as senior members of the family to return regularly to the empty house, open it up, greet their ancestors and offer food and small gifts. By doing this, there was no forgotten past, just a continuum of beings, generation following generation, and moving from one type of existence to the next.

In the kitchen, entrance halls and storage areas the floor was compacted earth at ground level. I was shown with glee an underground store pit where Satoko's grandma would imprison her daughters if they had been particularly naughty.

In one of the outdoor sheds hung a collection of old tools – for working the fields – that would have looked in place in a museum: long hoes, spades, shovels, picks, a back-pack made of woven reeds, and heavy shoes for working in the field.

Satoko's parents never threw anything out of their own home (Satoko had shown me a transparent PVC bag she had used as a swimming bag, thirty years ago, which was now hung in the kitchen to hold fruit) and not one single item had been discarded in Grandma's home. She could have risen from the dead, strolled in and found nothing amiss, misplaced or missing, carrying on her life without a murmur. That, of course, was the point. Her spirit was still here, and by being surrounded by the familiar, everyone believed she would remain happy and could continue to share an earthly life.

(Back in England, I remembered, even the last two generations of my family are scattered across half a dozen Oxford cemeteries. Forever apart.)

In the kitchen, blackened metal pots and pans hung from the walls and the crossbeams; water was still piped into the large granite sink. There were no cupboards – everything was stored on open shelves. A frail wall-mounted electric boiler had been fixed to heat water, and a gas ring sat on a wooden bench. (More often, food had been cooked over a bench-top charcoal burner.)

The electric boiler was a recent fixture. Satoko remembered how, as a child, the bath had been an iron tub heated over a timber fire. Fitted within the tub were wooden slats to sit without (hopefully) touching the hot iron. Sometime in the late 'seventies, electricity had arrived, a supposed sign of the revitalisation of the island but, within the blink of an eye, modern conveniences had come and then were needed no more.

Whilst the mourners sat crossed-legged in a circle – the men smoking and the women eating lemon cake and drinking cold green tea – Satoko and I walked through the village. Above us, unseen, we could hear granite being loaded with a thunderous crash on to trucks in one of the few remaining quarries being worked; granite used to build monuments, temples, shrines and tombs but which now was becoming too expensive to quarry in the face of cheaper imports from China. The industry had all but died out. Within a few years, the last quarries would fall silent. Satoko's family still owned several, leasing them to a mining company for a peppercorn annual income.

Around us, once thriving gardens were now choking under a heavy blanket of tangled foliage and reverting to a natural state. Houses too had been invaded, slowly crushed by spreading trees and creeping vegetation, collapsing little by little into piles of tiles, broken timber, clay and plaster. The village was disappearing into the ground: ashes to ashes and dust to dust. Nothing could stop its eventual death for the lifeblood of the village had gone. Closed. Everything was closing down. The village schools were boarded up; all shops and restaurants had battened doors – although a young doctor, who had a mission to minister to the elderly, ran a small surgery. So unusual and unexpected was this that he had been the subject of a TV documentary.

What elixir could tempt back young people to recreate a thriving community? I could think of no answer as we walked along a deserted beach. A beach that would make a perfect play area for kids, with expansive views across to neighbouring islands, with firm clean sand, rocks to scramble over, pools to hunt for crabs, and warm clear waters that lapped gently on the shore. We walked hand in hand, our bare feet making the first imprints on the sand certainly for that day, possible for many days.

The sky and sea had turned silver, merging imperceptibly at the horizon, and the nearby islands had darkened to lumpen masses. We watched our ferry continuing its slow circular journey, briefly linking communities together, and knowing in two hours it would return to Hiroshima and we would board it.

But, before catching the ferry, we'd one more stop to make. Satoko's father was uncertain of the route to take. Several narrow lanes we drove down finished in dead ends, and eventually we sought directions. An old man insisted he jump in the car to show us the way. He brought us to a lone grave at the back of the village of Enoura. The grave – like the one where we had just interred Satoko's aunt – was a mottled granite block, set squat in a raised bed erected not in a cemetery but in a field. On the grave itself, there was a simple inscription:

Eikoku Shikan Re-ki no Haka
Juichi gatsu nanoka
Meiji gan nen.

In English this reads:

The Grave of English Officer Lake
7th day of 11th Month of the first year of Meiji.

Alongside the grave was a hand-painted wooden sign offering a fuller explanation:

'Here lies the body of the British Officer Lake, a surveying officer who died in 1868 when his ship, the HMS *Sylvia* was sailing on the Seto Nai Kai Sea. His ship moored off Hiroshima, the nearest island

and they buried his body in a remote place on the western edge of Enoura village. After erecting a cross, they left. Then in 1868 a wealthy villager, called Okara Haju felt pity for the spirit of the officer, gave him a Japanese name Hasegawa Saboro Bei and registered his death at the local temple. He then erected this tombstone in commemoration.'

That I found this grave was remarkable and unexpected, but of greater surprise was to find it still well tended. For close on one hundred and fifty years, the villagers had looked after the grave, kept it weeded and ensured the granite was cleaned. We found it decorated with two vases of fresh flowers and a bottle of water.

Subsequently, I discovered that HMS *Sylvia* was a survey ship that sailed the Mediterranean and Pacific, mapping the shoreline and hydrographical details. When Japan allowed foreign shipping into her waters, British survey ships assisted in the chartering of her coastline. Whilst in Japan, the Sylvia also assisted Richard Henry Brunton (1841-1901), a Scotsman largely forgotten in the UK but who is celebrated in Japan as the founder of their lighthouse and lifeboat service. And the ship is mentioned in the diaries of A B Mitford who found refuge on board after being nearly drowned in a storm off Osaka in early 1868. No doubt, he would have met Lake.

Later, I found papers in the National Library of Australia, collected by an Australian writer, Harold S Williams, relating to the burial. I had copies sent to me and they provided more information and several different versions of what happened. According to the Nagasaki Press in 1899 for example, Lake died on board ship and his burial was arranged by the ship's captain, in ground belonging to the Ikowji Temple.

'Soon the wooden cross decayed and then Awaburi Tokuwan, chief of Ikwoji, Terawaki Kaemon, headman of the village, and other sympathizers such as Oka Ryohaku arranged for a stone monument to be built.

'He was reported as saying "Truly it would be a sad thing if the grave of our solitary guest from afar, who has become a spirit in a strange land, were suffered to pass out of all knowledge."

'It was completed on the seventh day of the eleventh month of Meiji 4 (1871). For years, the Japanese villagers tended the grave, and in April 1899, when this matter came to the notice of Sir Ernest Satow, the British Ambassador to Japan, he sent a letter of thanks to the Japanese Minister of Foreign Affairs.'

Another story recorded that the officer had drowned and, once his body had been recovered, buried on the island.

In a third article – also written in 1899 and appearing in the *Kobe Weekly Chronicle* (a paper that Lafcadio Hearn wrote for) – it reported the following:

'The grave is still kept in good order and preservation, the greatest care evidently being devoted to it. Mr Sim states that on his visit flowers had been laid upon the grave quite recently, and the old fishermen, accompanying the visitors, who was a lad of eighteen or nineteen when the body of the officer was interred, said that twice a year special services were held on behalf of the stranger and the grave put in good order and repair. Such an incident, entirely spontaneous in character as it was says not a little for the good-heartedness and sympathetic kindness of the people of this little village, and deserves recognition and acknowledgment by foreigners in general.

'In the relations of the people to each other, as well as in all their relations to himself, he will find constant amenity. Everyone greets everybody with happy looks and pleasant words; faces are always smiling; the commonest incidents of everyday life are transfigured by a courtesy at once so artless and so faultless that it appears to spring directly from the heart without any teaching.'

In 1967, Harold Williams visited the grave and found it to be still 'tidy and showing ample evidence that it is being regularly tended by villagers, with no less care than is given to their own memorials…there are two vases, one on either side of the gravestone, for evergreens which are frequently renewed, and a cactus has been planted on the left-hand side.'

Landing on the island, he found a thriving community of 3,000 people, and he reported that over £1.5 million worth of stone was exported. Nonetheless, he noted 'life on these small mountain islands is hard and offers few attractions and fewer opportunities for young men and women. There is therefore, a constant flow of workers to the large cities…the local policemen deplored that nowadays the young people are not much concerned with religion and show little interest in supporting the shrines and temples.'

Once again, I wondered under what circumstances I might return to this placid, gentle island and the more I pondered, the more inevitable it seemed that I would join the throng of spirits and *kami* that lived here.

The ferry pulled away with a shiver of its bulk. No hooter sounded, as if in deference to the peace we were leaving behind.

'Would you like to be buried next to the Officer? The two of you can keep each other company?' Satoko asked as Hiroshima receded into the distance.

'If I'm going to be buried here, it will be with you.' Death, I hoped, was decades away.

Once again, we crossed the Seto Nai Kai Sea, as placid as a boating lake, with its innumerable islands – over seven hundred, it is said – fading to invisibility as evening fell. When Rudyard Kipling was passing through the Inland Sea in 1889, he had written a letter that described it thus:

'That is to say, we have for the last twenty hours been steaming through a huge lake, studded as far as the eye can reach with islands of every size, from four miles long and two wide to little cocked-hat hummocks no bigger than a decent hayrick. Messrs. Cook and Son charge about one hundred rupees extra for the run through this part of the world, but they do not know how to farm the beauties of nature. Under any skies the islands—purple, amber, grey, green, and black—are worth five times the money asked.'

This tranquil nature had a hidden underbelly. Five hundred years ago, a fleet of violent, thieving pirates ruled the sea from these islands – Satoko's ancestors among them. The sea was one of the main trade arteries within Japan, and to China and Korea. The pickings were rich. The pirates were well known for their shipbuilding and seamanship skills, as well as being adept at making lightening raids before vanishing. Over time, the pirates were persuaded to use their skills to more productive ends, taking up positions as merchants and developing alternative industries on the islands. Hence, some of Satoko's ancestors turned to the peaceful and socially responsible occupation of quarrying granite.

But some continued as seaman. In 1858, when the Tokugawa Shogun despatched a delegation to the US to sign a treaty of friendship and commerce, most of the ship's crew came from these islands as they were thought the most capable of making the treacherous navigation across the Pacific. One of Satoko's ancestors was among them: a point of much pride in the family for not only was he one of the first Japanese to visit the West, but this was an indication of their cosmopolitan outlook.

When this first Japanese delegation arrived in New York in 1860, this heralded the start of direct and frequent contact and exchange between the Japanese and the US. In 1876, the Centennial Exposition in Philadelphia featured a Japanese Pavilion where the public observed objects crafted with hitherto unseen exquisiteness. The next year, President Grant met with the Emperor of Japan. In the 1880s, the writer and astronomer Percival Lowell – among several – travelled to Japan to observe customs, nature and art.

In part influenced by Lowell's *The Soul of Japan*, Lafcadio Hearn, then a young journalist, left the US and moved to Japan. Here he started to write, and his books on local life became best sellers in the States.

Hearn was a nomad, initially raised in Ireland, his father's homeland, before being sent to England for schooling. This was a brief stay for he then travelled to France for further education and by the age of seventeen was living in Paris.

By nineteen, he was living in Cincinnati and joined the Cincinnati Enquirer as a junior reporter.

In 1890, he accepted an assignment from Harper's to travel to Japan and write a series of articles. Once in Tokyo, he met Basil Hall Chamberlain who helped him find a teaching post – though not in Tokyo but over five hundred miles away in the city of Matsue. Here he met his future wife, Setsuko Koizumi, then aged twenty-two, (Hearn was forty-one) and they married in 1891, one of the few mixed marriages to have taken place in Japan. (At the time, it was thought that around 100 mixed couples lived in Tokyo.) However, her family insisted that Hearn be adopted within the family and take their name to ensure that the children would remain Japanese. (If he had refused, his wife and children would be said to have become foreigners.)

'For it has well been said that the most wonderful aesthetic products of Japan are not its ivories, nor its bronzes, nor its porcelain, nor its swords, nor any marvel in metal or lacquer – but its women,' he wrote in 1904.

Satoko, my Japanese wife, is a member of this same small select group. Of all marriages in Japan in recent years, only about one per cent annually or roughly 8,000 are between Japanese women and foreign men. Whilst few in number, statistics show that mixed marriages are increasingly popular – having increased six-fold since 1970 – and in cosmopolitan Tokyo the proportion is higher still with nearly ten per cent of marriages mixed.

As a British national, I discovered I was in a minority, one of only two hundred or so marriages recorded between a British groom and a Japanese bride in 1997 – the year Satoko and I married. My national pride was pricked when I learnt that American grooms numbered more than 1,300. Even accounting for the greater number of US residents in Japan this meant they were preferred.

Personal ads in *Metropolis* – a weekly English language magazine and a poor imitation of London's *Time Out* – emphasised this partiality.

'Japanese female working in Yokohama. I want to get to know warm
    hearted Caucasian American.'
'Japanese female 31 seeks sincere, smart, stable man under 36 from
    U.S.'
'Japanese female 29 seeks a marriage minded white U.S. man. Must
    have good job and be successful.'
'I prefer single, blond, romantic, fun-loving American banker or
    lawyer.'

There were as many as a hundred similar ads printed every week often with the caveat 'no playboys, serious only'. So why, I might ask, search for an American?

Perhaps I was verging on the obsessive but I was forever searching out viewpoints on mixed marriages and the very nature of love in Japan. Said one Japanese girl, twenty-six year old Sakakibara-san, when I asked about her marriage to a Korean, 'It happened naturally – we met, we went out and we got married, just like everyone else. I love him for he never lies. I hardly think of him as foreign and I would say that Japanese men of my age are not as usually as determined in their endeavours as he is.'

One night over dinner, I touched on the subject of marriage and relationships in Japan, with Akiko, a young artist.

'Our Japanese men never admit that,' she replied, after I had just explained to her that girlfriends had been a great influence on my life.

She continued, 'Men really want to be seen in control but in fact it's the reverse, they rely on their mothers, girlfriends and wives all their lives.'

When speaking, she tilted her head and looked at me through eyes heavy with gold mascara, a colour that complimented the elaborately embroidered silk Chinese dress she was wearing.

(This deliciously sexy dress, with a high collar and a long thin slit along the thigh was a complete co-incidence even though we were eating at The Red Star, a trendy proto-modern Chinese restaurant in Tokyo's Roppongi district – I recommend the Peking Sweet and Sour Pork, chunks of tender pork stewed in a rich dark sauce. Sublime. Anyway, to get back to the point, I hadn't forewarned her that this was where I planned to eat.)

'My news is that I lost my love,' she went on unexpectedly. 'I really have realized how tough it is to handle the damage of losing love when you get older. Well may be it's not true. Younger or older, it's damaging. We Japanese don't have much recognition that everybody depends on your love and you depend on their love.'

'You had a boyfriend?' I asked. 'I didn't know.'

She looked at me for several seconds, nodded and then began to eat without saying a word. It seemed best not to continue to talk about lost love so I asked about her students. (By day, to support her work as an artist, she taught at a high school for kids with special needs.)

'All my students have survived by clinging to a fictional fantasy they have made. But I'm quite sure that their expectations and dreams have never been met. So I always tell them just find a capable wholesome person, and then you'll sure to get somebody who loves you. Actually, they all live in a school dormitory so their fantasy of the opposite sex has just grown to sky high. Having fantasy can be an escape for getting out from a difficult situation. I let them go for that and I go for that too. It's an energy.'

I asked Akiko what she thought Japanese men sought in a girl. 'Japanese men are the same as always. They have a deep-rooted desire that good women are those who are young, pretty, and subservient. They want a girl who is *kawaii*.'

'*Kawaii*?' I asked. *Kawaii* is a Japanese word that can be simplistically translated as cute and applies, among many things, to the fluffy girly style of dress, modelled on Madonna's 'Like a Virgin' outfit, a fashion that would appeal to any man with a Lolita fetish.

'*Kawaii* is to them sexy. It's pretty, soft, feminine and communicates that the girl is servile. Actually, that's what men want. They don't want intelligent women who might argue and be better than them. They seek someone who is more stupid.'

What do girls look for, I asked?

'It's not only for men. Even some women prefer pretty or handsome guy, we call *ikemen*. Many women regard money and education background as most important. I think Japanese fashion magazine incite us to this situation. They write how a cute girl is precious and nice. They have never written anything good about intelligent women. Women's' magazine write about the type of women that men don't want. Women more intelligent than men, women that read the newspaper and not TV program, sports, and so on. I suppose Japanese men don't want women to leads others.'

Another girl, Junko, told me, 'Why do I prefer non-Japanese? It's simple. If I have a dinner party, foreign men offer to help with the cooking and clearing up. Japanese men never do.' She said this after – and despite – being cheated by an American, working for the US military in Tokyo, with whom she had first made contact through an Internet chat room. They dated for three months, a time of 'intense passion' as she put it, until he was posted to Rome. Before leaving, he pleaded with her to join him and they would then marry. Yes, she said, as soon as she could, but it might take three or four months for her to arrange everything to move to Italy. Okay, he would go on ahead and wait. She handed in her notice, started the process of obtaining a visa but just a week or two before she was to emigrate he confessed, via e-mail, he had found another girlfriend. Don't get upset, he told her, this was just a meaningless fling, he still loved her and when she came to Rome, they would marry. Fortunately, she decided against this – remaining in Japan – but she thought his confession showed honour and honesty, a trait she admired in her men.

'I still love him although he was bastard,' she told me. 'I'm thirty-eight, I want to marry and I don't want to marry a Japanese.'

'Will you change your mind and go to Rome?' I asked.

'No. I'll find someone else.'

Her *keitai* buzzed.

'It's this Japanese guy,' she said, 'he keeps texting me. Excuse me.'

'But you don't like Japanese guys.'

'When texting *keitai*, it's a courtesy to reply quickly, like within ten minutes or so, but I don't know what to say. What should I say?'

'No idea.'

'Yesterday, I was going to reply, but didn't for five hours and he texted again. This feeling that I have to be connected with him all day is tiring.'

'Tell him to bugger off then.'

'But it's fun. My first experience.'

'The American's liked what we called Export girls,' recalled an old man talking to me about the American occupation after the Second World War. 'They had broad faces and slit eyes whereas we Japanese liked girls with slim faces and high cheek bones.'

This disdain of Japanese girls having a relationship with, or marrying a *gaijin* (the Japanese term for a foreigner) lingers to this day, and not just among older men. There is an underlying and long-held belief that such girls amount to little more than whores. But then Western men suffer from a prejudice as well. 'He's only going with an Asian because no white girl will have him,' was a common sneering insult. Sometimes I thought it might well be true.

Whilst annually 8,000 Japanese women married foreign men, over 24,000 Japanese men took foreign brides, mainly Chinese, Korean and Filipino. Caucasian brides marrying Japanese men were, though, a rare match but three of our female friends, though, had done just that: married Japanese men.

'Most of my friends were surprised,' said one of the Japanese husbands. 'They asked if my foreign wife could cook a Japanese meal. They think an international marriage is going to be very different from an ordinary one.' He continued after pausing to think: 'In one sense it is. We have to compromise. That includes my family, my parents, as their son has married non-Japanese. They don't mind but they feel that in a small way they are no longer quite as pure a Japanese family as previous.'

Our own courtship and marriage provide an illumination into the collision and merging of the old and the new in Japan.

I met Satoko on a trip to Tokyo in 1995, and immediately succumbed to an unshakable crush on her, attracted by all sorts of silly things: the way she shook my hand, the exuberance with which she enjoyed eating and drinking without apology, her loud laughter, broad smile and sweet fringe. It was as close as things come to love at first sight – such is the mystery of love. She was no shrinking violet – nor *kawaii* – and no feminine defence mechanisms bridled when I talked to her. Of course, I also found her amazingly beautiful. At odds with something Hearn wrote:

> 'Beauty, according to our Western standards can scarcely be said to exist in this race, – or shall we say that it has never yet been developed? One seeks in vain for a facial angle satisfying Western aesthetic canons. Yet there is great charm both of face and form: the charm of childhood – childhood with its every feature yet softly and vaguely outlined, – childhood before the limbs have fully lengthened, – slight and dainty, with admirable little hands and feet.'

A month or so after we met, on our first date we clutched hands and descended into the Cavern Bar in Roppongi to see a tribute band, the Japanese Beatles, play. (They still do and they do it well.) At the time, I lived in Hong Kong but after our date, I flew from Tokyo to Penang for a holiday. I sent Satoko a postcard with a short message, something along the line that it would be great if we could meet for a second date, and adding my Hong Kong home address, reasoning that if there was no reply by the time I returned we were not to share a future together. On arriving home, a letter waited, bearing a Japanese stamp and I knew then we would become lovers.

Shortly thereafter, I moved to Singapore but we continued our long-distance love affair. Despite the novelty fun and romance of meeting across the globe (our jobs allowed us to meet in Australia, Thailand, London, New York, Malaysia as well as in Singapore and Tokyo), we reached a decisive point – two years later in 1997 – when we had to make a choice: to marry or to part. At the time Satoko was fascinated by William Morris, so on a trip to London I dropped into Halcyon Days and bought an enamel music box with a Morris motif as a design. This was despatched by courier with a straightforwardly direct message 'Will you marry me?' and a small portrait photograph of when I was eight years old with a goofy gap-toothed smile. Unfortunately, the package didn't go straight to Japan but was despatched – for reasons unknown – to Hong Kong instead. Halcyon Days phoned, confessed their mistake, but promised it would be sent on to Tokyo. Within two days the box had arrived but was impounded by Customs – they sent a note to Satoko's home, demanding import tax be paid. Of course Satoko was ignorant of the gift's significance. Annoyed, she phoned me asking whether it was worth paying the tax. Yes, I told her. But why, she said? It would mean the bother of visiting an inconveniently located office, filling out forms and she didn't have the time to do this. Work was too busy she moaned. A gift I thought you would enjoy, I said. When she had the time she would retrieve it, I was told. Several tense days later, three weeks after I had sent the message, she phoned again. Yes, she answered.

Having decided to marry, we agreed to live in Japan. Satoko loathed the idea of moving to Singapore. She found it small-minded and bereft of cultural stimulus. I too was bored with the petty-minded constraints of the City State (everything works but I had found how banal and one-dimensional that made life). In any case, it had been four years since I had been hit over the head with a tray and had vowed to live in Japan.

So far as I know, Japan is the world's easiest place to marry: the couple take their birth certificates to the Marriage Counter (and it is no more than a counter) at the local Ward (council) Office, fill out a form, pay a small fee and within days, a marriage certificate will arrive in the post. It's as straightforward as that. No need for witnesses to be present, and it takes a matter of minutes for the form to be completed and processed. Even with me as a foreigner, it wasn't much more complicated. I had to present my passport, and a document from the British Embassy stating that so far as they knew I was competent to get married (not that there was any test – physical or mental).

Such simplicity reflects the traditional nature of marriage in Japan, when marriage was no more than a business transaction. Marriages were entered into by the parents and arranged through a marriage broker. Neither the bride nor groom had much or any say in the choice of partner. The purpose of marriage was as a financial investment to ensure the continuity and economic well-being of the family. Love didn't enter into it. Hence, no more than a contract need be signed, as in any business transaction.

Old style formally arranged marriages may now be infrequent, but there is a huge matchmaking industry – companies that arrange events where singles can meet. But once a match is made, both families are consulted for their agreement, parents meet to discuss the proposal, and vigorous background checks are made to ensure the families are well matched socially and professionally. Employers as well are consulted. For men it's important they choose the right wife, one that won't hinder their career.

'In Japan, generally it is believed that to marry a nice guy is the most and only important thing in a woman's life because she will be taken care of by her husband and children and this is the easiest and safest life,' a disconsolate colleague once told me.'

'And love?' I asked.

'Affection and friendship more often. Women's status is weak in Japan. Marriage guarantees a woman's life. My father used to tell me from an early age that marriage is everything in a woman's life. Forget about a career, just worry about who you marry.'

Satoko's parents were shocked and confused when first told she was marrying a *gaijin*. (This in spite of her living and studying in England and Spain for a number of years, and having foreign boyfriends. And she was now thirty-five.)

She had become one of the small but increasing number of Japanese women who decided to shun convention and resist Japan's stifling restrictions. She had studied and lived abroad, and worked for a foreign company in Tokyo.

'I had concluded that I was strong enough to overcome the social pressures that would want me to marry to a salaryman, have children and live a conformist life as a compliant housewife,' Satoko said. This wasn't a rejection of Japan – far from it. Satoko was as fiercely nationalistic as the next.

'All I sought was to live in Japan on my own terms. Where I could balance a Western and a Japanese life, neither presenting a contradiction and nor would I end up as an alienated hybrid of the two.'

Before Satoko broke the news, I hadn't met her parents. Not deliberately but because of distance: their island of Shikoku a two-hour flight from Tokyo. I had never got round to travelling there when visiting Japan, and Satoko didn't press the need. No wonder they were shocked. What calamity had befallen their daughter? Not only was Satoko marrying a Westerner but also one they had never met, knew nothing about, and the marriage was taking place within a few months. But at least we planned to live in Tokyo and not in a distant country. A hasty meeting was arranged, to take place on neutral soil (in Japan, nearly all such meetings are held in a hotel).

We chose to meet in Kobe, a two-hour train journey for them, and a city where I would often fly to on business from Singapore. Fortunately and conveniently, only four weeks after Satoko had said 'yes' I was due to visit Kobe.

Having finished my meeting, I walked the short distance to the Bay Sheraton, Rokko Island: one of those identikit hotels, tacked on to the side of a large shopping mall.

Accompanied by Satoko and her niece Rikako, her mother and father were taking afternoon tea in one of the hotel's many restaurants. I walked in, not nervous as I knew we were to marry – come what may – but with some trepidation as I had no idea what to expect. Not that I imagined a row was about to break out. Despite what her parents and particularly her father felt, his inner feelings, his *honne*, would be overridden by his obligation to *tatemae*, the need to show harmony and avoid upset. Even more so in a public place. Her parents immediately knew who I was, stood and bowed deeply and seriously, even before I reached the table. Though retired, her father was dressed in a neat business suit with polished shoes that shone. Both he and Satoko's mother stood stiffly with arms held rigid at their side. What no doubt led to more discomfort was the fact that I towered over both of them (an intimidating figure); I was the first Westerner they had formally met and this brute of a man was about to marry their youngest daughter.

One of Satoko's delightful qualities is her ability to light up a room when she walks in. She injects energy and uplifts the spirit. As soon as we sat down, she immediately began putting her parents at ease by not being nervous herself but happily animated. Also, it was a masterly stroke inviting her eight-year-old niece as she provided an amusing distraction. Neither shy nor quiet, Rikako rushed round being curious and noisy. Everyone could fuss over her.

We first drank tea. Satoko acted as the interpreter but did most of the talking. There wasn't much I could say, other than describe my job and life in Singapore and I'm sure Satoko embellished the story as she replayed it to her parents. After tea — and to pass time before dinner — we walked round the adjacent shopping mall; look at that, someone would say, pretending it was fascinating when in fact the mall was the same design as any other that could be found anywhere in the world. Then we adjourned to my hotel bedroom to show Rikako a Western-style bed. She had never seen one before and delighted in bouncing on it and wriggling underneath the sheets. We teased her about her supposedly smelly socks (they weren't) so we could keep the atmosphere light and minimise tension and overcome the occasional lapse into silence.

'My father's still very nervous,' Satoko said to me, not needing to whisper because her parents couldn't understand a word of English. (But neither could I understand a word of Japanese.)

'And your mother's very quiet,' I added.

Later we had dinner in a private room off the hotel's formal Japanese restaurant, sitting on the floor around a low table, eating seafood and vegetables as Satoko's mother didn't eat meat. Rikako's favourite food was prawns. We teased her again, this time by asking if she wanted our prawns, and then refusing when she replied yes. Many flasks of sake were drunk, toasts called and, despite the language gap, Satoko's parents and I managed to hold a conversation. We spoke in different tongues and had no idea what each other was saying other than by a sense, by the look in the eye, the tone of the voice, the movement of a hand. The sake helped as well. To good effect. I smiled frequently, and kept reassuring them that I loved Satoko.

'My mother thinks you have a nice smile. My father thinks you are an honest boy,' Satoko said towards the end of the meal, 'and he is happy and confident that you will take good care of me.'

As he had been head of internal security on Shikoku Island, I knew I had passed the test.

'Did you know you look just like your father?' I asked Satoko before we went to bed. She thumped me.

The civil registration is the only form of legal marriage but signing papers in a utilitarian council office is hardly the most memorable and photogenic occasion and so most couples hold an additional ceremony, followed by a reception or party that often scale the heights of extravagance and kitsch.

Marriage is big business in Japan, notwithstanding that the marriage rate is declining whilst the average age of marriage is increasing. (Japan has the highest average marriage age of the industrialised world: thirty for men and twenty-eight for women, and Satoko and I were about to notch up the norm.) The cost of these ceremonies, the outfits and the parties is decadently expensive, running to forty thousand pounds on average, and most hotels (and many restaurants) wouldn't survive without them as a backbone for their business. Many hotels have established a special department dedicated to weddings: they sell wedding dresses, hire out morning suits, arrange the honeymoon, and many have an extensively stocked wedding gift shop on site. They will lay on the most over-the-top Las Vegas-style reception with light shows, karaoke, flaming candles, skyscraper wedding cakes and an appropriately themed pop song (Aerosmith, Elton John, Queen and Enya are popular) played at each and ever more elaborate stage of the celebration. Friends will sing, company bosses will look on with grim-faced approval and the bride will parade in several changes of outfit – in fact a centuries-old custom to signify that she is coming back into the real world, and is prepared to pamper her husband on a daily basis.

At the top of the pyramid perched the purpose-built luxury marriage centres like *Happo-en* or *Chinzan-so* (where we tied the knot). They are huge places, offer a variety of religious ceremonies, can and do churn out tens during the day, and provide on-site everything anyone could ever need to make the day one to remember. Such temples to the confluence of the commercial and sacred have been in existence since the early part of the twentieth century.

Our day was typical.

We opted for the Shinto ceremony – about a third of couples do. An alternative could have been the Christian wedding – the most popular – handled by a mock priest wearing mock priestly regalia, with the wedding, held in a mock church. (Any English-speaking Caucasian can take up the vocation of a marriage priest. Specialist companies that hire out priests use classified ads to seek recruits – though they are coy about admitting their provenance and [lack of] qualifications.) The money isn't bad and the work is regular, as John's grandma would say. A friend, John, earned his living that way, preaching a condensed version of the marriage litany.

'The couple don't understand a word I'm saying,' he confessed to me in his gentle Belfast lilt. 'It's a mockery. They stand rigid with fright, stumble over "I do" and they go away happy, thinking they have been married by a real priest. You would think they would wonder what all these priests are doing in Japan.'

How long does the ceremony last, I asked him?

'Fifteen minutes precisely. Not a minute more.'

'Do you sing hymns?' I was fascinated by all of this.

'Yes and they're sung in English but usually we have three professional singers who make most of the running.'

Now, you might question what sort of country, with no qualms, allowed a religion to be usurped and abused in this ridiculous way. I did but could find no satisfactory answer. Business is business, I suppose. Not that I am deeply religious but before I knew better it seemed slightly distasteful that this sham was sanctioned.

For our Shinto marriage was just as much a sham as the mock Christian ceremony. It had no foundation in the traditions of Shinto where the priest had no role to play in family events such as death and marriage. Traditionally, marriages took place in the bridegroom's family home, with no priest present.

Shinto is one of Japan's two main religions. The other is Buddhist and rather endearingly, statistics show an equal split of fifty per cent (with about thirty per cent in total claiming committed religious affiliation). The statistics obscure the full picture, as there are any numbers of new religions in Japan – a distinctive feature of Japan's religious heritage – as well as a thriving Christian church. A real one.

These new religions have emerged over the last two hundred years and whilst some maintain theological connections to Shinto, Buddhism or Christianity, others are entirely independent. Many are more than insignificant obscure sects and cults. They have a powerful presence; sometimes build anonymously secretive and imposing headquarters, and some go so far as providing parliamentary candidates. Most adhere to deeply conservative political and religious values. (The one exception is the radical Aum movement who attacked the Tokyo subway system with sarin gas.) Many preach the pursuit of happiness, including material success and all that goes with it whilst still stressing the importance of ancestor worship, as this is ingrained in society. Many of these religions are wealthy and it is naïve to judge them from a pious perspective as I did initially. They are not about priests leading saintly lives, wearing purgatorial sackcloth. The headquarters of one small sect shared the same building where I had offices. Their leader drove a silver-coloured 500 SEL Mercedes. With permed and dyed hair, wearing what used to be called 'sharp suits', he looked more like a member of the Mafia – some of whom happened to live in the same district of Akasaka – than a holy man. One day I caused an upset over parking. (I had inadvertently left my car in a place where it made it difficult for him manoeuvre his own). An argument ensued, which unsettled my staff, as they worried he might put a curse on us all. Maybe he did, and maybe it worked.

Our nuptials spanned two days. On the first, we held a Shinto ceremony for our immediate family. It was an auspicious day if only because the previous night the moon and six planets were strung across the sky like a diamond necklace, the first time in several hundred years. The following day, for family and friends, we threw a big wedding party with Thai food, and entertainment that included a *geisha*, rock band, two well-known actresses singing as a duet, a ukulele player and a transvestite singer.

Preparations on the day of the ceremony started early in the morning. For the only time in her life, Satoko was awake an hour ahead of me as her make-up and ceremonial *kimono* would take several hours to assemble. By seven a.m. I stood in a dressing room, being fussed over by three middle-aged Japanese ladies attempting to make the best effort of fitting a *kimono* to a *gaijin*, and a large one at that.

My *kimono* came in several pieces: a white under-robe, a black coat (*haori*), special trousers (*hakama*) which were striped grey and white, belt, socks, and a white tassel – a cross between a rabbit's foot lucky charm and a sporran.

Fortunately, the problem wasn't the size of the *kimono* – after all there were sumo wrestlers bigger than I – but making sure it fitted perfectly, hung straight without a wrinkle or bump, and that the correct amount of under-garment showed around my neck. For some reason the shape of my body made this an awkward task.

Eventually satisfied with the fitting, I was handed a small fan to hold, and a wedding hostess – charged with escorting me to the right place – led me to a waiting room. By this time, the *Chinzan-so* was filling with people. Think of it like a huge multi-storey shopping centre in the weeks before Christmas but entirely dedicated to marriage. Everywhere swarms of wedding guests rushed back and forth, seemingly panicked and without purpose. I felt I was swimming through a sea of giant plankton. Many women wore the most elaborate colourful *kimono*; in contrast, the men dressed – identically and immaculately – in black suits, black shoes, and white shirts with a white or cream tie. Forty-seven weddings were taking place that day so it was vital that everything ran like clockwork, that we were in the right place, at the right time.

As I was led to the waiting room, I couldn't help but conclude unromantically that this was a wedding factory and I was a minor and inconsequential component on a perpetual conveyor belt. My sense of being an impotent pawn was heightened, as I couldn't talk to any of the staff. I didn't speak Japanese and they didn't speak English.

Over the course of the morning, politely and with patient smiles, I was ushered around in the same firm manner. First to the dressing room, then to a waiting room, next to the Ceremonial Hall, followed by the photo studio until finally led outside to stroll round the formal gardens before being directed to lunch. I had no choice as to where I went and neither could Satoko assert control. Only the hostess was permitted to direct me – an example of the meticulously planned efficiency that lies at the core of Japan's daily routine – and I had no need to think or worry about what was taking place. Everything was taken care of and worked perfectly. As far as I could tell, not one single error occurred – a combination of ruthless, inflexible but unobtrusive efficiency by the staff, and the unfailing discipline of the guests to do everything they were told without dissent.

In the waiting room, our relatives and friends were seated. When I entered, everyone stood and bowed. Not a word was spoken. Even my parents followed suit. I bowed back and felt like royalty. I was directed to a seat in the centre of the room. On cue, and soon thereafter, Satoko appeared. Everyone this time stood and politely clapped. At first, I didn't recognise her, thinking (stupidly of course) that the wrong bride had been brought into the room.

She wore a heavy *kimono* of pure white cotton and silk. (Later she confided to me that it was so burdensome she could hardly walk.) It had a special name, *shiromuko*, and was the most formal of wedding *kimono*, worn originally by *samurai* families. The whiteness signifies that the bride was prepared to adopt the colours of the family she is marrying into.

'Dye me any colour you wish as I will conform to your family's social standing.' Satoko whispered and then laughed. She wore a traditional heavy wig. 'My neck aches already.'

'But it looks magnificent.'

'And it itches.'

Her face had been thickly powdered a pure white. No matter how long I stared, I found it hard to recognise her.

We sat patiently in the waiting room: a square, plain space with a thick, brown carpet, and three reproduction paintings on the wall. Long periods of silence were interrupted by flurries of conversation, and the click of teacups on saucer reminded me of balls being struck in a snooker hall. My father sat leaning forward, rubbing his thumbs, smiling broadly but understandably baffled. My mother also smiled as she looked for reassurance and glanced around the room. We had forty minutes to wait. One trick of Japanese competence is to make sure that everything is done well in advance so that last-minute snags are avoided.

Satoko took advantage of the wait to run through the ceremony procedures one final time: what I had to do, recite and when. This wasn't so complicated. My words were written phonetically on a sheet of paper and these I had practised for several days. I doubted that further repetition would make me any more word- or accent-perfect. A mediocre peak had already been reached but, for her benefit, I mouthed them once again.

Eventually, the guests were summoned to enter the shrine. Everyone stood; straightened ties, jackets, trousers and *kimono*, and loud conversation broke out.

Until they were seated, we hung back in the waiting room. Then our wedding hostess escorted us to the shrine's entrance, passing along long noisy corridors packed like the morning rush hour. I wondered whether a muddle might happen and the wrong people would end up in the wrong place. Another foolish thought. But even if they had what would be the problem? Each wedding was identical. The bride was unrecognisable. The ceremony didn't have any religious or legal significance. Choosing to attend a ceremony at random would mean missing nothing.

We both wore raised wooden sandals (*geta*) – the ones like clogs – which I was learning on the run, so to speak, to walk in without falling flat on my nose. Mine were of plain wood with black straps whilst Satoko's were colourful and ornate. The *kimono* was tightly wrapped around me, and the combination of this and the *geta* made comfortable walking impossible. I could only take staccato and unbalanced steps, presenting not a sartorial but a comical and absurd sight to anyone who had time to look.

As we approached, the doors to the shrine slid open. We walked side by side into a gilded ornately decorated hall, the guests sitting hushed – once again – in a row along the walls: Satoko's guests ranged along the left hand-side and my parents, sat alone on the right.

I glanced at my parents, their smiles had vanished and they looked as pale and utterly bewildered as I felt.

An elderly and unsmiling priest stood at the far end of the shrine accompanied by two young shrine maidens, or *miko*, dressed in white and red robes. He was dressed in full splendid costume and chanted in a murmur. Slowly we walked towards him and were stood behind a simple wooden table. At that moment, any thought I had that this was a novel and big game being played was forgotten.

He started the ceremony by purifying everyone present. The guests and we stood silent and still (except for Rikako who fidgeted and smirked broadly at what was going on or, most likely, at the two of us dressed in our wedding costumes, two of the more inappropriate people making a ridiculous attempt to appear traditional). The priest called on the gods to look favourably upon us. Satoko and I recited oaths pledging faithfulness and obedience to one another. No one sniggered but it was easy to imagine how ponderous and wooden I sounded. The spell was breaking; the charm and novelty of the Shinto wedding was wearing off as I thought how silly I looked: a *gaijin* attempting to imitate the Japanese.

Exchanging the nuptial cups, the *San-San-Kudo*, is the most important part of the Shinto wedding. In fact, it is the only formal and essential part of the marriage service. Three cups are placed on top of one another, on a small plain wooden stand. The groom takes the cup on top. A *miko* pours sake into it. Resist temptation. I remembered Satoko's instructions. Don't finish the sake in one gulp, Satoko had repeatedly impressed upon me. I had to drink the sake little by little, taking three deliberate sips.

Then I passed the cup to Satoko, it was refilled and she too drank by taking three sips.

Satoko then raised the second cup, sipped three times before it was passed to me, refilled and I did the same. Finally, I started on the third. Drinking and exchanging cups in this considered way has a profound significance: to deepen the relationship between husband and wife, symbolising the patience and care that a couple need to be successful in their relationship.

The final part of the ceremony was for Satoko and I to offer twigs of *Sakaki* – the sacred tree – in worship of the gods. Then, to signifying that through the wedding we were bound in unity, everyone drank sake.

In total, the ceremony lasted for forty minutes: short, sombre, and filmed on two video cameras slung from the ceiling.

When Isabel Bird travelled through Japan in 1878, she was once invited to a ceremony:

> 'The bridegroom is twenty-two, the bride seventeen, and very comely, so far as I could see through the paint with which she was profusely disfigured. Towards evening, she was carried in a norimon, accompanied by her parents and friends, to the bridegroom's house, each member of the procession carrying a Chinese lantern. When the housemaster and I arrived, the wedding party was assembled in a large room, the parents and friends of the bridegroom being seated on one side, and those of the bride on the other. Two young girls, very beautifully dressed, brought in the bride, a very pleasing-looking creature dressed entirely in white silk, with a veil of white silk covering her from head to foot.
>
> The bridegroom, who was already seated in the middle of the room near its upper part, did not rise to receive her, and kept his eyes fixed on the ground, and she sat opposite to him, but never looked up. A low table was placed in front, on which there was a two-spouted kettle full of sake, some sake bottles, and some cups, and on another there were some small figures representing a fir-tree, a plum-tree in blossom, and a stork standing on a tortoise, the last representing length of days, and the former the beauty of women and the strength of men. Shortly a *zen*, loaded with eatables, was placed before each person, and the feast began, accompanied by the noises, which signify gastronomic gratification.

After this, which was only a preliminary, the two girls who brought in the bride handed round a tray with three cups containing sake, which each person was expected to drain till he came to the god of luck at the bottom.

The bride and bridegroom then retired, but shortly reappeared in other dresses of ceremony, but the bride still wore her white silk veil, which one day will be her shroud. An old gold lacquer tray was produced, with three sake cups, which were filled by the two bridesmaids, and placed before the parents-in-law and the bride.

The father-in-law drank three cups, and handed the cup to the bride, who, after drinking two cups, received from her father-in- law a present in a box, drank the third cup, and then returned the cup to the father-in-law, who again drank three cups. Rice and fish were next brought in, after which the bridegroom's mother took the second cup, and filled and emptied it three times, after which she passed it to the bride, who drank two cups, received a present from her mother-in-law in a lacquer box, drank a third cup, and gave the cup to the elder lady, who again drank three cups. Soup was then served, and then the bride drank once from the third cup, and handed it to her husband's father, who drank three more cups, the bride took it again, and drank two, and lastly the mother-in-law drank three more cups. Now, if you possess the clear-sightedness, which I laboured to preserve, you will perceive that each of the three had imbibed nine cups of some generous liquor!

After this, the two bridesmaids raised the two-spouted kettle and presented it to the lips of the married pair, who drank from it alternately, till they had exhausted its contents. This concluding ceremony is said to be emblematic of the tasting together of the joys and sorrows of life. And so they became man and wife till death or divorce parted them.'

Chapter Two

The Pleasures of Ryokan and Onsen

'These good folk will be able, without any apparent effort, to make you happy.

'Really you are happy because you have entered bodily into Fairyland – into a world that isn't, and never could be your own. You have been transported out of your own century – over spaces enormous of perished time – into an era forgotten, into a vanished age.' *Lafcadio Hearn*

The delights of the traditional *ryokan* (inn) – and the horrors of public bathing in *onsen* – were a reoccurring motif within much of the writings of the nineteenth century, and still provide today one of the most unadulterated pleasures of traditional Japan (even if most Westerners crave reassurance that bathing is segregated – though, in the end, few actually make a trip).

Some might argue that the experience is no more than a pastiche of what it offered in the past. I would disagree. The facilities may be updated, the quality of the food better, the heating perfect, the arrival of a *gaijin* less of an event – although still a talking point – but I won't waver from the view that the pleasure of staying in a centuries-old *ryokan*, run through the generations by the same family, is one of the most sublime that can be experienced. It is a Fairyland experience, and one that cannot be found anywhere else in the world. (I think I've made my position clear on this.)

Satoko was the *onsen* authority. I tagged along carrying the cases. We had agreed that at the end of every year we had to escape Tokyo and spend a minimum of ten days recuperating in *ryokan*.

Not that there was anything satisfying or restful on the drive from Tokyo to the Izu National Park. It was my first *onsen* trip and as it was the New Year, our main route out of Tokyo, the Yamato dori, was locked solid with traffic. We crawled in fumes.

Once in the suburbs, the Expressway ran fast but as it was an overcast sullen day, the few attractive views we could have seen were wiped out by low cloud and drizzle. And the final twelve miles, from Exit 8 to the spa town of Shinjuzin, was a narrow rat run along Route 414: a single carriageway lined with car showrooms, flashing signage, thousands of flapping publicity banners, cheap fast food family eateries and gaudy pachinko parlours – a cacophony of colour that alone was enough to spin you into a delirium before blinding you with its luridness.

First impressions of Shinjuzin, the spa town where the Asaba Inn was to be found, weren't immediately favourable. The dour main street might make the uninformed turn round and drive elsewhere: run-down small shops stacked with dusty household goods, one or two dark uninviting coffee shops and several very tacky souvenir stores specialising in the sort of gifts you like to give to a mother-in-law, knowing she would actually appreciate them. Had Satoko erred in her judgement, I wondered to myself? This was my first ever *ryokan* stay and although I had high expectations I was ready to be disappointed.

But as soon as we passed through the ancient wooden gate to the Asaba Inn, stepped onto the delicate black gravel, we sensed an experience of release and transformation. For immediately, the tension knotted within our bodies began to slowly unravel. Our feet made a soft scrunch as we walked towards the main hall; the doors to the inn slid silently open, we were met with a calm smile, a deep bow, and ushered inside. The doors closed, we took almost faltering steps inside and we were at once aware a rarefied world had been entered: silent, tranquil, natural.

For three hundred and fifty years, the Asaba Inn had enjoyed a distinguished history, providing a haven of restfulness for travellers. Tucked under a densely wooded hill on the town's fringe, the inn nestled over a side stream of the Katsura River: a series of low wooden buildings, an elegant garden and the wonderful extravagance of the outdoor *Gekkeiden Noh* stage. Indoors, several *onsen* rooms ran off from the main corridor (separate facilities for male, female and for families). But the best, the most exhilarating, was outside: a large steaming pool (*Noten*) built by craftsmen in the early years of the Showa era: smooth rocks left in their original state and skilfully arranged to form the pool so that it appeared to be a natural not a man-made feature.

A maid who treated us like family friends whom she had known for years led us to our rooms. Once inside, we stripped off and packed out of view our Western clothes, slipped on *yukata*, the Japanese style of informal dress, slid open the windows, took deep breaths, listened to the gentle bird song and then sat down at a low table.

'I hear three tunes,' sighed Satoko.

'Bliss,' I replied.

'Can you hear them? The birds? Do you think they are speaking to us?'

'Maybe.'

'I want to take my earrings off. They feel heavy already.'

Tea and sweets were brought in, with steaming hot towels so that we could cleanse our face and hands. The tea leaves were stored in airtight copper caddies, one of many small details that made every encounter here a delight. (Later, we were told the caddies should be only be polished by rubbing them with bare hands. We also bought three.)

After tea, I sank into the clear waters of the outdoor pool, letting out long breaths as I adjusted to the temperature. Slowly I sank deeper until the water was up to my neck. My skin tingled from the heat. A heady aroma of *onsen* water and steam started to seep through me, coursing along my bronchia like fresh spring water, sweeping away the funk accumulated from months of living in Tokyo's polluted, dirty air. I was alone and, as I lay back, floating as still and silently as I could, allowing the peace to glide over me, I drifted far from the outside world. Stress, tension and discord dissolved into the waters.

I listened.

Hot water trickled into the pool through a wooden chute with a satisfying high-pitched burble. Alongside ran the stream, more robust in sound.

I listened.

To the complimentary melodies of the two flows of water, the only sound I could hear as daylight was extinguished. Overhead, the heavens gave birth to a million stars flickering like diamonds in a black jeweller's cloth. This, a perfect moment. I let my eyes fall in and out of focus as I gazed at the pinpricks of light, my worries floating away like foam on a river.

This bath I used most, relishing the invigorating and yet soothing contrast of cold air and hot spring water; floating in the mineral rich waters and then jumping on to a cold rock, the steam swirling from my naked body as I contemplated the surrounding gardens.

Despite the hedonistic temptations of the pool, we found our rooms equally satisfying. Large, sliding windows overlooked and framed the garden and, on the opposite hillside, the dense wood of bamboo, maple and cedar looked gorgeous during the day and was subtly and attractively lit at night by unseen spotlights. A continuum of nature ran from outside to in: the room, a mix of light-coloured cedar wood on the ceiling, the walls a beige plaster and on the floors pine *tatami* mats, blended perfectly with the nature outside. Simple rooms, unadorned with life's distracting trivia. Rooms where I could sit happily alone.

Before dinner, we did leave the room, and sipped champagne cocktails in the lounge. The wire chairs and glass-topped tables were classic examples of modern furniture and because they were simple, not out of place within the inn. At the entrance to the lounge hung a digital artwork by one of Japan's most internationally celebrated artists, Tatsuo Miyajima. In contrast, we could see outside a natural pool formed within the stream, illuminated only by candlelight, and beyond, the delicately lit *Noh* stage, a scene that would not have seemed out of place when the inn first opened those 350 years ago. If a ghost of a beautiful courtesan had been seen, gliding over the water, I would not have been surprised. Such juxtaposition of the old and new is a talent that few nations are able to show.

Dinner (and breakfast) was served back in our room. We waited in silence, wary of breaking the calm around us. Perfection went like this:

Champagne cocktail

Sesame tofu, creamy smooth and served in a red lacquer bowl

Sake aperitif drunk from wafer-thin porcelain cups

Crabmeat served with mountain vegetables in a lime cup

Crayfish

Tongue

Deeply smoked salmon

Sashimi roll

Noodles with River Crab

Sashimi of two local fish served in a brown glazed earthenware bowl dripped with a blue glaze

Grilled fish (grilled at the table) and then served on larva-black plates

Prawn

Eel wrapped in black rice grown in the local Shijenshi area

Mountain yam with sesame sauce served in an exquisite half-black and -white bowl

Minced chicken, local free-range and with all the flavour we had forgotten that chicken has. This, we sprinkled with 7-taste pepper from Kyoto.

A light miso soup with clams

Rice that arrived in a large wooden tub, and which we spooned into thick white bowls

For dessert, we chose *Kuzukiri*; fine strands of white arrowroot jelly, dipped in thick brown sugar syrup.

Finally, the chef carried in three silver pots of ice cream, and served scoops of pumpkin, Grand Marnier and ginger ice cream.

Some of the dishes might sound rather plain and ordinary but imagine them to be of simply the best ingredients, perfectly and delicately prepared so that you would taste food so beautiful nothing might ever compare again.

The maid serving dinner was both surprised and delighted that I could eat all the food. She clapped her hands in glee and said the chef worried when foreigners arrived as they fussed about the dishes and left a lot uneaten. I said to Satoko that I thought by foreigners she meant Americans – who won't eat anything, and if they do, dump half a pint of soy sauce on their dish. I was sure most Europeans enjoyed tastes that are more catholic. In that, I was wrong. John Morris wrote in the 1930s that he never took to Japanese food, and described a miso soup as tasting like 'a scoopful of deep-sea water heated up'. Tempura he did find delicious.

The way our meal was served can be found in the writings of Kipling, Hearn and Bird et al. This is from Kipling:

> 'The maidens came in with tea in blue china and cake in a red lacquered bowl, and they gave us chopsticks to separate the cake with. They returned with black lacquer stands a foot square and four inches high. Those were our tables. They bore a red lacquered bowlful of fish boiled in brine, and sea anemones. A paper napkin tied with gold thread enclosed our chopsticks; and in a little flat saucer lay a smoked crayfish, a slice of a compromise that looked

like Yorkshire pudding and tasted like a sweet omelette, and a twisted fragment of some translucent thing that had once been alive but was now pickled. After raw fish and mustard sauce came other sorts of fish cooked with pickled radishes, and very slippery on the chopsticks. After the bamboo shoots came a basin of white beans in sweet sauce. Some chicken cunningly boiled with turnips, and a bowlful of snow-white boneless fish, and a pile of rice concluded the meal. Here was colour, form, food, comfort and beauty enough for half a years contemplation.'

Next morning we curled under our warm duvets but the maid woke us and, with a smile, firmly chivvied us up. As we enjoyed a morning soak in the outdoor bath, she tidied our room and laid out a Japanese breakfast: mushrooms grilled over charcoal at the table, rice accompanied by creamed *wasabi*, soup, river shrimp, omelette, boiled and grilled fish, pickles and tea.

Following breakfast, I opened the *shoji* screens effortlessly with a fingertip, and marvelled at the perfect setting outside. If there was a place worthy of the name Shangri-la, somewhere you might choose to live forever, with none of life's petty intrusions, this was it. Not the smallest detail jarred. Even the guttering to the roof was formed not of plastic but copper, now oxidised and blending naturally with the environment.

Our instincts said remain in the room but we wanted to stretch our legs and explore Shuzenji. Our shoes waited in the lobby. They had been warmed on a heater so we could step straight into them and walk off with the minimum of effort and the maximum of comfort.

Shuzenji was typical of many old spa towns in Japan, down to the ageless, simple almost charming amusements provided for visitors: old-fashioned stores, their fronts open to the street, run by *oba-chan* (middle-aged women). We fired corks from a rusty air rifle at porcelain figures, tossed rubber balls at a pile of tin cans and played a mechanical version of pachinko. At the final tally, we scored a trifling ten points between us and won a china mug decorated with black and white cows.

The town straddled the Katsuro River, which cut deeply through the centre of town, forming a gorge spanned by bridges painted traditionally with bright red railings. *Ryokan* of various ages and qualities lined the banks. Inside we could see guests, mostly retired couples, sitting contentedly in their rooms, wives drinking tea, and husbands smoking. Exactly as Kipling had seen when visiting a spa town:

> 'Green bamboo pipes led the hot water to a score of bathing houses in whose verandas Japanese in blue and white dressing gowns lounged and smoked.'

In the centre of town and on the river, there was a free public bath: a circular bamboo hut that could be used by anyone. Little privacy was afforded, so the bather's nakedness could be spied by the passing world but this didn't bother the two men who were enjoying the hot waters.

'Apropos of water,' Kipling wrote, 'be pleased to listen to a shocking story. It is written in all the books that the Japanese though cleanly are somewhat casual in their customs. They bathe often with nothing on and together. The man led me to a beautiful bathhouse full of hot and cold water. There was naturally no bolt to the door any more than there would be a bolt to the dining room. Had I been sheltered by the walls of a big European bath, I should not have cared, but I was preparing to wash when a pretty maiden opened the door, and indicated that she would also tub in the deep sunken Japanese bath at my side. When one is dressed only in one's virtues and a pair of spectacles it is difficult to shut the door in the face of a girl. She gathered I was not happy, and withdrew giggling, while I thanked heaven, blushing profusely the while, that I had been brought up in a society which unfits a man to bathe *a deux*.'

When visiting *onsen*, it was possible to see the physiognomic extremes of the male penis. The film star David Niven once commented that in old age his penis began to resemble an acorn. In *onsen*, I had seen acorns on young men who were no more than in their early thirties. With some, it was impossible to see anything. No more than just a bush of black pubic hair. Conversely there were men, who must have been at least seventy, who had flagging bottoms, skin deeply speckled with age spots, thinning grey or white pubic hair, whose member was of a very decent size. Strange really, as a doctor told me, confirming David Niven's experience, that it is more common for older men to see their symbol of manhood shrivel and in some cases disappear all together.

Weedy men had big ones. Muscular men were lacking down under. There was neither rhyme nor reason to who had what.

Shuzenji was no Monte Carlo or Baden Baden. Here and there we saw a handful of picturesque old buildings: along one street, we found art and pottery galleries with gentle Japanese music playing from loudspeakers atop the street lighting and shops displaying delicate novelties made of coloured paper or straw, full of handcrafted and loving detail. But it was easier to find ugly newer buildings. Some hotels, more recently built to cater for the 'package group' trade, had already closed as business had declined because of Japan's economic recession. Left behind were decaying concrete hulks, with abandoned cars outside, creepers strangling the ironwork, and piles of unopened correspondence in the lobby.

One afternoon, we climbed a mile up a side of a steep mountain to admire the cherry and plum orchard at the top. Too early in the year for the blossom, we were told a magnificent view from the top still made the climb worthwhile. The walk was invigorating as we slowly hiked up a steep track through a dense cedar forest, the trunks perfectly straight, shooting upwards for hundred of feet into the sky. An eerie peacefulness surrounded us. No wind disturbed the leaves. The stream that in the rainy season would noisily tumble alongside the path was all but dry. The only sound that occasionally penetrated through the canopy was the angry cry of a crow, perhaps irritated by our intrusion.

On the way, we paused at the half-hidden graves of two *haiku* poets. My legs ached. This area had long been a favourite spot for poets to visit; now two rested silently in the forest glade with one final poem carved into their small moss covered headstones.

We wore traditional Japanese robes. The temperature was mild and, in any case, the steep walk kept us warm. But Satoko had gone one step further and wore wooden *geta* as well – I had walking shoes on – and I worried whether she might slip or find it too hard on her toes.

After an hour's solitary climb and out of breath, we reached the top, to find the summit crowded with trippers – all of whom had arrived by coach – dressed in thick winter clothes. Many stared at us, some pointed and who could blame them? We looked out of place and they must have thought us quite mad to be wearing such flimsy clothes in the middle of winter.

All of a sudden, I felt as if I were wearing pyjamas in the middle of Trafalgar Square. But, as promised, the view from the top was magnificent.

Over the surrounding mountains and in the distant west we saw Fuji's cone rise majestically: a divine being. This was how I imagined that one day I would see Fuji, a mirage floating over Japan. We stared at one of the world's most recognisable natural forms, finding its beauty inexhaustible before turning away and ordering green tea and Japanese sweets in the teahouse. But even here, we could still see Fuji, framed perfectly in the window, creating a living painting.

In 1896 Hearn had written on the Japanese ability to create simple pleasures for everyone to enjoy cheaply:

> 'Some locality is chosen on hill or coast by lake or river: gardens are made, trees planted, resting houses built to command the finest points of view; and the wild site is presently transformed into a place of pilgrimage for pleasure-seekers.'

In many senses, *ryokan* have changed little since they first flourished in the Edo period. Margaret Price, in her book on Japanese inns, explains how they started as places where the aristocracy rested on their journeys to Tokyo – a journey they were forced to make by the Tokugawa Shogunate as a means of being kept loyal and under control. They travelled with a large retinue and separate inns were provided for the followers, dependent on their status. In turn, as traffic increased along these routes, from travelling merchants, peddlers and tourists, more inns were established. Not surprisingly, men looked for entertainment and so would search the nearest town for food and fun, including women. In order to cut down on this lewdness, the Tokugawa Shogunate decreed that inns must serve dinner and thereby halt the need for men to leave the premises. Hence started the practice of serving dinner and breakfast as part of the stay.

When a traveller arrived, he would be shown to his room and offered tea. Before dinner, he could take a hot bath. After a dinner, a maid would clear away the food and lay out the futon for sleeping. In the morning, the guest would be woken for breakfast that again was served in his room.

This was Japan's *tatemae* spirit manifest as a way of life. Where everything was perfect. Both guests and staff knew exactly how to conduct themselves. For several days, we had lived a ritualised romantic life. And that's why foreigners are not encouraged to visit traditional *ryokan* and baths as it is felt that they will disrupt the *tatemae*. Not deliberately but because they don't know what to do. They will become embarrassed, do the wrong things, bathe in an incorrect manner, not eat the food, complain and disrupt the harmony.

At twelve o'clock, midday, the local clock tower chimed a sixty-second version of 'Green Sleeves'. We were in the heart of Kyushu, Japan's southernmost main island, staying in a small, but well-known spa called Yufuin, a town largely retaining its bucolic character and, because it was out of season, remaining pleasantly quiet. But our first favourable impressions weren't entirely accurate. The shops we admired from a distance on arriving turned out to be tacky souvenir and craft stores; a handful of coaches disgorged elderly but aggressive day-trippers. The lake, one of the sights to see, had a small but elegant wooden shrine on one side, traditional houses on the other but the largest building was a French restaurant looking like a prefabricated pastiche of a Swiss villa.

Close to this shrine, three girls stood shivering in the cold air, smoking cigarettes with snatched and hurried inhalations. When they saw me glance at them, they immediately stamped them out. Why were they embarrassed?

We stayed at the Tamanoyu *ryokan*. It first opened in 1953 as a rest home for a sect of *rinzaishu* Zen Buddhism. Later in 1975, it was reconstructed as a *ryokan* and was now a rustic but timeless complex of wooden houses, linked by covered passageways to annex, restaurants and pool. When we arrived, day tourists crowded around the outside, snapping pictures. To their profit, the *ryokan* now encouraged non-staying visitors by opening up the restaurants, and shop to visitors and not just guests.

Once we had weaved our way through the throng, our shoes were taken from us and we were politely shown into a lounge where a log fire glowed in a wood-burning stove. Over the last few years, I had experienced a log fire so infrequently that the smell of charred wood and smoke resurrected fond and hitherto forgotten memories of England. We were asked to sit down; a pot of green tea (*ocha*) was brought in, accompanied by small plates of *kaki* in syrup, and hot towels (*o-shibori*) so we could freshen our hands and face. Immediately we began to relax under a hypnotic spell.

Our journey had capped the year. As usual, Satoko was obliviously slow to get ready; we bickered and only just made the flight on time. At Tokyo's

Haneda Airport, the security team had confiscated my Swiss Army knife from my hand baggage due to some recently introduced and petty regulation. (This was the end of 1999, two years before 9/11.) That these knives were on sale at airports around the world, and only last week I had carried one on a JAL international flight just heightened my annoyance. Yes, at the other end, at Oita Airport, it was waiting to be collected when I emerged from the baggage hall but the principle grated and it continued to irritate me.

Fortunately, the onward drive to Yufuin was uneventful even if there was a constant drizzle of rain that made driving along narrow mountain roads more hazardous. We hired a Prius, the hybrid electric/petrol car then recently introduced by Toyota (and before it became fashionable): roomy, frugal with petrol, comfortable and a perfect car for my future retirement (a descendant of this particular model anyway as I didn't intend to retire quite yet.) Admittedly it was plainly obvious this wasn't a straightforward petrol engine and, from time to time, the engine noise and pull had traits more akin to that of a milk float but, despite initial misgivings, I found even going up the steep mountain roads of central Kyushu didn't stretch the car. The brakes were sharp, the steering accurate, and the road holding on the wet and hairpin roads surpassed what I expected. The only downside? Ugly little runt was the perfect description.

On the way, we stopped for lunch at a back street *Fugu* (Puffer fish) restaurant in the garish, seaside town of Beppo. An excellent start to our holiday: we ate thickly sliced (compared to Tokyo's thin) sashimi, all parts of the skin and organs and enjoyed thick, twice fried fritters of thick white flesh. As Kitaoji Rosanjin, one of Japan's most important twentieth-century potters wrote, 'The taste of *fugu* is incomparable. If you eat it three or four times, you are enslaved.... Anyone who declines it for fear of death is really a pitiable person.' The sashimi was arranged to resemble the petals of a chrysanthemum, the flower of death in Japan. About half a dozen people die every year from *fugu* poisoning, but if truth were told, they are amateurs who prepare the fish themselves and end up eating their Last Supper.

We also ate the liver; where much of the deadly poison is found. In most of Japan's prefectures, eating the liver is banned. But not here – though it needs a highly skilled chef to cut away the poisonous sacs. Fortunately, he turned out to be one such chef and I'm still alive. If he'd made a mistake, I would have been poisoned by the neurotoxin, tetrodoxin. Within minutes of ingestion, I would suffer from weakness, a tingling tongue followed by nausea, diarrhoea and sweating. Then paralysis would spread through my body and I would be thrown into horrible spasms and convulsions. Within twenty-four hours I would have choked to death as my respiratory system failed.

To accompany the meal we drank warm sake laced with black *fugu* fins. (Usually warm sake – as drunk in the West – is a bit naff but there are times in Japan when it is called for.)

Besides the food, the other marvel was the gnarled ancient microwave, possibly one of the first to be sold, whenever that was (thirty years ago or something?), and looking more like an ancient valve radio than a piece of high-tech kitchen gadgetry. I asked if it was still used and was told yes.

Back to our *ryokan*: after we'd finished the tea and sweets and signed the guest register, we were shown to our rooms. Our refuge for the next two days was a nest of warm and inviting smells: sweet tatami and cedar mixed with the steam that drifted from our own private *o-foru* (indoor hot bath) and which had been filled, ready for our arrival.

Our rooms overlooked a garden where the trees had lost their leaves, and the shrubs and grass pale and lifeless. As the sun disappeared (and didn't appear again for another two days), the already limp colours drained entirely: the boughs became a mesh of black against the greys of a darkening sky until even these colours disappeared to leave only formless black.

In an interview, I had recently read, a Dr Ryuko Ishikawa said. 'When you go to a foreign city like Tokyo – with its stifling crowds, people layered one on top of the other on trains, horrendous traffic and lack of living space – the entire experience grates on your nerves, exacerbates anxiety, and tends to force you to react emotionally.'

Stress is a noxious beast that manifests in many forms but has just as many ways to counter it. I found that for me, I had to find a sanctuary where I could contemplate the simplest things.

From this room, I stared for an hour, without boredom, at the drops of silvered rain trickling down the trees and listened to the rain beat an irregular tap-tap-tap on the roof; lying on the floor, naked, wrapped within the comfort of a thick duvet.

In the evening, we had our first *kisecki* (formal) meal of the holiday, sitting in our room whilst the rain continued to drizzle outside and a dense mist formed. The food was as healthy and as delicious as we would have expected:

luscious but simple dishes, with the minimum of preparation, based on local mountain produce: crunchy vegetables, '*jidori*' chicken, freshly stunned trout, a slab of local beef, glistening berries and fruit: both filling and cleansing at the same time.

On our first full day, we strolled alongside the streams that criss-crossed this small town. We stopped for morning coffee at a coffee house, run by an elderly woman whose daughter, she told me, enjoyed visiting England and travelled there whenever she could. The dainty interior was a mismatch of crafts and plants, ceramics and knick-knacks. She played a selection of Caribbean music on an early version of a hi-fi system. (I gained the impression, that Kyushu was a working museum of early Japanese electronics.) Accidentally, distracted from reading a map, I knocked my cup over and, without hesitation, she brewed another without charge.

Everywhere in Yufuin, we found a delightful innocence, a desire, so it seemed, to make the town the most pleasant in the world. Close to the *ryokan* was an art museum dedicated to Kei Satoh, an artist originally from Hiroshima but who moved to Yufuin after travelling round Japan. During his lifetime, he was practically unknown and only after his death from cerebral paralysis did his fame slowly spread but not far, for the sad truth was that his art wasn't that good. But nonetheless, this museum had been built.

The museum opened in 1991, designed by the architects' collective, Atelier Zo, and a perfect final resting place for Satoh's art; a place to wander, not to be intimidated. A wooden building based on sound ecological and energy-sustaining principles, it sprang out of yet merged with the earth. Within the grounds, a healing *onsen* had been built, albeit now a little decrepit and ragged round the edges, but faithfully reflecting the environmental concerns of the town.

Even the local evening paper was printed using a soy-based ink on recycled paper.

Walking through the town, we saw many feral cats; signs that said don't feed them, and rubbish containers designed to be cat-proof. The cats may be a constant menace but the sentimental, animal-loving inhabitants of Yufuin wouldn't have them destroyed. On the other hand, many houses kept dogs outside, securely chained but still capable of scaring off a cat – and tourists – with a ferocious bark.

The local river was a bird-watchers' paradise, at least for amateurs such as ourselves: we saw territorial waders, one with a yellow belly and then ten yards further down one with a black and white belly. Two competing slim elegant white ebus tried to scare off each other with a sound that sounded like and was louder than two drunks vomiting outside a pub. In contrast, there was a flock of politely twittering schoolgirl-like sparrows, and a haughty, schoolmasterly heron waited patiently for a fish to swim past.

On our final night, we ate not in our room, but in the *ryokan's* restaurant. The food was too good and too much. The grilled beef fell apart when eaten, the flesh sweeter and more tender than I'd ever eaten before. The vegetables, the local beer, the milky raw sake made for a memorable and tipsy meal which we finished by eating cake and pudding in the lounge, in front of that spitting and crackling fire.

The next day we travelled to the second *onsen*.

Unlike yesterday, the sun had appeared and as we drove along the almost deserted expressway, we could see tall rugged mountains jutting up from the plain, like a row of ferocious shark's teeth. We were noticing that in Kyushu, there was a greater sense of distance and space than seen in the countryside on Honshu (Japan's main island).

We hadn't planned a specific itinerary; we headed north-east and stopped at what seemed to be an interesting shrine on the outskirts of Usa. Not knowing what to expect, we discovered a complex so huge yet so simple that it was breathtaking. Being the middle of winter, there were few visitors. We could not only enjoy the buildings without distraction, most of which were restored to their original vivid and always shocking orange colour, but we could also appreciate in solitude the cedar and maple woods, the latter still densely cloaked in the most beautiful copper and red leaves. With such serenity surrounding us, it seemed indolent when we shook a branch to create an autumn leaf shower that fell around our shoulders.

That we should be jolted out of our idyllic peace was thus surprising. In the centre of the complex was a small lake. As we walked towards it, a group of geese didn't move away but instead loudly honked as if in warning. Satoko noticed first. She pointed to something hanging from a line over the water. I couldn't make out what it was; Satoko thought it might be a child's kite caught on an electricity cable that stretched to an island. But, walking closer, we saw a bird ensnared in a fishing line. A magnificent owl had become completely tangled, trapped several feet above the water, its wings and legs grotesquely twisted. As we approached it started to struggle, frightened by our presence. No, not frightened but terrified.

What could we do? Quickly we realised it was impossible to reach out from the bank; we might be able to wade in or if we could find a pole we might be able to snag the line and swing it towards us. But we couldn't find anything of sufficient length. Satoko then saw a group of workman. She dashed off to ask for assistance whilst I stayed and tried to reassure the owl by telling it that help was at hand.

It hung forlornly from the line, closing its eyes and I almost cried at its pathetic helplessness. As a nocturnal creature it must have become trapped a number of hours before. Now it was past midday and I was surprised we were the first to notice. Hadn't earlier visitors seen it? Cynically I thought perhaps they had but ignored the problem.

Satoko returned with a workman who, when he understood the difficulty, ran in to a nearby wood, returning a few minutes later with a long bamboo pole. He split the end and, with one deft swing, was able to hook the line and reel it and the bird on to the bank.

The line had wound tightly around the owl's wings, body, legs and talons. Gradually we cut and pulled it away, afraid, but finding that the fishhook at the end had not punctured the skin but had only caught in the feathers. The owl neither struggled nor attempted to bite us. Once all the line had been cut and the bird untangled, it appeared uninjured but no doubt shocked by the ordeal.

The moment of release would confirm if all was well. We stood back and, with a ruffle of its feathers, it swooped with massive wing beats into the wood and was lost from our sight forever.

As we strolled round the rest of the shrine, we felt we'd completed a good deed. If we hadn't spotted the bird, it would have surely perished within a few hours. (And I like to think, as well, that the geese were deliberately attempting to draw out attention to the bird's plight.)

But our good deed paled to insignificance when, on the final leg of our short journey, we stopped at the village of Yabaky to walk through a half-mile-long tunnel, cut single-handed through the cliffs by a monk some three hundred years ago. A monumental task of goodwill. In the seventeenth century, the village had only limited access to the outside world because of the high and sheer cliffs that blocked the route when the river, along which the village grew up, was swollen. The monk decided to dig a tunnel for the benefit of the villagers. Whilst the villagers ridiculed him for his efforts, he toiled alone for thirty years and, when his job was done, he was blind and crippled. Only then were his monumental achievements appreciated. The villagers made him an honoured citizen. Today his heroic story is told to all schoolchildren across Japan as an example of the moral perfection of man and, in the village, he is remembered with his own shrine and two life-sized statues showing a thin, bearded figure, one arm raised, holding a hammer. As we walked through the tunnel, carved out of solid rock, it was nigh on impossible to fathom the goodness of one man that did this and we talked at length about the virtues of man as we headed towards our destination.

The second *ryokan* was new, but built in a traditional fashion by the owners, a construction company. They used it as showcase for the artisan woodworking skills of their carpenters. At the basis of Japanese construction techniques is *tsugi*, a system of wood construction that uses dovetailed pliant joints that are extremely strong whilst being flexible in order to withstand tremors. The Tensui *ryokan* celebrated this craft from the massive posts and beams hewn from trunks that were the core of the structure through to the built-in furniture and the delicate *shoji* screens.

Our room had its own, private outdoor pool (*rotenburo*); and the first time I used it I was almost scolded when I slid in without poking a toe in the water first. A stupid thing to do. I jumped out shouting, my lower legs as red as a boiled lobster. By the next morning, the water had cooled down, my legs were less tender and I could float comfortably for an hour, dreaming of nothing and watching a copper-breasted bird preen itself.

The food here was simply overwhelming: both quality and quantity. By the end of our two-day visit we'd eaten turtle, sashimi horsemeat (lots of it), crab, lobster, giant cockles, tuna, tongue, beef, raw chicken, eggs, all kinds of fish, mountain vegetables, tofu of all varieties as well as local beer to wash it down. (This diversity according with the government's advice that people eat at least thirty different food items a day, recommended since the Second World War as a means of ensuring a balanced diet among the population.)

But what does raw horsemeat look and taste like? Thick, deep red, bloody and very, very rich.

After two nights, we left, stuffed to the gills, wondering how we could ever eat again.

Late afternoon. After several wrong turns, we reached the spa village of Kurokawa having driven through a deep and stunning valley to reach there: mountains and streams, rivers and trees tinted deep gold by the setting sun – when we stopped for an ice cream, the colours reminded both of us of our schooldays. But as we reached the area around Kurokawa, the countryside changed dramatically. The mountains lost their blanket of trees and were covered instead by tall brown pampas grass, a landscape I hadn't associated with Japan.

The *ryokan* was renowned for its pools, cut by the owner, into the mountainside (a modern day monk). No bad thing, it was the most traditional and basic of the three *ryokan* on this trip.

The first full day we spent in the inn exploring the pools and gardens. Two chickens lived in the grounds: one cock and one hen. I was told the hen supplied the eggs for breakfast but that struck me as untrue as the number of eggs needed would outstrip even the most productive bird. Sensibly, the chickens remained close to the water pumping machinery, enjoying the warmth from the steam leaking from rusting pipes. The cock was the bigger of the two, and the more inquisitive. I noticed that it had a huge swollen bottom, which looked as if weeks of shit had accumulated around it. Was it constipated? Should I grab the clump of shit and try to wrench it off? But if someone walked past and saw me naked, pulling at a chicken's bottom, lord knows what they might think.

Deciding not to explore the cock's posterior, I stretched out comfortably, naked (bar a strategically placed cloth), on a bench alongside an outdoor fire where two huge timbers glowed. The undisturbed chickens pecked for non-existent food around my feet, blindly pecking at anything – leaf, rock chips, and their own shit – incapable of differentiating muck from food.

I had just emerged from one of two hot pools found in the claustrophobic cave carved by the owner. A commendable achievement but once inside, with my vision obscured by steam, and sulphur scraping at my sinuses, my thoughts turned to the nightmare of being trapped behind tons of rock after an earthquake. I imagined boiling water cascading around me. How long would I last before being boiled alive? Or would I drown first or be suffocated by the sulphurous gases?

Cowardice convinced me to instead use the outdoor – and mixed – pool; a most unusual arrangement as usually they are segregated. Three kids noisily played there, disturbing the usual placid air: two young girls and their brother jumped on top of their dad, glistening bums riding in the air as they slipped over one another like dolphins. As I stepped into the water, they looked at me and shouted, in English, 'Hello.'

Mixed bathing has historic precedents in Japan but gradually died out during the Meiji era when the desire to westernise the country made such supposedly uncivilised practices undesirable.

Gradually it has been making a return – although the majority of *onsen* were still single sex – first among elderly couples but now among younger people too. Neither Satoko nor I were embarrassed at displaying our charms to an on-looking and curious world.

'I was worried about being stared at first,' said Suzuki, a girl in her early thirties, who was soaking next to me.

I would like to describe her in detail but only her head poked above the water.

'But I found people were friendlier and talked to each other,' continued her friend.

'Somehow the conversation is more interesting in a mixed *onsen*.'

'But I still don't tell my friends. They think that mixed bathing means strange sex.'

Until the family had left, the two women hung back in the shadows but they were now happy to move forward and hold a conversation.

'What do you like about *onsen*?' one of them asked.

I paused and rather than say something about the wonder of soaking in such a purifying manner I said, 'It's because this is the one place in Japan, that you're not handed a card when you meet someone. Here we are anonymous, naked and it really doesn't matter who we are or what we do. You don't know me from Adam and yet you're happy that we share this bath and soak. We have no pretensions here.'

They looked at me rather strangely.

In this simple inn, dinner was at six o'clock and could only be taken in the communal dining room. We sat among a group of all-male company workers loudly enjoying an end-of-year trip. They drank plum wine, beer, cold and hot sake (one swiftly after the other) and, although the meal had hardly begun, they were already bleary eyed, tousled-haired and red-cheeked. We cooked our food on an open charcoal fire. (That might explain the red cheeks of the men.) Big lumps of white-hot charcoal heated a thick iron plate: a quality of heat we would love to achieve – but never could – at home.

Fat river fish, swollen with roe, were skewered and set in the ash to curl and bake slowly whilst cuts of raw beef and vegetables were flashed grilled and sealed on the plate in seconds, then dipped in a sweet miso sauce. (This region preferred a sweeter sauce to that found in Tokyo.) Classic country cuisine, leaving us with a great sense of well-being.

On our second day, we visited a nearby pork farm, buying jambon and Spanish-style sausages that were surprisingly authentic; and at another farm, called the Guernsey Farm, we licked rich, soft ice cream and received the evil eye from a pissed-off sheep after feeding a goat, not the sheep, with the last piece of cone.

Close by was a beer village, a modern microbrewery, set on its own, on the edge of a mountain range with a wonderful view across the plateau and the distant ragged top of the Mt Aso volcano. The brewery was constructed almost entirely of wood and we sat and ate behind a large window, gazing out across the Aso-Kuju National Park – an area that was part mixed arable with traditional rice, tobacco and cereal crops, and part wild pampas.

They brewed four types of beer: a very light wheat, a typical pilsner, a brown ale and a dark brew rich in tobacco and nutty flavours. We sampled and enjoyed all four with, as a side order, three types of sausage and mustard.

Our waitress was short and, unusually in Japan, rather surly and perhaps because of this I noticed she wore heavy almost theatrical pancake make-up. Whether to conceal her age or an attempt to obscure unsuccessfully a big black mole, I couldn't decide. And, for such a short woman, she had large, thick-fingered hands.

That night, the sky was clear, with stars thickly pasted over it; perfect for stargazing. As we walked out of the inn, I banged my head hard – with a loud crack – on a low wooden beam. Attributing this mishap to the sheep's evil eye, I quickly dipped my head into a nearby pool of cold water, used a metal handrail as a cold compress and, in the morning, found I'd avoided severe swelling and bruising. Too bad, sheep, better luck next time with your curse.

Nonetheless, the stargazing experience was worth the immediate pain: the stars were magical, so abundant, bright and clear in the cold cloudless sky and, I thought, possibly better than I had ever seen before. But more than that, we both felt that we were closer to them than the earth. It was one of those simple pleasures that can mean so much.

This was the last night of our trip.

The next day we drove reluctantly, and at times in miserable silence, to the airport, passing through the mountains of the Aso volcano. Mt. Aso was not one but five peaks nestled in the middle of an almighty caldera 128 km in circumference. We took a cable car (or ropeway as they're called in Japan) to one of the peaks, Nakadake, topped by a very active, rumbling crater. Several times on the journey we lurched to a stop, everyone gasped as the wind violently swung the car, suspended in mid-air, above a terrain so bleak and inhospitable that only a coarse, purple coloured grass grew among the rusty pink rocks.

When we reached the summit, nothing could have prepared us for the force of the wind, so fierce that we were pressed against the low restraining fence. Normal movement was impossible, even to lift my arm to take a photo or opening my mouth to speak, and even if I could say something, nothing could be heard over the screaming gale. We clutched one another tightly to stop ourselves, as we imagined it, from being cast over the edge. Five hundred feet below, the bottom of the crater was filled with a steaming peppermint-coloured cauldron of water. This was my first visit to the top of a volcano; the sheer spectacle was humbling and the scenery more rugged and alien than I had seen before; the rock pummelled and ripped into jagged cliffs full of colour: coppers, purples, greens, reds, browns and yellows.

It was too cold to stay long and, in any case, the outer mountainous rim was cloaked with a heavy blanket of storm-laden clouds. Just in time, we started the final leg of the journey. As we drove towards the caldera's edge the wind raged and howled, pounding and bending double the pampas grass and bamboo, and torrential rain beat down making the windscreen wipers all but useless.

But as we broke through the western rim, the cloud suddenly disappeared and we were cast under the watery rays of the winter's sun until finally we reached the airport and the end of the trip.

I sat down in a small armchair and opened a book of photographs by Andres Serrano. Serrano had signed the first page, in a large untidy scrawl, with a dedication to the owner of the Tawaraya *ryokan* in Kyoto. Pictured inside were his most famous studies including photographs of corpses laid out in a morgue, people who had met violent ends, their bodies grey, bruised and mutilated.

I faced a window that overlooked a small, enclosed Japanese garden, in a small tranquil room, a place of almost complete silence, the walls lined with an enviable collection of books on art and architecture, many signed by the author.

As I turned the book's pages, studying another photograph of a murder victim, I wondered how many other guests had taken the opportunity to read it.

For most, including the many travel writers who had visited and then wrote their impressions, the Tawaraya was, as one said, 'a place where there are no rough edges'. So, had I found an edge after all? Why was a book of such violent and controversial images kept for visitors? This was so typical of Japan. Behind the perfect exterior, a place of peace and serenity, a remnant of old Japan, an escape from the world that it kept at arms' length through thick exterior walls, the casual visitor would stop seeing deeper. Most guests would fail to see the darkness beyond the faultless surface nor find this book; they would miss too the book by Robert Maplethorpe, photographs of naked black men with erect penises as hard as hewed teak. I knew this because both books showed scant sign of being read. Most visitors would only see and remember the conventionally beautiful – vases, flower arrangements, pictures – adorning the rooms and public areas, all painstakingly chosen to reflect the season. They would sit in the garden and not notice the grotesque eyesore – the apartment block – that had thoughtlessly been built to rub against the outer wall of the *ryokan*. They would not climb to the top floor, look out over the rooftops of Kyoto and see the city in all its ugliness, spoilt for eternity by the greediness of bureaucrats and corporations. But then sometimes, to contradict myself, I wondered whether this imperfection and blight was no more than a large-scale and modern example of *wabi sabi*, the ability to look at something worn, imperfect and still see, understand and appreciate beauty. An ability, in its purest form, to look at a worn piece of pottery and understand that this has come from the countless times it had been held. To hold the shabby fabric of a coat and understand it reflected the daily viscitudes of life. Or knowing the patina of an old piece of furniture was the history of a family who had sat round the table, eating their meals day after day, year after year. And the frayed desecrated skyline was the result of millions of people's lives being lived.

Wasuke Okazaki, a textile merchant, founded Tawaraya around 1700. Originally an outpost of his trading company – selling rice and cloth and, at the same time, offering hospitality to customers – over time, it became an inn and its trading role was lost.

The inn was still owned by the family, run by Mrs Toshi Okazaki Satou, the eleventh generation, and was lauded as one of the great hotels of the world, the best inn in Kyoto, if not Japan. Who could argue? The design faultless, the attention to detail so meticulous that it would be irrationally pleasurable to discover a mistake.

But we couldn't find one. How could you fault a place where, in our room, hung a scroll, on which one of the most famous gardeners in Japanese history – the gardener who had laid out the design in the Silver Pavilion – had written a poem in the most delicate calligraphy. The inn was full of such treasures: antique and modern, artistic and functional.

The bar of soap, for example, was milled exclusively for the inn: the fragrance filling the bathroom, mingling deliciously with the scent of the bamboo bathroom floor, the cedar bathtub and the bitter sweetness of tatami mats.

It is a rare visitor to Japan, that doesn't learn to appreciate the understated nature of their art and decoration. As Hearn wrote:

'After having learned — merely by seeing, for the practical knowledge of the art requires years of study and experience, besides a natural, instinctive sense of beauty — something about the Japanese manner of arranging flowers, one can thereafter consider European ideas of floral decoration only as vulgarities. This observation is not the result of any hasty enthusiasm, but a conviction settled by long residence in the interior. I have come to understand the unspeakable loveliness of a solitary spray of blossoms arranged as only a Japanese expert knows how to arrange it — not by simply poking the spray into a vase, but by perhaps one whole hour's labour of trimming and posing and daintiest manipulation — and therefore I cannot think now of what we Occidentals call "a bouquet" as anything but a vulgar murdering of flowers, an outrage upon the colour-sense, a brutality, an abomination.'

Our suite had three main rooms separated by sliding doors. Two were laid with tatami mats; the third carpeted in Western style, had chairs of a simple Scandinavian design but juxtaposed with an ancient wooden chest, covered with a rough strip of indigo-dyed hemp, serving as a table.

The larger of the rooms opened onto a walled garden. A cool refuge despite the street temperature rising above the mid-twenties, the sun – largely obscured by a canopy of bamboo and maple – restricted to throwing an abstract pattern of leaves on a wall, a series of grey washes like the most delicate of ink paintings.

If we wished to practise our calligraphy, we could do so with an ink stone and brush contained in a lacquer box. Modern pens and paper were found in a second lacquered box. A more up-to-date means of communication – the telephone – was covered and hidden with a patterned cloth. Much of the twenty-first century was disguised in this manner: the mini fridge, TV, the security box, and toiletries in the bathroom.

We had arrived before check-in time so we walked round nearby narrow streets, congested with traffic, hot, sweaty and overflowing with the commercial life of Kyoto. We strolled along the shopping street, Teramachi, a student haunt with cheap clothes shops, record and book stores, and then turned into Nishiki Street, famed for its hundreds of food shops lain out with fish, tea, spices, pickles, sweets and rice. Greedily, we bought rice and red bean paste sweets, to bring back to our room.

Check-in time at a *ryokan* was always at three p.m.; check-out usually at ten a.m. This left ample time for the room to be prepared. However, guests were always requested not to arrive too late as dinner was early and never delayed. This was all part of the ritual and custom of staying in a *ryokan*.

Having discarded our Western clothes, put on *yukata*, poured green tea, wiped the sweat from our faces and hands with the hot towel brought in by a maid, we lay down and ate the thick sticky sweets. Minutes later, mid-afternoon, we were fast asleep.

Before dinner, we soaked in the room's cedar tub. The bathroom was in fact three rooms: the first had two washbasins; off this were a separate toilet, and then a third room where the cedar tub and shower were found – this room also had a sliding full-length window that could be opened on to a small private garden of slender bamboo and twisted vines.

Our maid was called Suzuki. That night she served dinner dressed in a mustard-coloured *kimono*, tied with a turquoise belt and with a deep brown backpack.

We opened the windows so we felt we were eating in the garden and so that, other than the sound of our own voices, all we could hear was the trickle of water through a bamboo pipe into a stone trough.

After dinner, we climbed steep stairs to the roof, to look at a crescent moon suspended over the black rooftops of Kyoto. The modern city had all but disappeared into an untidy heap of flattened dark shapes, with no form or age to them. We might have been back in old Kyoto, at a time when it was the capital of Tokyo. We held hands and gently kissed, and then returned downstairs to slip under the crisp linen futon.

We stayed for one night. The next morning, as we drove away in a taxi, five of the *ryokan's* staff stood on the street bowing until the taxi turned a corner and we had disappeared from view.

Chapter Three

Escape to the Noto Peninsular

'I liked its vowel colour; I liked its consonant form, the liquid *n* and the decisive *t*. Whimsically, if you please, it suggested both womanliness and will. The more I looked the more I longed, until the desire carried me not simply off my feet, but on to them.'

In 1888, the writer and astronomer Percival Lowell had the fancy to travel to Noto, for no other reason than having seen it on a map and liking its name. When he asked friends whether they knew of the place, they all professed ignorance other than it was out of the way.

Satoko had not been there either. And when I asked both Japanese and Western friends not one had visited the region. So that was it. We decided to explore.

Why, when taking a long-distance car journey did we never pre-plan the route, I asked myself at the end of our trip? When I was a child, before every family holiday, my father would draw up his own detailed map listing road numbers, towns, villages and landmarks, even if we had made the same journey many times before. Forty years later I could still recall, for example, the sequence of towns to North Devon: Oxford, Farringdon, Swindon, Devizes, Frome, Shepton Mallet, Glastonbury, Taunton, South Molton, Barnstable and finally Muddiford. When my job demanded I flew on business trips, I would ask my secretary to type up a detailed itinerary with flight numbers, car pick-up times, hotel names, addresses, telephone and fax numbers, contact details of all the companies or people I was going to meet, times of meetings as well as any social arrangements that had been booked. Call it retentive, but I never missed a flight or an appointment in fifteen years of intense travel. But this morning Satoko and I loaded the car with two suitcases: warm clothes (for it was winter), champagne and caviar to celebrate

Christmas, a laptop and other sundry items. Lowell had taken canned food, a bottle of whiskey and beer, as well his own bedding – he preferred to sleep under sheets and blankets rather than a futon. And, of course, he had to take his passport that carried details of his route. Both of us had cameras and books.

I started the engine and only then keyed our destination into the satellite navigation system, discovering for the first time the route and how far we had to travel. As we were about to experience (again, I might confess), modern technology was a seductive tool that perniciously builds a lazy habit of total reliance that can catch you unawares.

The suggested route to Ishikawa Prefecture and the Noto Peninsular – on the west and opposite coast – appeared on the screen: a blue line superimposed over a map of Japan, skirting close to Yokohama, Nagoya and Kyoto, before turning north towards Ishikawa. The distance was over 550 kms and the computer gave an estimated arrival time of seven-twenty in the evening (it was now just after ten in the morning). An unpleasant surprise. We had expected to arrive mid-afternoon. The computer's recommendation was too indirect and long, we snorted to each other, so I keyed in another city, one sure to take us in a northerly direction from Tokyo and then west over the backbone of the Japan Alps. Annoyingly, the distance remained over 500km, and the computed arrival time still in the evening. 'Rubbish,' said Satoko again, 'it's wrong, we should arrive by three.' (As this second route seemed intuitively less circuitous, we decided it was the better of the two.) It was also the route that Lowell had taken.

Off on holiday: eight days of relaxation and indulgence; visiting four different locations around the Noto Peninsular, and spending as much time as we could, luxuriating in hot springs and eating good food.

Soon we were to escape Tokyo, we told each other with knowing nods and smiles, and quicker than Lowell – who on the first leg of his journey had missed the train.

Following the navigation system's instructions, we joined the Expressway at Meguro, just minutes from home. Tokyo's Expressways are elevated dual carriageways that carve through the city, their route dictated by where they could be built and not by traffic needs. Even outside Tokyo, they were often elevated above ground, nearly always no wider than a two-lane dual carriageway, and their routing indirect – although this a function of immovable mountains that foil construction. Despite their limitations, I hoped to remain on them for most of the journey. Driving would be significantly easier as regular A roads in Japan are notoriously clogged with traffic.

Finding the Expressway clear of traffic, I pushed my foot down hard on the accelerator, exhilarating in the sense of speed, with sun streaming through the windscreen with a characteristic – for winter – cloudless blue sky overhead. Our holiday had begun and we were flying along at a pace rarely enjoyed.

An hour or so later, our out-of-date car navigation system left us stranded in the middle of Saitama, a depressing outer suburb of Tokyo. The Expressway had abruptly stopped without any warning, the navigation system was in a muddle, the automated voice in a panic, and we were on single-lane urban roads clogged with cars and lorries, and with traffic signals every fifty to a hundred metres. An alternative Expressway was less than fifteen miles ahead but took more than an hour to reach. (The Japanese Government might spend trillions of yen on construction to boost – ha-ha – the ailing economy but their road-building programme was hopeless. Tokyo still can't claim a decent complete arterial or ring-road system). Once reaching it, we were confident we were now on the correct road, one taking us over the backbone of the Japan Alps towards Niigata, after which we would follow the coastline down to our first night's stop at Kanazawa. The irritation and frustrations faded quickly away. Driving in Japan was nothing if not an emotional, steering-wheel slapping roller coaster.

To our left, we could clearly see the distant snow-covered peak of Mount Fuji; Satoko said it was a good omen when the peak wasn't covered in cloud. Ahead of us, the undulating foothills of the Alps were bathed in the slanted slats of a winter's sunshine. Not before long, they had been reached and the road started to ascend into open countryside and towards high peaks. We had driven for three hours from Central Tokyo and had only just left its outer fringe, we were behind schedule and had at least another 350 kms ahead of us.

As we made our ascent, thick grey clouds were quickly descending, obliterating the higher slopes. From their colour, it was obvious they were pregnant with snow. One minute we were enveloped in warm sunshine, the next snow began to fall and the higher we drove the thicker and more fatly globular it became.

Having only just left bright sunshine, we thought it impossible the snowfall could last for long. We were wrong. Soon the fields and forests around us looked impenetrable. Not that this made driving difficult, for as heavy as it was to our side, on the road the snow melted and traffic moved with little hindrance.

Until we joined a slow-moving queue. Had there been an accident? Was it because of deteriorating road conditions? Some minutes later, we reached a police checkpoint. They inspected the tyres of every car. Those with winter tyres were waved through. Those without had to put on snow chains in a nearby service area. We weren't short-sighted enough not to have packed chains, and that morning, I had watched, at Satoko's insistence, an instruction video on how to fit them. (After all, men hate to watch any type of instruction. Don't we know it without having to be shown?)

Although I wouldn't admit it to Satoko, it was fortunate I had, otherwise I would have floundered. The procedure was first to stretch the chains – actually, rubber and steel nets – by standing on one part, gripping the opposite side, and then heaving upwards to stretch them so they were bigger than – and could be slipped over – the tyre. Fortunately, I managed to fit the two chains over the rear wheels with ease, within minutes we were on our way, and I felt self-satisfyingly pleased with myself on accomplishing the task so quickly.

Still, I wondered, why the bother of fitting the chains? The road surface was still relatively clear – even if the snow was falling furiously – and ordinary tyres would have gripped without assistance.

'You're not an expert,' said Satoko, 'the police are. You don't have conditions like this in England.'

The surrounding countryside had turned into a classic picture-book snow scene: unblemished and pure white, the darker branches of the forest trees forming a tracery like delicate marguetry. As it looked so pretty I asked Satoko to shoot a video.

A few miles on, the snow unexpectedly turned nasty, now falling as if being hurled from the sky by a demon. All of a sudden, we saw fewer cars on the expressway; maybe many had decided to turn off and end their journey. Their absence was eerie and discomforting. Inside the car, we felt warm but the temperature outside had fallen to below zero – from 12°C when we left Tokyo. It was a horrible sticky wet snow, our wipers hardly cleared the windscreen and I knew now the chains were vital to stop the wheels skidding.

Then we reached a second police roadblock. They told us we had to remove the chains because we were about to pass through a long tunnel – they didn't explain why. We were directed off the road. I got out and froze. The wind had whipped up, and I had to kneel in snow as I stretched and pulled at the chains trying to manoeuvre them off. As easy as they were to put on, they were proving to be as difficult to remove. I had to yank and tug at them, both from the front and back of the wheel, stretching them bit by bit until they were bigger than the tyre, and then I could roll the car forward to remove them completely. That was the plan. In the video this took no more than a minute or two, but in real life, I was making little progress.

In the end, I had to jack up the rear of the car. Whereas everyone else made the switch in less than five minutes, I took half an hour. My jeans were sopping. My sodden gloves proved useless at keeping out water, and I threw them away in disgust.

Back in the car, at least I warmed up quickly and we set off through the tunnel. Yes, it was long and took us ten minutes to get through at something like a steady sixty km/hour. Perhaps the chains had to be removed to protect the road surface. It was annoying and I felt it unnecessary. They're the experts, Satoko kept reminding me. They know what's best. What do you know about winter driving? My hands tightened on the steering wheel.

Emerging at the far end of the tunnel, we were met with a wall of snow and once again directed off the road. To continue onwards we had to replace the chains. On, off and now on again. The snow was falling so heavily I could hardly see the other cars alongside me. My arms ached. My knees were sore, stiff and cold. The ground was covered in a thick freezing slush that once again I had to kneel in to fit and lock the chains over the wheels.

And once again, I had to laboriously jack up the rear of the car, first one side and then the other. As I'd thrown away the useless gloves, I had only rags to wrap around my hands so I could grasp the chains without them cutting into my flesh. I muttered a stream of invectiveness aimed at the police. Now one of the chains wouldn't tighten properly. The locking mechanism was crushed; perhaps I had run over it. I struggled to pull the chain tight, heaving it around the tyre, scraping my hand on the wheel arch, and swearing ever louder at the police, Japan and myself. Satoko was by now fed up with me. As far as she was concerned, I hadn't done my homework correctly and I was blaming everyone else for problems of my own making.

'Do you know best?' she asked.

'Yes I do.'

'As usual. What do Englishmen know of mountains?'

Of course, she was right but, instead, I told her how unhelpful she was being.

The car door slammed.

Finally, the chains were fixed in place. My legs and feet were soaked to the bone, and I could hardly move my fingers, they were so wet and cold. Back inside the car, I spent some minutes warming up before setting off. A few hundred yards on and a terrible rubbing noise erupted from one of the back wheels. I pulled over to the hard shoulder and discovered it came from the nearside wheel, the one wrapped by the chain with the broken mechanism. The chain was unwinding itself and was already half off. I had to try and get it back on and somehow lock it in place.

Despite increasing fatigue, this I managed – or so I thought. But the noise soon returned. We had no choice but to continue onwards; we couldn't turn round on the Expressway. Our only option was to drive to the next turn-off and decide what to do once there. Maybe it was best if we bought new chains. I kept a slow and steady forty km/hour. This didn't stop the chain flailing against the inside of the wheel arch with an awful racket but it seemed an optimum speed, making at least some progress whilst not having the chain spin off.

Neither of us spoke now. I just listened to the din hoping that if nothing else it would remain at the same level and not reach a pitch that could only mean trouble.

Perhaps a half-hour later we came to a junction, with a tollgate and a long queue of traffic. Were all cars and lorries left on the Expressway now doing the sensible thing and getting off? Clearly, the snow was causing havoc. High drifts had formed on both sides of the road and the road's surface lay hidden under impacted snow. But if we passed through the toll, we had no idea what would then happen. By now, it was late afternoon. We could be stuck in the traffic jam for hours; there was no indication how far the nearest town was from the tollgate and it was unlikely that we would easily find a shop selling chains. Another option: we could look for a hotel, stay the night, and continue the journey the next day in the hope that the snow had cleared but we didn't know if there were hotels close by.

Reluctantly we joined the end of the queue. Then I saw a car park. I pulled in and decided to attempt another temporary fix. I heaved and tugged; I didn't know whether I'd improved matters but something inside me told me to continue the journey and not leave the Expressway. I didn't want to be trapped here, in the middle of god knows where, with no idea whether the weather would be any better tomorrow. I spoke with Satoko and we decided to press on although what would happen if we broke down or got stuck we had no idea. At least the chain now made less noise.

And then luck was on our side: after a few miles, the snow began to fall less thickly until it stopped altogether. We were starting to descend the western slope of the Alps. I judged it unlikely that we would experience the same snow levels again and as soon as I found a safe place to pull up, I did and removed the chains, throwing them in to the boot of the car.

Lowell had enjoyed a less hectic journey. It had meant several overnight stops, and the train didn't go all the way as the engineering obstacles to build a line over the highest part of the mountains proved too much. So for part of the journey he had to take a horse, ferry, and stay in some inhospitable inns. Everywhere he stopped, he had to show his passport to a local policeman; he had to haggle with boat and carriage owners but also he found everywhere he went curious but friendly fellow travellers.

By now, it was sunset. We had a further 250 kms to drive.

Satoko worried we would hit snow again. At times, we both held our breath and daren't say anything when flashing orange and red overhead signs warned that chains were needed up ahead. I ignored them. The rain might have been heavy and made for grim driving but it was only rain. We kept going and eventually at eight p.m., ten hours after setting out, we reached the city of Kanazawa and our first stop, the New Grand Hotel. The car navigation system had been right after all with its estimated time of arrival. I joked (or was it choked) that miraculously it had anticipated the snow. Satoko shouted at me.

The New Grand Hotel in Kanazawa had a top floor restaurant with a sweeping view over the city. It had French pretensions and was grandly called Roi. As breakfast was included in the price of the room, we ate there both mornings listening to piped music: a strange arrangement of classics (the sort voted as Listeners' Top 100) interspersed with birdsong. Sometimes the birdsong would continue over the tune before fading out and then coming back as the last bars were played. Before the next melody, the birds would twitter for a minute or two and then a new tune would start.

(We could chose between a Japanese or Western breakfast. Lowell dislike Japanese breakfasts, describing them as 'the most cold, the most watery, and generally the most fishy in the world'. Only of the latter would I agree, and I was happy to have poached and grilled fish to start the day. No different than eating kippers.)

The restaurant's kitsch matched the rest of the hotel. On the outside, it looked boring and plain but on the inside, it had been transformed into a cringing cheap pastiche of European luxury. In our bedroom, hung from ornate brass fittings, thick brown velvet drapes, adorned with gold tassels, framed the window. The wallpaper was heavily embossed. There was a large French-style sofa upholstered in purple velvet. The room was separated from the entrance area and bathroom by an etched glass panel set in decorative metal work. All very *fin-de-siècle*, and clearly someone's ill-conceived idea of elegance and sophistication. But fun nonetheless. (We later saw a TV commercial for the place that pronounced it the most stylish wedding venue in Ishikawa Prefecture.)

Kanazawa's English language tourist brochure read, 'The city escaped bombing during World War 2 and so was able to preserve many old neighbourhoods and customs.' What a cheek. Most of Japan had been destroyed (including almost all the old neighbourhoods in Kanazawa) not by bombing sixty years ago but by the relentless demolition of old buildings and replacing them with tat. But then Japan suffers an irritating habit of shifting blame on to others for its own ill-doings.

After breakfast, we strolled round the old neighbourhoods and Kenroku Koen Garden, said to be one of the three most beautiful gardens in Japan.

Certainly, the name was apt and beautiful: Garden of the Six Sublimities. The six sublimities, the attributes of a perfect garden, were spaciousness, seclusion, artificiality, antiquity, water and broad views. This garden had them all in abundance. A panorama of scenes unfolded one by one as we walked round. Each had a special charm, bringing forward to the spectator a cycle of wholly natural vistas. Graceful pines might dominate one; the next had moving water, ponds and waterfalls; a third had paths winding through dense shrubs and opening on to lawns of bright green moss. (Isn't it odd that the Japanese know how to make any plant attractive whilst we in the West have a rabid desire to eliminate moss from our gardens?) At this time of the year, there was the added pleasure of Japanese Black Pines tied with *yuki-tsuri* (maypole-like poles and rope supports). A straw rope draped from a central pole tied and supported each branch for protection against the snow. They looked as though large umbrellas had been part opened, an effect rather like a 1950s' film-set for a Gene Kelly musical, and one that added further interest to the overall look, for this man-made spectacle, wholly functional in purpose, could still be made to look pretty.

To my untrained eye, Japanese gardens can look all too similar. They are built on a series of principles that had not changed over hundreds of years, repeated from one garden to the next. Sometimes I would succumb to a 'oh, not another bloody garden' reaction. But it didn't last. The serenity and perfection in these gardens – the natural planting, a ripple of water, a hidden teahouse and the mystery of the stone lanterns – ultimately never bored and instead I was left in awe. The Kenroku-en was no exception. Everyone who has visited Japan is seduced by its gardens. Hearn wrote,

> 'Each day, after returning from my college duties, and exchanging my teacher's uniform for the infinitely more comfortable Japanese robe, I find more than compensation for the weariness of five class-hours in the simple pleasure of squatting on the shaded veranda overlooking the gardens. Those antique garden walls, high-mossed below their ruined coping of tiles, seem to shut out even the murmur of the city's life. There are no sounds but the voices of birds, the shrilling of semi, or, at long, lazy intervals, the solitary plash of a diving frog. Nay, those walls seclude me from much more than city streets. Outside them hums the changed Japan of telegraphs and newspapers and steamships; within dwell the all-reposing peace of nature and the dreams of the sixteenth century. There is a charm of quaintness in the very air, a faint sense of something viewless and sweet all about one; perhaps the gentle haunting of dead ladies who looked like the ladies of the old picture-books, and who lived here when all this was new. Even in the summer light — touching the gray, strange shapes of stone, thrilling through the foliage of the long-loved trees — there is the tenderness of a phantom caress.

These are the gardens of the past. The future will know them only as dreams, creations of a forgotten art, whose charm no genius may reproduce.'

'In a Japanese Garden', *Atlantic Monthly*, July 1892

Visiting this garden was the sole reason we came to Kanazawa in the first place. Originally we planned to stay at a traditional *ryokan*, but they had messed up our booking, had taken a high-handed attitude about their mistake, and so Satoko decided we would instead stay at a cheap hotel for a couple of nights. (The *ryokan* had subsequently apologised and delivered a gift of cakes but even so Satoko refused to relent.) Despite the traumatic journey and the kitsch hotel, the garden had made it worthwhile.

The next morning I dumped the useless chains in a skip, and we began our drive along the west coast of the Noto Peninsula. No snow was forecast and our route didn't take us high into the mountains. We were cautiously optimistic that we would have an incident-free drive and no need of chains.

Initially, the coastline was flat and monotonous, the land separated from the sea by low-lying wind-blown sand dunes. At one point Satoko told me to take the Beach Driveway. I followed the signs to a long expanse of sand, the type of beach where land speed records were set sixty years ago and now the only beach in Japan where you were permitted to drive. This might have been fun in the right car – a four-by-four for example – but the Lexus wasn't built for such conditions and after the trauma with the snow chains, I wondered why Satoko wanted to attempt this. But the sand was firm, and I decided, so long as I maintained a steady speed, kept away from the water but not too close to the dunes, I would be safe.

(Though I couldn't escape the worry that at any moment the wheels could start to spin followed by the car digging inescapably in to the sand.)

I tried to assess the firmness of the sand as if with an expert eye. I kept a tight grip on the steering. I wanted to feel the movement of the wheels through it. I couldn't relax and enjoy the drive. After ten minutes, we eventually came to the exit road. I was audibly relieved as we drove back on to tarmac. 'That was fun,' I lied.

Further on, the coastline turned wild: steep cliffs of gashed red rock, with the sea rising up, pounding against their base and sending clouds of spray hovering in the air like dense smoke. Screeching seagulls and hawks wailed overhead, more hawks than I had ever seen in one place. We stopped at several designated scenic views, one of which was a favoured suicide spot: a spur that jutted over the sea with a drop of several hundred feet. It was a short walk from the road and, along the path, signs beseeched would-be suicides to turn round.

'If you are courageous enough to commit suicide you can face life,' one read.

We walked out onto the rock – it was like a large flat fingernail pointing accusingly across the ocean – but dared not stand closer than a few feet from its edge. A strong wind was gusting and we didn't want to become an unwitting statistic.

Far out to sea we could see one lone fishing boat being tossed in the heavy swell and on the horizon, a large cruise ship or ferry which, from this distance, looked to be making poor headway against the wind. Satoko thought it was probably en route to Pusan, Korea. For some reason this made me think about being on the far side of the Asia-Europe landmass, and I was momentarily struck by a sense of time and vast distance from home in England.

At the cliff's base so mighty were the waves hurling themselves against the rocks that at times it felt that the earth itself was heaving with some unspeakable pain and we might be shaken into the sea. I was glad to return to the sanctuary of the car.

Lowell had come to a similar place where the cliffs dropped sheer into the sea. He said that it was known as *oya shiradzu, ko shiradzu* a spot where the father no longer knows the child, nor the child the father as the fear of danger, of an unholy death by drowning, obliterates any other senses.

Inland, the countryside was one of the most unspoilt I had yet seen in Honshu. The Noto Peninsular was known for its heavy rainfall, and the bamboo, pines and agriculture were dense and vivid lush greens. The houses were large, grew from the ground and many were built in a traditional style: massive planks of unpainted wood formed the walls, and black glazed tiles the roofs. They were set in neat villages, nestled among the forest with none of the neon signs and the piles of discarded junk that disfigure many Japanese villages.

In a paradoxical way the countryside was a welcome contradiction to a recent quote from Koichi Kato, a prominent member of Japan's ruling Liberal Democratic Party. He admitted, 'Now there are no trees on our mountains. There are no vegetables, no woods, no fish.'

But, in fact, for most of the country he was right and the Noto Peninsular an exception. Later, in the middle of 2002, a scandal emerged that undermined Japan's environmental credentials, and in small part explained the deforestation that had been happening across most of the nation. It was discovered that forestry authorities on the island of Hokkaido had ignored illegal logging by Yamarin, a lumber company, in exchange for the company employing retired forestry officials. (The practice of bureaucrats being hired by companies and industries that they formerly supervised is known as *amakudari* – descent from heaven.)

Japan's answer to its economic woes was and continues to be construction. Build, build, build. For years, it had gradually destroyed the countryside and coastline through unplanned, unzoned industrialization. Across most of Honshu, the countryside was hideous and characterless.

Shortly after making his remarks on the desecration of Japan's beauty by construction, Kato's private secretary was charged with a tax evasion scandal. Saburo Sato was suspected of concealing several hundred millions of yen of income received from a transportation company and a talent agency that he owned. The authorities also believed that Sato received money from, yes you guessed it, construction firms, who bribed him in the hope of obtaining political favours and winning bids for public works.

Yet, whilst this despoilment continues apace, the government is promoting, harder than ever, the need for the country, particularly the young, to be more nationalistic and take greater pride in their country. Shouldn't a nation's nature be a fundamental part of this?

As we drove on the final leg of that day's journey, we passed through alternating patches of sharp sunshine and squalls of murky rain. The backdrop of cloud was a blue-grey, the sun was behind us and I told Satoko that these were perfect conditions for a rainbow. On cue, a fully formed and perfectly banded rainbow appeared, arching across the road, with its feet in the adjacent rice fields. At times, it drifted very close. Once it almost seemed we were right beneath it and that indeed we could leap out of the car, embrace it and unearth the crock of gold.

It was late afternoon when we reached the small town of Wajima on the northern and furthermost edge of the peninsular. This small fishing port was famous for being the 'Home of Lacquer Ware'.

Many small lacquer studios lined the main road into town but, disappointingly, most were closed. Today was the Emperor's Birthday and a national holiday. Eventually we found an open showroom, one that had a rather formal and hushed coffee shop attached to it, where even the public phone had been lacquer coated. We sipped coffee that cost seven pounds a cup, from plain lacquer cups that cost over £100 each if bought in the showroom. Even the sliver of a sugar spoon cost thirty pounds. However, the coffee was faultless and the cream pastries delicious.

In the showroom, a set of five black rice bowls, with a fine gold design of bamboo was priced at Y1, 000,000 or close to £1,500 apiece. The lacquer (a resinous sap) had been painstakingly applied, smoothed and polished layer after layer, and then gold, silver and mother of pearl added to create a rich lustrous finish. These were heirlooms that would last for centuries.

In contrast to this splendour, the *ryokan* was simple. For one night we didn't need anything fancy. From the outside, it looked much like a typically unattractive modern house. We stepped into the lobby and found ourselves in an amazing state of transformation: its walls and ceiling had been covered entirely with natural coloured washi paper, creating an effect that was splendidly graceful and serene. An old man, whom we assumed was the owner, came to greet us. Stooped and heavily lined, he looked over sixty but had attempted to hide his age by wearing one of the nastiest toupees I have seen. Maybe a dog had gnawed at it as it didn't have the appearance of hair but was more like a heavily chewed dirty carpet. To my annoyance, he asked me to move my car and park it in another parking space. There was no reason why I should do this, at least none that I could fathom; just one of those inscrutable Japanese things. So, I moved the car one parking space over.

The rooms were simple, austere even, not as pretty as the lobby and the *onsen* itself just a narrow pink tiled tub in a small shower room overlooking an untidy back yard. But we weren't fussed. All we were interested in was eating fresh crab.

Before dinner, we walked round the town. I was sure that normally the town was bustling and lively but because of the holiday, most shops were shuttered and the hundreds of trawlers in the harbour were forlornly empty and motionless, save for the slow creaking of timbers as they rubbed against one another. By five o'clock, it was all but dark save for brilliant, sharp rays of moonlight that punctured through the clouds. Everyone was at home, screens pulled tight over the windows.

On our walk we came across a quoin construction site. Quoins are huge and ugly lumps of lobed concrete dumped on beaches supposedly to protect the coastline. Because of their size, they are hugely expensive to transport, they spoil the look of the coastline and they are more likely to cause rather than prevent sea erosion. (This was a futile example of the government's cynicism, pumping money into these useless objects, fattening the accounts of construction companies, doing nothing for the economy whilst destroying the environment.)

The following morning we were, as usual, the last guests to check out – we're always the slowest to get up and pack. We paid in cash. Like many less sophisticated places in Japan, credit cards weren't accepted. Before leaving, Satoko phoned the next *ryokan* to find out if snow had fallen. No, they reported.

From Wajima, we took a northerly east direction to the outer tip of the peninsular. The coast road was empty. The rocks on the shore were gleaming with minerals: reds, blues and greens shining like Fabre's iridescent beetles. The villages remained undeveloped and unaffected by modern life. Most of the houses were wooden; we passed few convenience stores, petrol stations or other intrusive signs of contemporary living. Of the few people we saw, most were old women, wearing thick pyjama-type working clothes, peaked cloth hats, and bent double as they walked along the road, using pushchairs for support but also to carry food and household goods. Because of the infrequency of shops, we came across several old women who clearly had to walk miles, up and down sometimes steeply undulating cliff roads, to buy their daily provisions. Tough old boots, them.

Neither did age stop them working in the rice fields, weeding and hoeing the land, or scraping seaweed from the rocks. The winter's air was harsh and cold, at least for us, but when Satoko spoke to one of the seaweed gatherers she was told the winter was too mild. This meant the seaweed's colour didn't grow as dark as the market liked.

We were charmed by this peninsular. With the prospect of winter storms rushing from the sea, the villages were wrapped and protected by tall fences of dried bamboo. Many snuggled under huge sheer cliffs, a tangle of houses, boats, rice paddies, vegetable patches and salt pans, all squashed together and tightly sandwiched between rock and sea on a narrow spit of land. If we stepped out of the car, all we heard was the plaintive whistles of the circling hawks and the lap of the sea.

Eventually we reached a bigger town, Suzu. We stopped for lunch and bought petrol. Satoko asked the attendant what would be the best route to leave the Noto Peninsular to avoid snow. Pursing his lips, he advised that we stick to Route 129 before joining the Noto Toll Road. But this journey we would make in two days' time.

Despite its moderate size, there was little activity in Suzu. Like most seaside towns, anywhere in the world, it was dormant in winter. Shops closed tight. Streets empty. Life boxed up and put away until the summer.

The couple that ran the Coffee & Pub confirmed this. Nothing happens here, they told us and by the look of the pub, trapped in a style that was fleetingly fashionable in the 1980s we could see that. They were a young couple, the husband looking even younger than the wife. She might have been in her late thirties; he looked young thirties. Sat at the bar, was their daughter, a teenager, neatly dressed in school uniform, typing out labels for their New Year cards. Why she was in her uniform I don't know. It was the school holidays after all. The pub had one beer tap and a limited collection of gins and whiskeys. There were two slot machines and a karaoke player. This is one of the most exciting places in town, they laughed. As it was Christmas, they had mounted a small silver coloured artificial tree at one end of the bar. On the TV, the same variety show we had been watching as we ate lunch continued. But the coffee was good and tasted similar to the coffee I drank in the early 1970s, at the late Robert Maxwell's bookstore in Oxford – though why I should remember this I wasn't sure.

Earlier, we had eaten lunch in a snack bar, a modern extension built at the back of a dusty, ramshackle grocery and general store. This wasn't just any old lunch but our Christmas Lunch. We guessed Dad was doing the cooking, whilst his mother and a high-school-aged daughter served. The daughter studied me through thick pebble glasses with undisguised and unembarrassed interest. I assumed that *gaijin* visitors were rare. Perhaps she was interested in the way I ate or the clothes I wore but she looked at me with such intensity that I wondered whether she was reading my thoughts. I thought of white knickers and then a naked girl but she didn't flinch so I must have been wrong.

Like all cheap restaurants, a TV was switched on. And if you didn't want to watch the lunchtime variety show, you could read a selection of *manga*.

For Christmas lunch, I ordered plain chicken *udon*, and Satoko, a plate of curry rice, a peculiar Japanese manifestation of curry, similar to the packet variety sold in England under the brand name Vesta. Curry rice was always served on a shallow oval platter. Precisely one half was white rice, the other a very mild brown chicken curry and, on one side, a small mound of pickled vegetable.

I quizzed Satoko about the format of the TV show. Very little was happening: a handful of celebrities horsed around, playing the occasional silly game such as passing a balloon from one vacuum cleaner pipe to another. The purpose wasn't to have winners or losers but just to let the audience howl as their favourite stars played the fool. It had been the same for thirty years, Satoko told me, its very purpose to be unchallenging and familiar. Japanese TV is at its most undemanding during Christmas and the New Year, she explained, relying heavily on the talk-show format, quizzes and news reviews.

'Just like English TV, uhh?'

This year I had already seen too many 'big eating' shows (where contestants had to gorge themselves, eating the most or the quickest) and any number on magic (but where the theme was to show how tricks were done) and unexplained phenomena. Every TV channel copied what the others were doing. It was rare that any would go out on a limb and broadcast something original.

As we strolled through the town and then shopped in the supermarket, I decided there was a predominant facial type present. An oval face: not ugly, just plain, as if centuries of harsh sea winds had smoothed out all characteristics and irregularities. In the eighteenth century, ten types of Japanese female facial form were described. Women with oval faces were called (and still are) *tanuki-gao* or badger faces: round, wide, and chubby with a flat appearance: their eyes widely set, round and low; eyebrows thick and short.

That evening, our first meal at the Yoshigaura *ryokan* was memorable both for the quality and sheer amount of food. Having eaten simple *udon* for Christmas lunch, it seems churlish to complain but at the end of the meal, we groaned with bloated stomachs. Among the many dishes were a huge steamed crab, lobster and tuna sashimi, tender abalone sashimi with its guts as a rich accompaniment, grilled steak (the meat marbled with fat), tai soup, paper-thin fish carpaccio, a vegetable and chicken stew, succulent prawns full of roe (*botan ebi*) eaten raw and which literally melted in our mouths, five small bowls of assorted fish and vegetables, grilled buri fish, rice, a second type of miso soup with tiny clams, lobes of uni, air-dried scallop and marinated fish. Eating started at five-thirty p.m., finished at eight p.m. and then we fell straight into bed (or rather the futon on the floor).

A repetitive tapping woke me next morning. I opened a screen but no one was there. Was a Christmas ghost visiting? The tapping continued and I realised it was coming from the upstairs room. I went up, slid back another screen, and startled a big crow that jumped back, flew off to another window, and started tapping with its beak on that one. When eventually a screen was slid open, the crow flew to another and started tapping all over again. Clearly, it had learnt the trick of waking people up in the morning, although for what gain I didn't know. To irritate humans? Was it expecting some reward?

Anyway, the disturbance didn't matter: it was seven-thirty a.m. and breakfast was at eight. Fortunately, not so daunting a selection of dishes: rice which I ate with raw egg and seaweed; crab soup, seaweed soup, rice porridge with crab; sashimi cut from a small herring-like fish, pickles and assorted vegetables. All the guests ate in one big room. Most were youngish couples all, we included, with that Hugh Grant just-woke-up-sleepy-ruffled hair look. Whereas the night before everyone was talking, conversation this morning was muted.

Afterwards Satoko and I soaked in the outdoor hot pool hoping this would speed digestion. We had another day here and we had no idea how we would be able to eat anything again.

Only our heads emerged above the steaming water. The water temperature was 45°C whilst the air was 3°C. After five minutes, our bodies had turned pink like lightly boiled lobsters (indeed the Japanese call this ideal *onsen* state, *yudedako* or boiled octopus), we slipped out of the water and sat naked on the side of the pool cooling down before sliding back into the water again. We repeated this every few minutes. On the third or fourth cycle, as I lay in the hot water staring up blankly at the sky, I noticed a crow fly by with something large wedged in its mouth. They've stolen something, I thought with a wry smile. Only later, when I returned to our room did I discover two pieces of wrapped cake – left on the wooden veranda to keep cool – had gone missing and they were what I had seen in the crow's mouth. (The other missing food saga that I will quickly touch on was the tin of caviar we brought from Tokyo, an indulgence we were going to enjoy with a bottle of champagne. It mysteriously went missing. No idea where or when and we never found it.)

The *ryokan* was idyllically located in a small cove, hemmed in by tall cliffs. We had to leave the car at the top of a headland and walk down with our luggage. To reach the headland, we had driven a half a mile from the main road along a rough track and Satoko was worried about whether we would be able to get back on to the road if it snowed. Fortunately, there was no sign of snow. Cold but bright.

The *ryokan* was a cluster of four neat separate buildings, sturdily constructed in a traditional style. The owners were the fourteenth generation. The inn itself was founded in 1574 when it provided rooms for fishermen sheltering from stormy seas; the location was on the confluence of the inner and outer Japan Sea, where opposing currents make the water particularly rough. Of course, over the years, the buildings had been rebuilt, renovated, and upgraded so that now it was a luxury inn. It was built abutting – and some few metres above – the water. There was no beach. The sea crashed against rocks that came right up to a low protective wall, sending up spray that gently rained over us, whilst a breeze caught the salty ionised smell of the sea.

Our rooms overlooked a shallow decorative pool that bordered the rocks. I felt we were floating over the sea and that if I stretched out an arm I could catch the waves. We slept in a lower room. Upstairs, in the floor of a smaller room, charcoal logs burned in an open pit fire (*ironi*). The fire was lit day and night and from downstairs, we could hear the erratic but soothing spit of the charcoal embers. The rooms were simple but elegant.

At night, when the rocks and pool were lit with gold and blue lights, and the screens had been pulled across the windows, the inside of the room was like a theatre set with coloured opalescent light softly filtering through the *shoji* screens.

Before turning over to sleep, I would listen to the roar of the waves, a thunderous deep-throated roar of the night sea. (It sounded different from the sea during the day.) I could remember looking at the waves during the day, watching them swell, creating cavernous mouths that tried to swallow the rocks, spiting out foam that dribbled along the fissures and, when repulsed by the immovable weight of stone, were then sucked back through the very channels they had carved over millennia. The wind rattled the glass, shrieking like a demon as it rushed over the tiled roofs.

What was it about the sea that holds such hypnotic fascination? Why could I stand at the window and gaze pensively at the ocean's horizon as if trapped by some inescapable dream? What draws men and boys alike to be fixed on a distant fishing boat, making up tales in their head as they watch it pitch and wallow in the swell, their pulse quickening as they imagine the fishermen battling on the boat, forever headed seawards towards the black, swirling horizon? Do we imagine we can embark on a long voyage with them? Does some primeval DNA draw us to the sea?

Our final two nights were spent at the Araya-Totoan *ryokan* in the old spa town Yamashiro; a four-hour drive south.

Religiously, we stuck to the route recommended by the garage owner. There was no snow and the journey was uneventful.

Satoko told me she had been dreaming of coming to this *ryokan* since she booked it three months previously. It was particularly renowned for its crab. She wasn't to be disappointed.

Our first evening meal was served in our room at six-thirty p.m. We sat on the floor, dressed in blue and white *yukata* and turquoise socks, at two low black lacquered tables. Dish by dish, the waitress brought in the food. She was quite thickset for a Japanese girl, with heavy fingers. She was talkative and we discovered that unusually she had moved away from Tokyo rather than the other way. 'I'm a gypsy,' she told Satoko.

Our meal started with an aperitif of cloudy, unfiltered sake (*nigori-zake*). Higher in alcohol than regular sake, with a creamier but less refined underlying taste, the opaqueness comes from unfermented rice solids left in the brew. Little of it is brewed, hence it is more difficult to find particularly in shops. I always enjoyed drinking it and wished I could find it more often.

Assorted meat and fish appetisers accompanied this, followed by crab sashimi, which we dipped into coarse Noto sea salt. Incredibly delicate and light, the meat looked like newly unfurled fern fronds.

Then we enjoyed a small dish of steamed lotus bulb and crab, a diminutive mound of intricate soft and hard textures.

Next, a whole crab was brought in and grilled on a tabletop charcoal burner. We cut the legs with scissors, extracted and mixed the sweet white flesh with the slightly bitter tasting brown guts of the crab.

That was only the first whole crab. The second arrived steamed and the third was boiled in a hot pot on our table. They were big crabs too: red, long-legged, and called locally *beni-ʒuwaigani*. During the November-to-March season, when the sea is at its coldest, they're at their best.

Finally, we finished with a bowl of rice mixed with miso, sake, egg and seaweed.

Each dish was prepared to perfection and each was stunningly delicious but afterwards, I didn't want to see another crab for months. (And this time I meant it.)

After dinner, too full to walk or to fall asleep, we watched a TV programme about Harry Potter, featuring two Japanese (a teenage schoolgirl and a middle-aged author) visiting London, Edinburgh and Cornwall retracing Harry's journey — and seeking the influences on J K Rawlings. Harry Potter's popularity was as high in Japan as anywhere else in the world. If not higher. The first film had just been released. Satoko told me that Japanese bulletin boards on the web were devoted to similar journeys, the home of experts who pass on the most detailed knowledge. (For many centuries, there has been a habit of becoming obsessively interested in a single subject, knowing more about it than anyone else and hence demonstrating a certain degree of superiority.)

Quite why we watched I don't know as neither of us had read the books or been touched by the Potter phenomenon but it was worth it just for one sequence shot in the Edinburgh Academy. Two teams of children, aged, I think, twelve years old, set each other questions on the stories. The winners had on their team a girl who was a remarkable expert. Not only was it a delight to watch the shy smugness with which she answered the most difficult questions but also the mounting irritation of the opposing team.

'She should be disqualified,' said a sullen boy eventually.

'Why?' asked the teacher?

'Because she's read the books too many times,' he replied.

After the Harry Potter programme, we watched another on French pop stars of the 'sixties. I recognised very few whereas Satoko knew all of them and kept telling me what big stars they were. This I didn't understand until she explained that many enjoyed huge hits in Japan. Patiently I pointed out, that when I was a kid, with one exception, French pop music was laughed at in England – with some justification as I was now being reminded – as the songs were slushy sentimental ballads. (The exception being Jane Birkin and Serge Gainsborough's *Je t'aime*.) But the programme taught me one thing: now I could understand why Japanese pop music was still rubbish as, clearly, the success of the French in the 1960s has had a sustained influence on the nature of songs here. (Just as an aside, Steve Davis, the snooker player affectionately known as Mr Boring, is a world expert on French progressive rock of the 'seventies and 'eighties – which says it all really.)

The French stars were interviewed. Forty years on, they had aged little and were testament to how the French prize their outward appearance. All the women were beautiful. None wore anything vulgar, none of that glittering tasteless display of wealth seen so often with Hollywood stars of yesteryear. They were the epitome of elegance and good taste.

Going to *onsen* is a lifestyle-defining ritual in Japan. Everybody does it – some very frequently – as a way of obtaining health, both mental and physical. The hot, mineral-rich waters bring serenity, peace and harmony, as well as a perfect complexion and the smooth workings of all bodily functions – including bowel movements and libido. Eggs that are par-boiled in *onsen* water will stay fresh for weeks. Is this also the secret of Japan's long life expectancy?

Because Japan is one vast range of volcanoes, it is fissured end to end from which bubbles a constant supply of steam and hot water. *Onsen* are found all over Japan and I would say that every single Japanese person in the country visits one at least once a year. Companies organise annual outings; TV programmes and magazines are devoted to describing them. The most popular are booked months in advance and planning an itinerary was always hard.

I found the only sour note was the amazement of the Japanese that a *gaijin* could stay in the hot water for more than a second. How do you do it, they would ask me and I would smile and say it was easy and then stay in longer than they could. (A ridiculously painful thing to do.)

Chapter Four

Adoption

'Adoption, with us [the West], is a kind of domestic luxury, akin to the keeping of any other pets, such as lap-dogs and canaries. It is a species of self-indulgence which those who can afford it give themselves when fortune has proved unpropitious, an artificial method of counteracting the inequalities of fate.' *Percival Lowell from The Soul of the Far East.*

Conversely, as Lowell recorded, in nineteenth-century Japan, adoption was a very different thing. If the head of the household had no children, or the children were all girls, it was his duty to adopt a male into the family. Unlike the West, where generally infants (or sometimes children) were adopted, age was of no importance in Japan. Grown men would be adopted into the family. Lowell continued, 'The simplest procedure in such a case is to combine relationships in a single individual, and the most self-evident person to select for the dual capacity is the husband of the eldest daughter. This is the course pursued. Some worthy young man is secured as spouse for the senior sister; he is at the same time formally taken in as a son by the family whose cognomen he assumes, and eventually becomes the head of the house.'

Has this practice died out? Not at all. This was exactly what Satoko's father had been happy to do. As a second son, his family's name was secure. He'd been adopted into his wife's family and taken the Okada surname as Satoko's mother had only sisters, the brothers having been killed in the Second World War. And that created a connection and point of reference as I too had been adopted – as a baby.

Chapter Five

Shikoku

Covered completely from head to toe to protect themselves from the sun's violent heat, old women toiled in the fields surrounding Satoko's parents' house. It was the rice planting season – once, that is, the rain fell and filled the reservoir that serve the concrete aqueducts and irrigation channels which, in turn, would flood the rice fields, transforming the ground from as dry as an Arizonan desert to a muddy swamp. In the meantime, the old women, bent at right angles from the hip, laid out plastic trays of seedlings. Timing was crucial: not wanting to keep the rice seedlings under the sun for too long as they would shrivel and die, yet the rice had to be planted quickly once the paddy was submerged under water. Rain was forecast to arrive tomorrow.

We arrived in Marugame yesterday and we will stay for three weeks. It's so rare that we visit, we thought we ought to devote proper attention and act like good children. In any case, I like Marugame as I like the unsophisticated small-town atmosphere.

This morning we walked past the schools Satoko attended, and the stores where she bought sweets and buns, or had her cycle repaired. Of these stores, only the last was still open – the others with metal shutters down were shut forever – and it was the same man – who repaired her bike for free, thirty years ago – who threw a double-take when we walked past, half-recognising Satoko and at the same time confused by the appearance of a Japanese/Western couple. No greetings were exchanged.

Her parents live on the fringe of town, their detached house raised above and overlooking a jigsaw of small fields marked not by hedgerows or fences but by deep irrigation channels. Both Satoko's mum and dad had fallen foul of them: once her mum tripped into one, and her dad drove his car into another, although this wasn't an incident much talked about.

Some thirty years ago they had built a one-storey house. Subsequently a second floor had been extended into the roof. Downstairs there was one small Western style-living room with air-conditioning, two small sofas and a desk. This was my room – although how they anticipated my arrival those three decades ago is anyone's guess. Having a Westernised room in a house had – since at least the 1920s – been an indication of culture. Then, existing Japanese houses might tack a Western room on the side or back of the house, lay wood on the floor instead of tatami, and fill it with foreign style furniture. But the rest of the downstairs was pure Japanese: a small kitchen where we ate around a table that could fit four people at a squeeze, two tatami-mat rooms, a bathroom and the bedroom area. Upstairs, where we slept, were another small bathroom and three tatami rooms. (Obligingly, the toilet had been retrofitted with a raised plastic seat over the Japanese-style squat toilet, just so that I would be comfortable.) Surrounding the house was a small Japanese garden in which Satoko's mother had infiltrated some European plants. In common fashion, the perimeter wall was tall so that passers-by couldn't look in.

Once, this house had been surrounded only by small farmhouses, but slowly the aging farmers had sold, piecemeal, plots of land to property developers. Modern housing and flats encroached on all sides, none attractive – particularly the one painted a shocking purple. The farmers or their families couldn't be blamed for selling out. Hard work, the returns decreasing, and the sun hotter. Consequently, young people won't work the fields. They seek a university place and an office job, leaving only the old and very old to labour. In the house opposite, the eldest girl has been trying for three years to get into the right university that will lead to a career in the diplomatic service. She failed and had to work in the town hall.

Besides new housing, a new road was being built: a wide incomplete road that abruptly stopped in the middle of a field. Even if it could continue, we couldn't figure out where it could connect. What's going on, we asked Satoko's parents but they were as bemused as us, and said that no one knew why the road was being built but it was unlikely to be completed as the council had run out of money and couldn't buy any more land.

Dominated by its port, Marugame was a small industrialised city, producing chemicals, textiles and salt and was the sort of city that young people left as soon as they could. When Satoko moved to Tokyo she was typical, and she was determined never to come back to live

With an aging population of around 70,000, it ranked twenty-third in the Japan for the quality of its life. Someone living there would describe it as quiet and conservative, its fame limited to the manufacture of round fans (*uchiwa*) and the remains of a once splendid castle. But Marugame was now decidedly shabby, its port withering away, along with associated industries. Even manufacture of the famous *uchiwa*, designated a 'national traditional handicraft', was an industry in slow decline.

Into its easternmost flank came the Great Seto Bridge, one of the world's longest, and the first permanent link connecting Shikoku to Honshu. By eliminating the awkward ferry ride, the plan was to stimulate the local economy. This had failed. The tolls were priced too high and now there was a movement to petition the government to lower them. (This would mean the government would have to further subsidise the cost of the bridge.)

Beyond Marugame, the land became increasingly isolated, mountainous and magnificent. Shikoku was famous for its rivers, gorges, papermaking and shipbuilding industry and *haiku*. (Shikoku was also famous for dog and bull fighting but that was something not talked about much to visitors.) It was famous for an ancient *kabuki* theatre, for being the birthplace of Kenzaburo Oe, the 1994 Nobel Laureate for Literature and, in Utazu City, the 'Charm Station: World's Toilet Museum' where a twenty-four-carat toilet was proudly displayed, containing twenty-four kilos of gold and said to be worth Y60 million.

Most famous of all, were the eighty-eight Buddhist temples, popular as places of pilgrimage. These ancient temples were scattered across the island. Japan's Buddhists hold a lifetime's ambition to undertake a pilgrimage to each, the most faithful on foot and in a single journey. We saw them walking along a road, dressed in white pilgrims' clothes, wearing a wide white hat, ringing a bell as they walked, and chanting a pilgrim's canticle. The less zealous might walk the route in several stages over a number of years or, heavens above, drive from temple to temple. The laziest booked a two-week coach tour and wore sportswear and sneakers – although it was said it doesn't matter how the pilgrimage was undertaken so long as the pilgrim retained the essential spirit. The Shikoku Pilgrimage known as *Shikoku-henro* was the most famous pilgrimage in Japan and followed the trail that the monk who introduced

Buddhism to Japan, Kobo Daishi, walked in his youth whilst searching for the Truth. It takes around sixty days to cover the 1,647 km. Close to Marugame were several of the shrines including the Kotohira Shrine (one of the more important) dedicated to Kompira, the god of fishermen and sea travellers. Before the advent of cars, trains and planes, many of the pilgrims arrived and departed by sea through Marugame and this had added to its wealth.

Whether a Buddhist or not, I could understand the attractiveness of undertaking the walk. Not that I was seeking enlightenment, nor was I prepared to devote time learning the Buddhist scripts but I could easily imagine the spiritual tranquillity that would come from walking along deserted country lanes, through muddy fields full of the earth's fragrance, standing under the eaves of old houses when it rained, listening to the sound of birds and running water and the clack of a walking stick on the ground. Within the temples, the pilgrim would hear the ringing of bells, the murmur of chanted sutra, and the whole trip sounded unquestionably romantic Accommodation was said to be excellent in and around the temples. At one time, the charming custom of *zengon-yado*, of giving pilgrims free bed and board, was practised. A child was sent out to the nearest temple in the evening to find one or two pilgrims to take in that night. In return, the host expected only that his *osame-fuda* (the name card he carried) be offered at the temple by the pilgrim. This mindset of *osettai*, the kindness that pilgrims receive, is something the people of Shikoku are proud of.

On my first morning, I paid my respects to the two grandmothers kept in silver pencil cases within the family altar: I clapped my hands and made a short prayer – to their ashes, of course, interred in silver boxes, the same shape and size as the wooden pencil cases we owned as children. Were we really so diminutive when reduced to ash? No. I was wrong in thinking that these were the complete ashes. They were a sample. Some had been interred in the family plot; others had been given to other relatives.

Before breakfast, I strolled through the paddy fields. I had found sleeping on the floor uncomfortable. I stretched my limbs by waving my arms in the air and kicking out my legs.

The croak of frogs was close to deafening. Satoko had told me this was because they were waiting for the rain and could sense its imminent arrival. For all their noise, they were only little bright green tree frogs, just an inch or two long. They sat on leaves or hugged stems; some were sitting on the garden gate. Overhead the sky, looking like greasy piles of rags, hung as if about to collapse on to the ground. Minutes later, rain fell and the frogs croaked so loudly I dubbed them the amphibian equivalent of Phil Spector's Wall of Sound.

Satoko's mum was an excellent cook. For breakfast this morning we ate grilled fish, boiled bamboo shoots, tempura, rough country tofu and boiled squid. Eating such food would lead to regular bowel movements and we would feel cleansed from deep inside. Natural colonic irrigation I called it. Because we were on holiday, we drank Asahi 'happoshu' beer, a recent phenomenon in the beer market – just a small glass as otherwise I would have fallen back to sleep before the day had begun. Over the last year or so *happoshu* has gained around half the market. *Happoshu* looked and tasted similar to regular beer but because of a lower malt content, tax was lower and consumers paid less – around one third less than proper beer – and in recession-hit times, it had proved popular. The taste was acceptable – although I found it sweet, lacking the bite and edge of real beer – but at around a pound a pint, I understood the attraction.

We had to book beforehand to visit Noguchi's studio – writing in with a preferred date and time. Isamu Noguchi is one of Japan's most celebrated artists – albeit his mother was the American poet Leonie Gilmour, and his father the Japanese poet Yonejiro Noguchi. He was born in Los Angeles and spent most of his working life in the US, only in his later years coming to Mure, an hour's drive from Marugame.

A young girl dressed in obligatory art gallery black, led us on a one-hour tour. We were instructed not to take photographs, as the sculptures' images had been copyrighted by a New York foundation. I found this absurd, and discreetly snapped away. How could someone stop me taking photographs for my own use and enjoyment? The sculptures were displayed in the open air. This was plain copyright madness.

The studio was on the edge of Mure, a town that had grown over hundreds of years on the artisan skills of stonemasons. Huge gashes, from centuries of the granite being quarried, cut across the surrounding hills, and the streets were littered with stone and rocks stacked around the stonemasons' factories. Mistakenly, I had an idealised picture that Noguchi's studio would be found in the middle of desolate countryside and was surprised to find it hemmed in by houses. Not that this detracted from the experience. On display were many individual works, some finished but most incomplete, left scattered *in situ* from the time of his death in 1988. Ignoring the museum's 'No Touching the Artwork' rule, I wrapped my body, arms and hands around the stone. Some of the sculptures' surfaces were smooth; others left rough or dimpled, or with holes tunnelled through them forming a pattern of scars like the tattoos on a Maori's face. An arousing experience: absorbing heat and cold, stroking and caressing the surface, hugging the immoveable weight.

The sculptures ranged from mere fragments to enormous blocks, displayed in the open within a stone circular wall – a wall, I sense, built to preserve Noguchi's shy personality. Left in the studio were his implements – hammers, chisels, power tools – as if he had just put them down after a day's work and I found the contrast between the beauty of the sculptures and the hard, dusty, everyday banality of the tools (unlike the delicacy of the painter's brush) intriguing, blurring the line between craftsman and artist.

He lived just outside the studio, in a house now also preserved: so simple and refined, only a genius could have lived there. This house reflected Noguchi's presence more than his studio, better capturing the harmony of the man, between his work and the nature that inspired him, and his ability to take something natural and, rather than transforming and removing the wrinkles of imperfection, gently changing the form to offer another facet to what was there all along. Noguchi didn't fight nature; through his hands, he became part of it. As I looked through a window (we weren't allowed inside), I pictured him sitting cross-legged on the floor, in the corner of the main room, leaning over a low wooden table, reading a book or sketching a design under the dim light.

Breakfast: raw cabbage and boiled egg, followed by slices of sweet bread and tea (we had brought our own English tea bags) after which Satoko and I read the newspapers, her father took a nap and mother attended to correspondence. The frogs were silent but two screeching crows, sitting on a nearby telegraph pole, replaced their noise with one louder and more intrusive.

Once everyone was happy to face the day, Satoko's parents drove us to a public *onsen* in a neighbouring town across the mountains. Showing how quickly things change from one valley to the next, we went from Marugame, a sprawling, shiny, corrugated city to Noi, a country town, whose urban limits were shredded by large areas of agriculture including colourful orange and peach groves. Not that long ago, each valley community was all but cut off from the next and knew little of its neighbours. Only with the advent of the car and the cutting of tunnels were communications between valleys eased. But the sense of distinctiveness and unique character remained.

This *onsen* was a modern municipal building perched high on a hill. In the men's section, I found four large indoor baths each capable of seating comfortably at least twelve, an outdoor bath, and a huge sauna with a TV set in the wall behind a Perspex screen. In the large public rest areas, most of Noi were sprawled on the floor, taking naps, drinking beer, smoking and enjoying the opportunity to both rest and gossip. If I had to choose a single reason to retire to Japan many years hence, it would be to use the public *onsen*. For a few pounds, it was possible to enjoy magnificent spa facilities that elsewhere would costs hundreds of pounds. And I could stay all day. And if lucky, I might catch a glimpse of a breast – as I did. A young mum, wearing a loose cotton top, leant forward to pick up her baby, exposing a small firm breast topped with a dark pointed nipple. (Such snatched delights might be important for an old aged pensioner.)

The only drawback? Smoking wasn't banned and the air was acrid and murky but maybe that will change over the next few years.

I had brought with me, the writings of Isabel Bird. I lay down on a *tatami* and opened a marked page. She hadn't been here – not anywhere close – but except for the modernisation of the facilities, the atmosphere and way of life she found was still to be seen today:

'The village consists of two short streets, 8 feet wide composed entirely of yadoyas of various grades, with a picturesquely varied frontage of deep eaves, graceful balconies, rows of Chinese lanterns, and open lower fronts. The place is full of people, and the four bathing-sheds were crowded. Some energetic invalids bathe twelve times a day! Every one who was walking about carried a blue towel over his arm, and the rails of the balconies were covered with blue towels hanging to dry. There can be very little amusement. The mountains rise at once from the village, and are so covered with jungle that one can only walk in the short streets or along the track by which I came. There is one covered boat for excursions on the lake, and a few geishas were playing the samisen; but, as gaming is illegal, and there is no place of public resort except the bathing-sheds, people must spend nearly all their time in bathing, sleeping, smoking, and eating. The great spring is beyond the village, in a square tank in a mound. It bubbles up with much strength, giving off fetid fumes. There are broad boards laid at intervals across it, and people crippled with rheumatism go and lie for hours upon them for the advantage of the sulphurous steam. The temperature of the spring is 130 degrees F.; but after the water has travelled to the village, along an open wooden pipe, it is only 84 degrees. Yumoto is over 4000 feet high, and very cold.

Last night it rained, a day later than forecast, but then I always found Japanese weather forecasts unpredictable. I woke to find the irrigation ditches swirling with water, sluice gates had been opened and the rice fields starting to flood. A hive of activity has already broken out. Tractors churned the dried earth, letting the moisture soak in, a creamy scum forming on the surface. Rice seedlings were readied for planting in a mechanical sowing machine. White ebus skipped from field to field, grabbing worms emerging from the ground, and the farmers plugged leaking gaps in the concrete retaining walls as the waters rose higher. The picture was a mix of the modern contrasting with methods and tools that had not changed for hundreds, maybe even thousands of years. The women worked as hard as the men, knee-deep in the gloppy mud, no task too heavy for them. (No gender distinction exists in agriculture.) The only distinguishing feature between the men and women was that the latter were covered from head to toe to protect themselves from the sun: wide brimmed hats, scarves tied around their heads, long sleeves tucked in to gloves and long trousers tucked in to rubber boots. Like a pioneer racing driver, with only the eyes exposed.

Marugame Castle, the three-storied *donjon* on top of Kameyama Hill made a fine landmark, dominated the town and was rarely lost from view. Satoko and I walked to its summit at lunchtime and, when looking out from the top of the castle tower, I was reminded that Marugame was a sea-town: a port now less significant, but still with two huge tankers moored on a quayside alongside numerous smaller cargo and fishing vessels. Otherwise it was something easily forgotten and up until now I had thought of Marugame more like a country town. I pointed this out to Satoko but she didn't agree. But for me, it lacked the smell and distinctive seaside features found in an English seaside town.

Designated a national treasure, the castle's three-hundred-and-fifty-year-old remains were nonetheless scruffy: knotweed sprouted from the giant buttress walls (the *ohgi no kouba* or fan-shaped slopes), grass was left uncut and there was a general air of neglect. But it was a perfect spot for a picnic, with a commanding 360-degree panoramic view over the city (even if a pair of crows did steal our wet tissues: I can only imagine mistaking them for food – unless they were particularly hygienic). In 1926, the castle's site was purchased by the city, and laid out as a park with a library and museum, a baseball ground, swimming pool, amusement park, small zoo and gardens.

Until the 1950s, the castle had massive double moats but then the outer moat was filled and the area used for building. Much of the rest of the castle had also disappeared although there were two fine massive wooden gates: *Ote-ichi-no-mon* (First Front Gate) and *Ote-no-mono* (Second Front Gate), both built in 1670 and now Important Cultural Properties.

Castles around the world have their legends and tales: Marugame was no exception.

The ramparts of Marugame Castle, the tallest in Japan, were an impressive sight and when local people talked about them, they might mention the tale of Naked Juza, the mason who built them (naked for the simple reason he always worked naked).

With the castle nearing completion, the lord, whose castle it was, sang the praises of Juza.

'What a wonderful fortress he has built for me. No wonder he prides himself on being the best mason in the country. Juza is a genius. None but flying birds will be able to breach the walls.'

The lord sent for Juza and said, 'True, you are a master in the art of masonry. But you would not be able to climb the walls of your own building?'

Juza answered, 'Yes, I think I could, if you'd give me a pair of iron rods one foot long.'

A pair of iron rods were brought and before the startled eyes of the Lord, he climbed the walls as easily as a monkey climbs a tree.

A few days later, Juza was ordered to measure the depth of a well. He climbed down to the water's level, when suddenly a heavy stone fell on him and killed him outright.

What is said to be his grave, a simple stone, is in Jukaku-in Temple.

Later we came across Sue-chan, a domesticated crow, kept at a coffee bar run by The Master, a friend of Satoko's. He made the best Irish coffee in the world and if this is a particular obsession, it's worth travelling around the world to taste his.

Inside, the décor had a rustic Mediterranean touch but had been left untouched for many years and was scruffy; two tables sat four and six people respectively and counter-seats another six (Sue-chan lived outside, perched under an umbrella). The bar was open most hours of the day: from early morning to early morning. Helping was a waitress, aged I think in her mid-thirties, who today was wearing a pair of pink hot pants, and knee-length black leather boots. She sat at one end of the counter, long legs loosely crossed, drawing very slowly on a menthol cigarette she seemed loathed to take out of her mouth.

The Master's favourite method to prepare coffee was using two glass bowels placed on top of one another. A naked flame heated the water in the lower bowl; this bubbled up a tube and filtered through the coffee in the upper bowl. There was something particularly sensual in this, as if an alchemist was turning lead into gold and I suppose in a way this was exactly what happened: coarse brown beans were turned into a golden liquid.

Coffee was taken seriously in Japan. It was hard to find a bad cup.

'Do you know they even make instant coffee in England when you go to a coffee house?' the girl in hot pants said to me as she cleaned the table. By the way she said it you might have thought she had observed five year old children being sent to work down mines.

The son of Tam – another childhood friend of Satoko – had caught the crow. This son, whom Tam observed was growing up because his dick was growing, was not the academic type, preferring to skip school to fish or hunt. To make matters worse, he had been identified as one of a group of bullies making low-level extortion demands from fellow pupils. Tam sighed when she told us these stories. Her dream was for him to leave school as soon as possible and enlist in the army.

Tam and the crow had become local celebrities after appearing on TV in a five-minute slot. Apparently, domesticating a crow is difficult and rare. The city was fascinated by how the crow adopted Tam as her mother. Not only did Sue-chan nestle up to Tam, at any opportunity she also went for walks with her. Such is the nature of fame in Marugame. But Sue-chan's celebrity life was tragically cut short when she was run over by a car outside the bar.

Two granite spheres, like two giant eyeballs stood next to one another, framed within a concrete bunker. Impassive, they stared out over a headland; and the sea and far islands were caught in a reflection on their polished grey surface. The installation by Walter de Maria was called *Seen/Unseen* and formed part of the Naoshima Contemporary Art Museum. The museum, owned by Benesse, a Japanese publishing company, was to be found on Naoshima, a small island sandwiched between Honshu and Shikoku. Whether by design or otherwise, Benesse had established one of the most unique museums in the world.

To get there, Satoko and I had taken a well-worn ferryboat that wheezed and wallowed as it sailed from island to island. The voyage wasn't long, about an hour. Naoshima was the first stop of several. For the small number of people on board, the ferry was too fat and wide, an overweight old sea-salt. It could have easily carried a thousand people, maybe the sum total of all the islanders who lived in this part of the Inland Sea but today, there were a handful of foot passengers, and a similar number who had driven cars and vans on board.

The museum was more than just a single building, although its centrepiece was Benesse House, a small but imaginative building atop a headland. There were, for example, outdoor sculptures dotted along the coast, many taking dramatic advantage of their setting. But the most imaginative idea was to be seen in one of the nearby fishing villages, where several houses had been skilfully restored and converted to show off an artist's work. The most striking was by Tatsuo Miyajima who installed his underwater *Sea of Time '98* in a storehouse. There it was possible to sit in semi-darkness and watch numbers flash on and off in a shallow pool. It was one of the most peaceful but thought-provoking experiences I have known.

'What surprised me,' wrote Miyajima, 'when I visited Naoshima was the wonderful art existing among nature and co-existing with people's lives. Inherent in all excellent works of art is the question of human life and death and how we live our lives. In that sense, Naoshima Cultural Village is an environment in which we naturally keep asking ourselves questions about the way we live. Such places are rare in Japan.'

In another, but new building within the village, a room of almost complete blackness had been created. We walked in, our hands nervously outstretched trying to touch something so we didn't inadvertently walk into a wall and smash our noses. We had been told to find a bench and sit down. In the distance (it was impossible to say how far ahead), two faint lights reflected off a surface, suggesting the room was the shape of a parabola narrowing to an apex. But that was all we could see: just light, nothing solid. Initially it was so dark we couldn't even see a hand waved in front of our faces. Over time, our eyes became accustomed to the darkness, the form of the room slowly emerged, not as some strange parabola but an ordinary rectangle with two benches on the far wall where we sat. It was a magnificent deceit.

More of Naoshima's houses were being turned over to art. Like many small fishing islands, it was in decline because there was increasingly less economic benefit in fishing. Boats were too small, their catches not large enough to make a decent living. As old people died, their houses were left empty. Their families had no desire to return, and no market for the houses existed. Most of the old houses had walls a mix of plaster and charred cedar board – the latter a popular building material in the Seto Inland Sea, resistant to insects and fire. But left unsold, because of their simple structure, the houses would quickly collapse becoming victims of the intense weather extremes.

To my mind, Benesse was one of the world's great contemporary art museums not because of the stunning architecture and location but because of the overall concept of creating a harmony between man, art and nature. The main museum housed work by some of the world's leading artists and displayed them exquisitely. Indeed the whole experience attempted to bring an element of surprise: a unique dimension was created to display art in a stimulatingly new way.

Anyone could stay overnight at the museum, either comfortably in a hotel, or camped in one of the Mongolian tents erected in the grounds. Satoko chose the second option because, she said, before meeting me she had always enjoyed camping. Twenty tents were arranged in a field. Ducking through a low wooden door, we entered a spacious tent that could sleep four people on beds. Carpets covered the floor, and the furniture included freestanding cupboards, a dining table and an air-conditioning and heating unit (all mod cons and not like camping at all). The high roof curved upwards in a frame of stays, and was painted a multitude of bright colours. Supper was served in an annex – where spotlessly clean toilets and showers could also be found. (As I said, not like camping at all.)

At the time of our trip, it was the rainy season; I also caught a stomach bug and spent most of the night running and slipping across the wet field, clutching an umbrella in one hand and a torch in the other. (Now that's more like camping.) I had no doubt that this was the most unusual way to visit a museum.

If this was a surprising cultural find, then in Marugame itself there could be found two outstanding contemporary art museums: the Marugame Museum of Contemporary Art, and the Hirai Museum – housing a small but stunning collection of contemporary Spanish art. In MIOCA (or the Genichiro-Inokuma Museum of Contemporary Art to give its proper but unused name) they were holding an exhibition of the work of Jan Fabre, a radical and unsettling Belgium artist. In one documentary about his life and work, a curator talked of Fabre's rage and determination to overcome all obstacles to show his work. Another film highlighted how Fabre's genius came from his ability to separate himself from his audience and having no hesitation to expose his inner self in all its raw emotions. This was best seen in his performance work but, in the exhibition, it was still possible to capture some of this angst.

Angel and Warrior – Strategy and Tactics was the title of the show. On display were objects (if one merely regards them as objects) that were some of the most remarkable things I had seen: dresses, spheres, and pieces of armour and asses' heads, all made out of beetles. The objects were life-sized. The beetles had been laid on steel mesh to form amazing iridescent shapes. He had drawn captioned illustrations with his blood, in the style of medieval monks; in another work, a dead warrior had sunk into (wax) mud and regiments of beetles prepared to eat the decaying body. *Angel and Warrior* itself was a suit of armour covered in angel hair and resting on a large mirror.

Stacked up against a wall were wooden crosses like those found on the fields of Flanders, drawn over with Bic ink that changed colour with the angle of viewing.

The museum was a dramatic and inspiring space, a relic of the bubble economy. Finished in 1991, an eminent Japanese architect, Yoshio Taniguchi won the prestigious Murano Prize for his design. From the front, it appeared to be an open box from which tumbled large sculptures. In the English language brochure, it was called 'one of a kind'. I'll buy that accolade – in part because of the virtuoso design but also because of the location next to a drab JR station, where drunks sat by the side of a fountain, and adjacent to a run-down barren shopping area. That such a radical space sat in the middle of ordinariness was a miracle. Indeed just being built at all in the sleepy port of Marugame was remarkable.

Not far from the MIOCA was the Hirai Museum. Another noteworthy building. Designed by the Spanish architect Alfredo Arribas its stunning bold looks were also in contrast to its drab location: off one of the main thoroughfares through the town, and surrounded by a jumble of factories. Arribas had designed the opening ceremony for the 1992 Barcelona Olympic Games – a highly unusual commission for an architect – and the Hirai Museum was one of his most interesting pieces of work outside Spain. It housed an important collection of contemporary Spanish art including major works by Irazu, Villalta, Gomez, Barcelo, Sevilla and Urzay among many.

The centre of the complex was an oval sculpture garden, bordered by a low building with a cafe and a gallery for temporary exhibitions on one side, and the eight-storey main building on the other. Like the sculpture garden, the main building also had an oval ground plan, from which an extremely dynamic elevation was developed: an ovoid tube, with butterfly wings formed at the top and an outer framework of galvanised metal. Arribas intended the building to be an architectural sculpture; contradicting the opinion still held by many artists that architecture should be nothing more than a neutral container for their work. Arribas said that he designed the museum so that it was 'alternating conceptions of architecture as a setting for artworks and as an expressive symbol in its own right'.

There was nothing announcing the museum's presence. No signs on the street. Even the local tourist guide failed to mention it. Once we arrived, we had to walk around the building several times before finding the entrance. A security guard hunched in a small cubby hole looked up from the portable TV where a baseball game was playing, saw us and beckoned us in. We then discovered that the building was the headquarters for a broadcast and publishing company and they owned the museum. Three floors of the eight-storey building were devoted to showing the work. An amazing collection: small and concentrating on Spanish art executed in the late 1980s and early 1990s by a young generation of artists. Some fifty works were exhibited and, when there, we had the space to ourselves. (The café was more popular, particularly at lunchtime, but if Arribas had seen the interior, he might well have had an apoplectic fit. It had been turned into the most banal space.)

We were not surprised to discover that Rikako – our niece – who lived in Marugame who attended the best high school in Marugame, who had won national art competitions, had never set foot in either of these places. Neither her parents nor the school had ever thought to take her. She was an unfortunate example of the apathy that exists towards art both by people at large but also by the education system.

There was one more museum to see. (Today was our Museum Day.) In the town's Nakazu Bansho Park (a small but exquisite garden) we found a gallery devoted to the paintings of the Barbizon school of artists such as Millet, Rousseau, Corot and Courbet. The gallery was dingy, makeshift in appearance and felt damp inside but its collection whilst small was rich. Satoko and I walked around the park, built in 1688 by Lord Kyogoku II. Unusually, it centred on a large pond, spreading through most of the garden, a miniature of Japan's largest lake – Lake Biwa. And, although now surrounded by docks, by industrialisation (you could hear the rattle of freight trains as they passed nearby), it possessed a composed air of serenity. The pond was a haven of wildlife among which was a two-metre-long blue snake that swam up to where we were standing, raised its head out of the water and hissed, frightening the wits out of us. More pleasing were the fish leaping in to the air to catch insects on the wing, and the heron, ducks and koi.

We spent two hours walking round, leisurely crossing the pond over the bridges and islands – named Sails, Wild Geese, Snow, Rain, Mist, Bell, Moon and Evening Glow. Once again, we were impressed by the extensive collection of trees: small bent and twisted pines, and the conical 600-year-old pine, trained to resemble Mount Fuji, the only one like it in the world.

So why, in this single prefecture, one off the beaten track and with little artistic heritage, can some great art can be seen, located in dramatic and unique spaces, the likes of which can be found nowhere else?

Patronage and money from the bubble economy are the answers. In the 1980s, Japan was awash with money to the extent that no one knew what to do with it. One decision was to spend money on culture. This was done both publicly and privately. Municipal governments wanted to boost their status and local companies were roped-in to assist. The catalyst for the Hirai Museum was the visit of Marugame school children to San Sebastien in the Basque region of Spain. This led to a series of sustained links between the two cities. When a local media company took the decision to build new headquarters, they agreed, with some pressure from the municipal government, that it would be beneficial if Spanish elements were incorporated within the design. This escalated to hiring Arribus and including, within the building, gallery space for contemporary Spanish art. It was a means by which an undistinguished town could buy prestige.

Chabo, a Japanese friend living in London, arrived in Marugame last night.

Unlikely as it sounds, we embarked on an *udon* pilgrimage. For just as there were eighty-eight temples for the faithful to walk to, we discovered eighty-eight *udon* restaurants that should be visited, Shikoku being famous for the quality of its noodles. These were marked on a special map and you could collect a stamp from each to prove you had visited; Chabo also bought two books describing cult *udon* restaurants on the island. Our goal was to visit five in a morning.

Accompanied by another friend Mitarai — who volunteered to navigate — I drove the four of us round Marugame's nearby countryside. Our first stop was at a small store — no more than a roadside shack — and, although only a few minutes after ten, we were not the only aficionados already on the road. At the entrance hung a sign that read '*te-uchi udon*' which meant '*udon* kneaded by hand' — said to give a better taste than machine-kneaded noodles. Ten others were eating or rather sucking the long threads of noodle noisily from the bowl. The practice — as it was in several of the others we visited — was to serve yourself. Taking uncooked *udon*, we plunged them for several seconds into boiling water, then added what ever ingredients we wished from a selection on a side table: stock, soy, onions, leeks fishcakes, vegetable tempura, raw eggs among them. The décor was simple and informal: a few rough benches and chairs, nothing fancy. The kitchen – where the *udon* was made, the vegetables chopped, and the stock simmered – was open for all to see.

All the ingredients were totally fresh and this first bowl of soup was easy to digest and didn't leave us feeling full.

We were thankful for that, for by two-thirty p.m., we had completed our goal of five – albeit now with heavy stomachs. Each restaurant had distinctive characteristics: one, for example, was famous for the quality of the water it used and it did seem the *udon* tasted lighter. Another was renowned for the hard chewier texture of its *udon*. Certainly there were discernable – if sometimes subtle – taste differences at each, and from being wary when I'd started out in the morning, I found instead I'd enjoyed the experience.

We had consumed ten large bowls of both hot and cold *udon* and yet the final cost for each of us was only Y600. This had to be one of the best bargains in Japan and, not surprisingly, many friends later made the same pilgrimage.

Before returning home, we stopped at the vast and sprawling temple complex of Kobo Daishi (774–835). One of the greatest men Japan has ever produced, Daishi has been named the father of Japanese culture and civilization. In just forty years, he amended the fundamentals of the Japanese version of Buddhism, while making significant achievements as a scholar, poet, artist, calligrapher, sculptor, architect, educator, social worker, inventor, discoverer and civil engineer. Phew. He had time to do all of that?

By the age of seventeen, he was studying in Kyoto. At the age of thirty-one, he was in China.

After he returned to Japan, he introduced measures and rules, Chinese medicine, new varieties of seeds, as well as the arts of dyeing, of making Indian ink and writing brushes, and new building techniques for temples, bridges and riverbanks. It was said he was the first Japanese to have learnt to grow tea and process it, to use coal and petrol, to prepare *udon* and *tofu*, and to make cakes and candies.

In 828, Daishi founded the first school open to the poor. Teachers, who were also given free meals if necessary, gave poor children free meals and a sound education. The thirty-volume dictionary, which Daishi compiled for the pupils, was the first dictionary in Japan.

It is widely believed that Kobo Daishi invented *hiragana* (Japanese syllabify) and created *katakana* (another syllabify) through his knowledge of Sanskrit. Until then, reading and writing were restricted to scholars and aristocrats – who could spend a lifetime learning thousands of Chinese characters. These new alphabets enabled common people to write their language phonetically.

In the spring of 835, Daishi announced the day he would die – 22nd April. After bidding farewell to the Emperor, making his will, and naming those who would take over his responsibilities, Daishi confined himself in his tomb. He informed his disciples that he would come back when Miroku, the future Buddha, the saviour of the world, returned to earth, and that until then he would always be watching people from the Pure Land of Miroku.

The most unlikely tale I had read in a long-time.

My own enlightenment in the temple came from a group of schoolgirls. Each looked identical, dressed in white polo shirts, blue tracksuit bottoms, no make-up and with shoulder-length straight hair. Three were stroking a cat and I took a photograph. Immediately, half a dozen more jumped into frame and shouted, 'Photo photo.' They squealed with glee when I took one. Then they asked where I was from and, when I said England, they chanted, 'Bikham, Bikham.'

Remembering I had David Beckham's photo on my digital camera, a long-distance shot taken in Sapporo when England played Argentina in the World Cup, I showed it to them. They went wild, almost pushing me to the ground as they jostled to see it; their squealing reached a crescendo, even though, in the photo, Beckham was no more than a white splodge, and there was no way anyone could identify who it was without being told.

Marugame's city centre was suffering the same fate as many small provincial towns and cities: the rise of out-of-town shopping and the lack of public transport was killing the centre. This was a mid-Saturday afternoon and yet the lanes in the shopping mall, opened with a fanfare in the 1970s, were all but empty of shoppers. There are no famous brands here – no Louis Vuitton bags or Christian Dior belts.

Nowadays migrant workers have to be brought in to undertake manual labour. Many are from China and they live in dormitory blocks and keep themselves very much to themselves. They cook their own meals and all spare income – most of their income – is sent to mainland China. They don't bother to shop for fancy goods. They need only a bicycle to get them to and from work, T-shirt and jeans.

Although Marugame was in decline, it boasts an Internet café where we signed up as members and spent a couple of hours checking e-mail, none of which – at least for me – were of great interest as most of my 'hotmail' was spam.

'Become debt free.'

'Grow your penis by an extra 4 inches.'

'My personal incest pictures.'

Since I last reviewed my e-mail six days ago, 124 of them had accumulated, by-passing the 'junk mail filter' system.

But none proclaimed, 'Two prawns too big to eat.'

We ate at a family restaurant specialising in jumbo prawns. Glutton that I am, I thought I might need more than the two prawns served as a portion. Wrong. Confronting me were two whopping prawns, eight inches long and at least an inch and a half in diameter. (Where did they source such monsters other than from prawn farms adjacent to nuclear reactors? Or had these prawns read one of my spam mails?) Served with a scoop of potato salad and a small pile of shredded cabbage I was full, bloated and overstuffed, once finished.

But being overwhelmed by two prawns wasn't the only shock. From the outside, the restaurant was a concrete nonentity, part of a roadside bowling ring and *pachinko* parlour complex. But once past the entrance, the décor – if you looked closely – could have been straight from an innovative, cutting-edge Scandinavian design studio. Funky, chunky chairs with curved wooden backs patched with leather. The tables and modular low partitions were simple plain wood, forming complex geometric patterns. If the collection of beer posters, china figurine figures, Bavarian beer mugs, vases and other fiddly tat had been cast aside, the interior would have graced the pages of that bible of style, *Wallpaper* magazine. Who had taken the care to design such an interior and what motivated them to do it?

With the planting of the rice seedlings complete, the fields around us have transformed from grimy brown to a sparkling green. Each paddy was now submerged, and in the water swarmed black and brown creatures that look like tadpoles but weren't. They swam upside down, little legs whirring like fans. Sticking above the water's surface were the black shells of a freshwater mollusc. Satoko told me that once they used to eat them as a delicacy, boiled with miso, but they had to stop, as there were too many chemicals in the water. (Farming may look like some agrarian idyll but, in reality, it is heavily intensified and as opposite the organic end of the spectrum as can be found.)

Overhead, defiant swallows battled against the buffeting wind, straining to make forward progress as they caught insects on the wing. (Later when evening came, bats were on the hunt as well but, by then, the wind had calmed and they swooped with easy abandon.)

We walked to a nearby *onsen*: this time a private, not municipal, bath. Whilst showering, I noticed for the first time that a large scabby mole had emerged on my scalp. (There must be something about *onsen* that is leading me to examine my body thoroughly.) I'm certain it hadn't been there before, at least at this size, the size of a penny. Immediately I thought of skin cancer. Certainly, the relentless sun may have caused it to blossom. It didn't itch or bleed but crumbled when rubbed.

The *onsen* had two saunas. In one, the temperature was 104°C, the hottest I'd ever been in and within seconds my body was belching sweat. The other cooler, and with a tub of coarse sea salt that I rubbed all over my body. It stung. A lot. I also gingerly lowered myself into the bath with an electric current running through it – recommended for those with arthritis, and a weird and unpleasant sensation. My limbs jerked into uncontrollable spasms and I could only remain in the water for a matter of seconds.

This was not an *onsen* to indulge pleasures. Japan's TV game shows, where contestants are humiliated by being made to undertake extreme challenges, are laughed at the world over. This was my very own programme.

In spite of being on the edge of countryside, daily life in Satoko's parents' home was far from peaceful: this morning a light plane droned overhead playing pre-recorded advertising, read by a high-pitched female voice. One was for a local optician; Satoko said it hadn't changed for twenty or thirty years. Dogs barked constantly from their kennels, birds grittily twittered, neighbours chatted loudly on the street, cars over-revved their engines and motorbikes raced past. Indoors, almost too many clocks to count marked the hours and quarters by ringing out melodies and clanking chimes. Think of Pink Floyd's 'Time'.

My gold filling had fallen out on Saturday, prompting a visit to the dentist. It cost only Y2500 for the filling to be re-fitted (by a dentist, who didn't wear gloves and whose stained and antiquated dental tools looked as if they had been washed hastily in washing-up liquid). But then we walked in off the street with no appointment and waited only for five minutes so I shouldn't complain too much – unless I catch something nasty.

After spending two hours with them, I have concluded that Akuta's parents are the world's experts in making vile food. (Akuta is another friend of Satoko's from her schooldays.) Her mother had already brought to Satoko's parents a jar of pickled and fermented aubergine that, after one taste, I had pushed to one side. This afternoon, we visited their home and not only ate more fermented abominations but the vilest set of drinks I've ever tasted.

Akuta's parents once owned a timber company but sold it some years ago and retired whilst still in their late fifties. This gave them the opportunity to travel the world and, in one room of their home, they displayed a staggering collection of souvenir knickknacks: masks, dolls, cheap ethnic jewellery, daggers, embroideries, paintings, ceramics, sands, minerals, crystals and so and so on – so much that they must return from each trip weighed down with suitcases of the stuff.

Shown photo albums, each page an identical pose of both standing in front of a well-known landmark, I wondered if they actually saw anything of where they went to, or whether they merely leapt from the coach, posed for a photo and then rushed to the souvenir stand.

Akuta's father infused his own liquors by steeping fruits, seeds and petals in brandy and other alcohol. Most tasted horribly medicinal but the worst was the little trick he played on us, asking we sample one, and then guess what it was. The liquor was a pale colour, with a slight greenish tinge. Tasting musty and dry, I guessed it came from a hard fruit like an apple but was far from sure. Satoko couldn't decide either.

Any hints? No, he said. After we gave up, he fetched the bottle. He carried it in, wrapped with paper and when unwrapped we saw coiled inside a dead snake. Yes, we had drunk dead-snake liquor. I felt queasy. Even more so later, as the liquor left in the glass began to smell faintly of a dead body.

'The snake was a bit putrid when I found it,' he joked (maybe). 'Would you like some more?'

'No,' I said, perhaps a bit too forcibly, as I slammed my hand over the glass.

I wasn't unhappy to leave. He handed us gifts: a selection of liquors, which I passed on to Satoko's dad, warning him that one was snake. Straightaway, he fetched a small glass, and, I thought, rather enjoyed the experience.

I do mind if I never go back. Despite being a foreigner, despite that, when I'm there, Marugame's residents both see me but don't see me, I find a resonating comfort in the straightforwardness of life in this unsophisticated city. How long will the Contemporary Art Museum be able to afford to mount internationally important exhibitions? One day it will be holding school painting shows. The Hiraii Museum has now long ceased adding to its collection of Spanish art, and so the way of life here will continue to slide towards even greater simplicity. Not that the towns will become more beautiful. Marugame's shopping mall will one day collapse on itself and the port will finally disappear, leaving behind an empty basin save for a gaggle of small pleasure boats.

Maybe the young who hurried to Tokyo will tire of living among thirty-one million people and want to return, to spend their days in the municipal *onsen*, sprawled across a tatami mat, reflecting with no pleasure on the glittering future they had once sought but had never found.

Chapter Six

Otaru

On the train from Sapporo to Otaru, a young man, Gary from Nuneaton sat opposite us. 'Me 'ead's shattered from the beer. Feels like a bag of broken mirrors. Where the fuck am I going? Can you tell me when we get to Otaru?' he said with a phlegmatic slur in his voice.

Four little maids from school sat opposite us, perfectly uniformed in black laceless shoes, white ankle socks, and blue pleated skirts, white short-sleeved blouses, blue under shirts and blue and white striped neckerchiefs. All four had centrally parted, shoulder-length hair. They swayed, like flowers in a row and giggled, hands at their mouth, as they talked: about me, and the boy who had sat beside me, still moaning about his head.

'I just downed four cans on the platform. God I was thirsty. So hot here. I thought being in the north it would be cooler.'

I asked if he was a visitor. No, he told me, teaching English in Otaru.

'Been here for two years. You don't get many English in Otaru. In fact I haven't seen any since I arrived.'

I thought that was a long time not to have seen a single English person. 'Don't you travel in to Sapporo from time to time?' I asked. 'That's a cosmopolitan place.'

'Too expensive,' he said. 'Eight quid each way…I only go once in a while.'

In fact, it was eight quid return but it didn't seem worth correcting him. Later he said that he had been in Otaru for only two months. As he was drunk, it was clear his power of thought was failing.

'Nothing to do in Otaru,' he continued. 'No English TV or newspapers. Only the Ruskies. Miserable sods. But the money's good and I like the students. They're so polite.'

'How long will you stay?'

'Some people stay for ten years or more. I might do the same. The pay's great, you know.'

His eyelids slackened. I let him fall asleep, and nudged him awake when we arrived at Otaru.

'Want a drink?' he asked.

'No, we have to get back to the hotel. Sorry.'

I left him at the station, slumped on the steps at the entrance.

Otaru is a small port on Hokkaido, a town famous for its fish, crab, uni and cod roe; some of the best in Hokkaido hence, Satoko was ready to proclaim, some of the best in the world.

On our arrival yesterday, the local express train from the airport took us directly to Otaru, through Sapporo and then alongside a rocky coastline, tightly sandwiched between a sea the colour of dishwater (the weather was cold that day, even though it was June) and the bottom of a low mountain range.

In spite of the cold, a few brave and hardy families sat on the pebbles, huddled around portable barbecues. Not many, mind. When it comes to taking advantage of the sea air, no matter the weather conditions, the British win hands down.

The Grand Hotel, Otaru was on Sushi Alley, a nickname given to a street full of brightly lit seafood shops selling big red spider crabs, sticky thick red roe and a vast assortment of mirror-scaled fish laid out in perfect rows on beds of ice. A line of tour buses were parked in front of the stores, engines humming, their passengers allowed a precise ten minutes to crowd into the open front, poke and prod at the seafood, and buy produce to be shipped home.

Besides its well-deserved fame as a gourmet's paradise, Otaru was known for a collection of historic buildings. One hundred years ago, the town's fortune was built in part on its being the key port in Hokkaido for the export of coal, and for the export of fish to the rest of Japan. For a while, this was the richest city on Hokkaido. Banks erected stern gothic facades. Rich merchants built sham Italianate houses in an American style – not surprising, as most of the architects were American and America was the key influence at the time. Now the mines have closed, the fish and other manufacturing industries are in decline, and the town is slowly withering, supported mainly by tourism – trippers attracted by the seafood, in winter for the nearby skiing – and the occasional visit of cruise ships.

Today, it's easy to sneer at Japan's fascination and pride for a non-descript jumble of buildings only a hundred years old. Of no architectural importance, outside of Japan they would merit no interest at all. And yet here, they deserved large explanatory signs written in Japanese, English and Russian, detailing, with some trouble, the building's history and architectural distinctiveness.

'This building is constructed of a wooden frame and soft sandstone. It is distinctive because of the two arches at the front.'

But little historic secular architecture has survived earthquakes, the ravages of war, and relentless commercial development. This group of buildings, scattered along a few streets close to the sea front, were nigh on unique.

But there was one fly in the ointment. Despite unabashed civic pride, no attempt had been made to preserve them or their immediate environment from the encroachment of garish modernism. The streets had been turned over to a series of cheap shops, faced with ugly bright signs, selling tourist tat: glassware is popular here. Even the historic buildings had been badly repaired, the stucco peeling, updated insensitively and plastered with intrusive signage. Why, beyond the obvious answer of corruption and ineptitude, were Japan's planners incapable of implementing strict planning regulations?

Or should the West be blamed for this shambles?

Hearn wrote of the foreign concessions, that had sprung-up during the 1870s and 1880s:

> The foreign concession offers a striking contrast to its far-eastern environment. In the well-ordered ugliness of its streets one finds suggestions of places not in this side of the world, -just as though fragments of the Occident had been magically brought overseas: bits of Liverpool, of Marseilles, of New York of New Orleans.

In contrast, he described the Japanese city as little more than a 'wilderness of wooden sheds – picturesque, indeed, as paper lanterns are, but scarcely less frail…there is no great stir and noise anywhere – no heavy traffic, no booming and rumbling, no furious haste'.

The most famous of the historic buildings were a series of warehouses lining a narrow canal that separated port from town. They can be seen in every view, picture postcard, phone card, and poster. (And the local TV station had erected a web cam.) In the publicity material, I noticed that all the photographs had been taken either at night when the warehouses were floodlit or in winter when blanketed with snow. Being told that this was the oldest part of town, I imagined an area similar to The Rocks in Sydney.

We knew we were close when we saw an excited crowd, a horse and carriage, rickshaw and several commercial photographers.

But then, disappointment. In broad daylight, we were confronted not with the picturesque view we expected but with no more than a collection of four tattered warehouses, backing on to a fetid canal. Neither the buildings nor the canal were in any way handsome, out of the ordinary or historic – deserving not even a second glance. And yet here were hundreds of tourists, excited and clamouring to have their photograph taken against this backdrop. Aping Paris, artists erected stalls along the canal walk, offering a wide range of sketches, watercolours and oils of the scene. Photographers offered to take a large-format sepia-toned photograph. I smiled that so much excitement could be built upon such a silly and misleading premise.

After a lunch, we walked to the port, coming to an area where three Russian and one North Korean boat had moored: rusting hunks of battered metal, huge iron plates welded together – with none of the grace of a ship's line – putrid bilge water spilling out, the decks awash with grease and dirt. When Kipling travelled through Japan, he too came across a Russian steamer. He called the Russians 'Bad People' and described how filthy the ship was. So nothing had changed.

On the quayside, some of the sailors sat cross-legged on the ground, others rode bicycles in lazy circles whilst a few sprawled on battered sofas, smoking, and drinking an unrecognisable liquor from oily bottles. Vodka maybe or a spirit distilled from the engine oil.

'Why do Russians look so Russian?' asked Satoko, a question that I couldn't answer. They eyed us suspiciously. No hint of a greeting or a smile as we walked past. Just malicious suspicion. I felt conspicuous and awkward holding my camera. Their business was to ship used merchandise back to their homeland. The Russians specialising in second-hand cars, air-con units, used car tyres and fridges; the Koreans in boxes of twisted metal scrap; a trade that's been going on for centuries between Otaru and the countries across the sea.

Later, when we eat dinner, the chef/owner of the restaurant moaned about the Russian boats who fished illegally, and the Russian mafia buying up crab from the *yakusa* at inflated prices to sell in Moscow. (Otaru has more than its fair share of big Mercedes with darkened windows, all but masking the faint trace of someone inside, a cell phone stuck to an ear.)

'It's damaging the stocks as well. They over fish,' he told us.

Did we know it took at least fifteen years for a crab to reach a decent edible size, we were asked? 'The illegal fishermen poach anything and everything.'

Behind Sushi Alley ran a warren of narrow streets lined with clubs and hostess bars. No doubt, they thrived when the fishing port and harbour were stuffed with visiting trawlers and ships but, particularly today, it was difficult to see how they could all keep business afloat. The fact that the hostesses, some of whom we saw walking through the streets on their way to work, had an average age of sixty underscored that better days had been seen.

Somewhere in the middle of this faded soapland was this restaurant – Satoko had visited once before. Not much to look at – so forget first impressions – but the most incredible seafood was her assessment.

After backtracking, we found it at the bottom of a covered alleyway, the last door of three. I pulled back a sliding panel to reveal a tiny room. Inside it was dark, heavily tobacco-stained and looked filthy. There were tables but no seats; we had to sit on the floor, covered with a threadbare and stained carpet.

'Don't worry,' promised Satoko, 'the food's good.'

On the walls hung various fishing artefacts, a stuffed turtle – four feet in length from snout to tail and no doubt a protected species – and torn tourist posters of Japan. We sat at the far end, in front of two large aquaria, looking like they hadn't been cleaned in years. On the counter, dirty plates and dishes were stacked high, and behind them worked the owner. He looked forty-something, swarthy and with leathered brown skin. He bought or caught, prepared and cooked the seafood, his day starting at four a.m. and only finishing when the last customer left. His wife took on the responsibility of waitress. She looked much younger, no more than her early thirties and with her was their twenty-month old daughter – who walked confidently and was not too shy to come to our table as soon as we sat down, to say hello. She wasn't even intimidated by my *gaijin* looks or English language.

We began with *uni*. Mum came over to the aquaria, pushed away two pieces of wood, plunged in her hand and pulled out two black spiky sea urchins. She took them to the counter, handed them to her husband and a few seconds later they reappeared on two dishes, split in half and ready to eat. Inside was gleaming orange flesh. I took a spoon and lifted part of a lobe to my mouth. It was heaven: soft, creamy, the caviar and truffle of seafood. I had never tasted such fresh sea sweetness in my life. Fresh? It was alive.

More of the freshest seafood followed, served to that simple formula I now knew well: use the highest quality ingredients with little adornment and minimal cooking.

The crab was cooked half on one side (I think for seconds) but left raw on the other. The cooked half had meat that had swelled through cracks made in the shell, not at all like the meat we associate with boiled crab. A grilled air-dried fish was exquisite, the salty slightly pungent flesh falling from the bone. We had thirty-year-old shellfish, once common but now rare. They were divine: a richness and depth of flavour I had not tasted before from such creatures. If we'd ever tasted the sea's true flavour it was here.

The food on its own made it a memorable experience. But only in part.

Halfway through the meal, the daughter, who up until now seemed not like a baby but a child, insisted she was hungry. Without a hint of embarrassment, the mother sat on the floor close to our table, lifted her jumper and breast-fed her baby. And not just once, but again later.

After which the little girl decided she no longer wanted to wear her nappy and was sent to the toilet, on her own, to change. She took it off, cleaned herself, reappeared naked from the waist down and wandered round the restaurant like this for the rest of the night.

Mum and Dad didn't care. Nor concerned when the little girl – actually her name, as she told us, was Yuki – helping to clear up the empty plates, dishes and *sake* cups from the table and counter, also helped herself to dregs of *sake*. Picking up a cup, she knocked it back with one swallow. Now I doubt that much was left in the cups but she drank as if she had been on the gin all her twenty-month life.

In a few years time, she would be out-drinking everyone. Let's say by the age of five.

Chapter Seven

The In-Between Land

Only half-past-nine in the morning but already a noisy flock of *oba-chan*, (middle-aged housewives) were drinking Kirin beer and pink sickly Japanese wine, laughing at stories of past trips.

We shared the same Green Coach #9, hurtling between Tokyo and Kobe on Hirari 117, the *Shinkansen* that departed Tokyo on time, to the second, at 9.07 a.m. (although the higher priced coach was neither green on the outside nor inside: the reclining seats were brown velour, the carpet and curtains a thick beige whilst the exterior was painted white).

I was making one of my frequent trips to Kobe.

Most of my other fellow passengers were silent salarymen, all wearing a finely pressed sombre grey or black suit, and immaculately groomed from head to toe: hair slicked, hands scrubbed, nails polished and stubble eliminated. Fashions had changed but not the attention to perfection. When Kipling rode this line in 1889 he described his fellow passengers as wearing neat tweed suits, with fawn-coloured overcoats, with paper and celluloid collars and white cotton gloves, 'and they smoked cigarettes from fairy little cigarette cases'.

This was a non-smoking carriage. The few more diligent souls among them tapped on laptops – making final preparations for their forthcoming meetings – but most slipped off their black shoes and slumped back asleep. Those less knowledgeable about Japanese work habits might be surprised by this lack of diligence and application to work. Surely, the salaryman worked at every opportunity? But, no matter the Japanese toil longer hours and take fewer holidays than their Western counterparts, they've been found to be no more productive than other industrialised nations; in fact, they come quite low in the league table. Robotic work-automatons they are not.

If it weren't for the chatter and the snoring, the bullet train would be virtually noiseless. There was no rat-ta-tat clacking of rails, just a slight but unobtrusive whine from the electric turbine, sometimes a faint grumble from steel wheel on steel track and the occasional dull thwack as the shockwaves of two trains travelling at over 300 km/hr in opposite directions collided. For most of the journey, the ride was so smooth, the carriage so stable, that if I did decide to work it was easy to write without my pen jerking in an illegible scrawl across the page or the laptop sliding off the table.

I always caught the train when travelling to Kobe. I could fly – the door-to-door journey marginally quicker – but on the train, I watched a fascinating panorama of Japan slip past (and grabbed the chance to doze).

A young girl walked past me pushing, with an effort she tried unsuccessfully to hide, a metal serving trolley laden with drinks and snacks. She wore a candy-striped apron, a yellow blouse, an orange scarf – a medley of colours that add to the sense of holiday I always felt when on the train, and a further reason to prefer travelling this way.

In broken singsong English, she asked if I wanted to eat anything. Pointing with a finger, I chose an *Arare* set, a box of savoury, soy-flavoured rice crackers, best eaten with beer but, at this time of the day, I stuck to a plastic bottle of cold green tea.

Sat next to me a middle-aged man had fallen asleep. He had taken off his suit jacket and meticulously hung it so it didn't crease. In the lapel, I could see his company pin, the company logo, and a mark of group identification, loyalty and belonging worn by many employees.

To shade his face from the morning sun, he'd pulled the curtain.

Up until today, it had been raining steadily and monotonously for five days. Japan's rainy season started Saturday night at the precise moment I stood on a balcony looking over the southern sprawl of suburban Tokyo. Inside, a party was taking place hosted by a gay couple: one German, the other Chinese. As the rain fell, the rooftops gradually disappeared under a grey shroud that dampened everyone's spirits.

(Since the party, the couple had acrimoniously split up. The German ran off with a younger man, and the Chinese partner moved to Los Angeles to start life anew. Everyone's sympathy was with Shin; Jorge tarred as the bad guy. Shin was good-looking, young, tall, slim, and intelligent – so no one could understand what Jorge, a rather dumpy but, we thought, pleasant German had in mind to run off with a younger boy. Maybe better sex someone suggested. Or was it, speculated someone else, because Shin's still mixed up – once heterosexual and married, and with a very cheeky daughter whom he would have to visit from time to time.)

It was only a mild exaggeration to say it was one endless mass of buildings from Tokyo to Kobe but then, even by the seventeenth century, Japan's arterial highways ran through village after village where all boundaries had been lost to ribbon development. A journey through an area known as the Pacific Belt – where most of Japan's industry had developed since the Second World War – took a smidgeon over three hours. From the train, Japan looked like a country where someone had tipped, from the sky, a giant Lego box, scattering buildings with abandon.

From time to time, it was possible to snatch a glimpse of the Pacific Ocean – a shimmering blue – between the piles of tangled buildings, an ugly sprawl of pre-fab houses, aluminium-clad factories, pachinko parlours, love hotels, cars, roads, pylons and the detritus of metropolitan living. Just occasionally, the train cut through paddy fields, rattled tea bushes and bent the slender bamboo that grew in dense groves alongside the track. And if lucky, on a sunny and clear day like today, I might see Mount Fuji from base to summit, a perfectly smooth heavenly cone, although, more often, its white peak was enveloped in heavy cloud cover.

When Kipling had taken a train along this same route – a journey that had taken twelve hours for a distance some two-thirds of mine – he complained ironically about how varied the scenery was: a 'blinding alteration of field, mountain, sea-beach, forest, bamboo grove and rolling moor covered with azalea blossoms.'

Now the speed of the train blurred what little variety was left.

Very few of the towns or villages were, in the remotest way, pretty. More like upmarket shantytowns. Instead of the houses being neatly and amply spaced, they were heaped together in a random and haphazard pattern, often too close to one another and with only the smallest of gardens. Most were prefabricated kits of concrete, glass, plaster, metal and plastic. Some might be tiled in a traditional manner but, in the hundreds of miles between Tokyo and Kobe, no local characteristic peeped through. Localised building features as we recognise in England, like Cotswold stone or the flints of East Anglia, were absent. Just like the salarymen slumped around me, all signs of difference had been squeezed out and eliminated.

We sped past a car park where the neat ranks of hundreds of cars appeared to be of only three colours: white, silver and black – thoroughly washed and sparkling in the sun, but not one with a distinguishing element of individuality. Every opportunity to add personality and character to the design had been shunned.

No wonder this morning my attention was grabbed by a yellow VW Beetle waiting at a traffic signal. Not only did the colour shout out, but also I could take the design, reduce it to three simple three curves and yet most of the world would identify its shape. This was impossible with a Japanese car. At forty paces who could spot the difference between a Honda, Nissan or Toyota? I couldn't.

The train reached Shin Kyoto station, an ugly concrete bunker blot that spoilt the centre of the city. Nowhere in Japan is there one example, historic or modern, of an attractive railway station.

The *oba-chan* nudged and jostled each other off the train, shuffling along the platform in a tight protective pack. Too many Japanese women and girls shuffle with toes and knees pointed inwards. Whether this is physiological – after all they have short legs – and I read that penguins waddle because of their short legs – or cultural – as wearing a *kimono* and clogs preclude any other manner of walking and somehow this has assimilated into the natural gait – I don't know but they shuffle. Once, I heard a Taiwanese female VJ – she worked for MTV – comment that Japanese girls walked on carrot legs. But then I also read that an old Japanese term for the shape of women's legs was '*daikon ashi*', meaning legs like a giant radish.

On leaving the station, the *oba-chan* will maraud around the temples, restaurants and coffee shops of Kyoto; their husbands had been packed off to work, the golf course or the cemetery, his salary or legacy commandeered and now wilfully spent.

A wife took responsibility for the husband's salary and handed him pocket money. I heard it often said that she wasn't too fussed whether he returned home in the evening or not. At every chance, and if she had no children to look after, she would have fun with her friends. Forget the Western misperception of a meek and mild wife waiting dutifully at home with dinner on the table. No wonder the salaryman sought solace in the company of a hostess, groping a knee, feeling a tit, scratching his balls, falling horribly drunk, and pissing and vomiting in the street. With his mind-numbing routine at the office, working at a cramped work-station set in rows like the office in a Dickensian novel, with no personal privacy and under the constant gaze of his boss and workmates, and a wife who enjoyed her freedom on his money who could blame him?

Two further stops down the line I stepped out at Shin-Kobe, exactly three hours, seventeen minutes after leaving Tokyo and arriving precisely on schedule.

Down the stairs, through the ticket barrier and on to the concourse where I hailed one of the many waiting taxis to take me to Rokko Island (a man-made island, built a few hundred yards from the shoreline with rock quarried from Mount Rokko, a mountain overlooking Kobe).

I had been coming here on business since 1993. Then the island was in its early years of construction and much of it was wasteland. Within ten years of the first rocks being dumped in the sea, most of the island's infrastructure had been finished and it was home to tens of thousands of people. Indeed, completion would have been quicker but for the Great Hanto earthquake of 1995 when construction resources were diverted to rebuilding Kobe, and when the open ground on the island was used to erect some of the thousands of temporary housing units that sheltered earthquake survivors.

Many friends lived on the island when the earthquake happened. At precisely 5.46 a.m.

They spoke of a sense of total helplessness. As their world shook to pieces, they described being bounced helplessly like rag dolls; all they could do was lie on the floor or in bed, waiting for it to stop, gripped by the terrible belief that their apartment block was about to collapse.

For twenty seconds they listening to the crack of plaster and cement, and the crash of breaking glass and china as their possessions fell to the floor.

Then it stopped. For a moment, silence. They spoke of not being able to move at first, paralysed by terror, expecting the shaking to start again, not knowing what to do. They were trapped in darkness, the sun had yet to come out and the electricity had failed. Then crying broke out. Those with children stumbled around, tripping over furniture as they went to their children's rooms to find out if they were safe.

Then their thoughts were to get out of the building before it collapsed.

They threw on clothes and rushed down the emergency stairs. Many of the children now cried hysterically.

For the first two or three days, they and the other islanders lived in a school hall, shut off from the mainland as bridges connecting island to shore had collapsed. Walking around the island was possible – although often having to walk through deep mud due to the liquefaction of the ground – and they discovered that Rokko Island was relatively unscathed; no building had collapsed. Across on the mainland, they saw fires raging, black palls of smoke, the elevated Expressway that had keeled over, and toppled buildings. Overhead was the constant whine and roar of helicopters. Most weren't rescue but belonged to the media. Portable radios were the only means of hearing news of the devastation, listening with horror as the names of the dead were read out, always wondering as lists were updated whether the name of a family member or friend was among them. After-shocks raised more fears, everyone waited for the next big one and few people could restfully sleep.

Within three days, evacuation began by ship, moving everyone to nearby Osaka. Not one life was lost on Rokko Island but elsewhere the earthquake claimed over 5,500 lives and 35,000 people were injured.

A number of factors contributed to the severity of the damage. Notwithstanding the size of the quake itself, extensive damage was caused by the concentration of many old buildings in Kobe, the fact that much of Kobe over the last 800 years had been built on landfill and a series of unusual geological land structures focused and amplified the energy of the shock.

Later, I found a comment written by a Japanese student who survived the earthquake.

Takeo Funabashi wrote: 'I was dreaming. I was sound asleep and deeply dreaming. And the dream was a good one, but this dream was broken and I never saw it again…. . Dark, it was really dark and more it was somehow a horrible darkness. No other darkness was as fearful as this darkness.'

Five or six years on, only vestiges of the earthquake could be found on the island and then only if searched for. In places, pavements had slipped and remained unaligned, or a road sign or bollard was off centre. (But pointing them out to less knowledgeable but enquiring visitors left me feeling like a voyeur.)

In Tokyo, I experienced many minor earthquakes and several that were a sudden hard jolt, dislodging books, knocking over vases but never damaging anything significant. I learnt how impossible it was to react once the trembling started: I was fixed to the spot, only thinking how long was this going to last, how big was it going to be?

Rokko Island was the Disney Land of all urban developments, a town planner's utopian dream, and the type of place that in the 'fifties and 'sixties was proclaimed as the vision of how we should all live in the future. Through its centre ran a paved pedestrian zone, a shallow watercourse with fountains, and an overhead monorail. Mothers strolled safely with babies, toddlers paddled happily in the water, unattended children played games without risk of being run over or abducted, and old women walked to the shops without being mugged.

This was a wholly self-sufficient community served by a large hospital, several schools catering for all ages and nationalities, two hotels, several shopping malls, a multi-screen cinema, enough restaurants to satisfy most tastes including a Wendy's, Starbucks and a MacDonald's, and a fashion museum. It was a place where, every weekend, barbeques, keg parties and treasure hunts were held. For good measure, not all was perfect: the loss-making fun fair quickly closed, and the Seagull, the only decent bar on the island, shut after local residents objected to the noise.

To me, Rokko Island was the nightmare made real of the urban future: clean, efficient, safe, orderly, and sterile with none of the uniqueness, and quirky character of Japan. The antithesis of everything I loved and hated about Tokyo. Most of all, it was place where you didn't have to think.

I was awake with the sun at six a.m. Outside my hotel, seventeen floors below on a plaza, over a hundred kids lined up in front of a track-suited adult. What were they doing? Some stragglers rode up on their bikes, dropped them to the ground and ran to join the end of a row. A few others gathered in small groups, a little distance from the main pack.

The adult began to jump up and down. The kids followed suit. I couldn't hear any sound from behind the triple-glazed hotel window. Spellbound I watched for the next fifteen minutes: these kids jumping up and around, waving their arms in the air, bending over and touching their toes. Then it stopped, and like ants madly running in all directions from scalding water, the kids dispersed. The plaza was empty.

On a return trip from Kobe, we had stopped at a station, it was early evening and I heard an awful unexpected screech from the front of the carriage. Not a mechanical one. Human, but inhuman like a trapped animal. I took no notice until I heard a second, louder than the first. Everyone in the compartment stood up. At the front stood two uniformed train officials, standing over someone sat in the first row of seats. An argument started. Whoever it was, and I guessed it was a girl, shouted at them. They shouted back. The officials were joined by a third and suddenly two of them lunged at the girl, she was pulled from the seat and dragged from the compartment. She was young, in her early twenties maybe, shouting at the top of her voice but I couldn't understand a word said. As soon as they manhandled her off (and it took a matter of seconds to drag her from the carriage) the train lurched forward. I looked out of the window. The girl was held, with her arms pinned behind her back, by two of the men whilst the third spoke into a walkie-talkie.

I don't know what caused the incident. Perhaps she hadn't paid the full fare. Who knows? It didn't warrant this rough treatment. I wrote a letter of complaint but never received a reply.

I sat back; disgusted by the way the girl had been manhandled; in strange contradictions to the rules of social behaviour in Japan, which said that everyone should show restraint and politeness at all times. Rigid rules, with great importance placed on them being observed and up until now I had never seen them broken in public. The concept of *wa*, the way of creating harmony among individuals where the group is more important than the self. (*Wa* is also used as a prefix to identify things Japanese from things foreign.) I had never seen anyone argue in the street, in a shop, or at an airline check-in counter.

Nothing wrong with good manners and restraint, of course. The French philosopher Andre Comte-Sponville argued that good manners were the foundation of good morals. However, he argued further that whilst politeness was essential as a child grew up, in adulthood, too much politeness was insincere. 'It is better to be too honest to be polite than too polite to be honest.'

There was a school of thought at Oxford in the 1960s that emphasised the virtue for individuals to be good rather than relying on good acts. In Japan, I was discovering it was not the true nature of a person but the good acts, the right behaviour, the giving and receiving of a gift that were used to define character. In other words, you could be a complete idiot but if you abided by the rules you were seen as good, and any defects of character forgiven.

Japan, for me, should not be celebrated as the land of the rising sun but that of the setting sun and the golden transformation of the country.

It was half-past four. I sat on the *Shinkansen* returning from Kobe.

We passed over the languid estuary of a river, the water reflecting a deep opaque blue. We flashed past trees of the darkest green. As the sun dropped towards the horizon, shadows darkened and lengthened, their colours becoming more saturated by the minute. The shadows fell on ground that had dried out, the grass dead and brown but in the sunset, it turned a dull gold. Distant mountains faded behind a veneer of haze. At this time of day, the rural side of Japan was accentuated over the urban: the evening light transmuted the edge of buildings, roads, and telegraph poles. Hard shapes evaporated.

Outside I imagined the air was perfectly still.

An old man walked his dog along a raised path cleaved through the paddy fields. I noticed him, but he would never have seen me. On another path, a woman carried two bulging bags of shopping, one in each hand. Neither she nor the man was in a hurry to return home. I was reminded of school days. Of autumn evenings when returning home, the colours the same coppers and gold, skipping along the road with no cares or worries, knowing tea was on the table but not rushing indoors. The air was warm without being stifling. It was pure, chilled with a slight zing. Sounds were muted. Those days I thought I could play forever.

But it was remarkable how few people I saw in this semi-rural hinterland. Few bicyclists on the road, few people walking along streets or lanes; school playgrounds empty, and workers locked inside the factories. Nobody tended their gardens. Cars, construction equipment and lorries looked abandoned.

Life had stopped. Suddenly the sun dipped behind a mountain and the sky exploded into a sweep of mottled greys, oranges and reds, as if frail curtains of fire hung from the sky.

Mount Fuji's giant cone soared in the distance. (Not one volcano but three lurked in its bowels.)

Ironically, one of the world's most pleasing mountains, a father to Japan, when seen up close, suffers from a terrible blight at its base: criss-crossed by electricity pylons, red and white striped chimneys belched smoke, land had been pock-marked by quarrying, and an elevated road was under construction. A rash of shopping malls and *pachinko* parlours crept slowly up the lower slopes like an advancing eczema

Why doesn't the mountain erupt and incinerate this disfigurement?

If it does (the last large scale eruption was in 1707), it has been predicted that within twenty-four hours, ten square kilometres of Fuji City would be buried under larva. The key transport arteries, the Tokaido Shinkansen line (which I was travelling on) and the Tomei Expressway would be severed irreparably at several points. Tokyo would be covered in eight centimetres of ash; Haneda and Narita airports paralysed. Over a million households would be without electricity and the total cost of damage would exceed Y2.5 trillion. Is it possible that Fuji could erupt again? In recent years repeated, albeit minor earthquakes within the mountain, remind the world it is still an active volcano.

We passed by. There had been no eruption. In fifty minutes, we would arrive in Tokyo.

Chapter Eight

Welcome to Tokyo

"—You wonder why I hate Kumamoto. Well, firstly, because it is modernized. And then I hate it because it is too big, and has no temples and priests and curious customs in it. Thirdly, I hate it because it is ugly. Fourthly I hate it because I am still a stranger in it, — and perhaps because I can't get literary material. But Settsu [sic] made me post my letters of application in the table-drawer and wait. She says it is better to stay here another year or two, — that it might be much worse elsewhere. Perhaps she is right. She thinks, like you do, that the only trouble is I can't understand these people." *Lafcadio Hearn in a letter written in 1893.*

When Hearn wrote this, he might have equally said the same thing about modern-day Tokyo.

But then it may do no more than show the contradictions that any foreign resident in Japan faces, not only then but also now. The longer you stay, the more you find that you are a stranger because, far from finding that a lengthy sojourn makes you accepted, you find that the longer you stay in one sense the less accepted you become. If you visit as a tourist, you are a mere temporary being that hardly impacts upon the nation (even today Japan receives less than five million tourists a year), and can be safely dismissed. But to stay?

Foreigners were objects of curiosity and distrust even when the country was opened to the West after 1868. They could only travel through the Japanese countryside with passports stamped and with the route predetermined. Before arriving in Japan, visitors had to contact the Japanese Foreign Office with details of the route, age, profession, and a personal description. On arrival at a main port, the appropriate papers would be ready for collection.

Little had changed. In the weeks prior to the 2002 World Cup kick-off, scare-mongering by the British and Japanese media was rampant. Announcements were made that over a thousand fans – read hooligans – were subject to Football Banning Orders, surrendering their passports and prevented from travelling. Even the British Foreign Office assumed only trouble would occur, and the embassy in Tokyo issued warnings of what a spell in a Japanese prison would be like. Not very nice was their verdict. Furthermore, two Japanese immigration officers had arrived in England, analysed intelligence reports, concluding that at least a further150 people would be denied entry if they landed on Japanese soil. I worried that Japan's police force would lump all English fans into one big pot called 'hooligan', viewing us all as criminals, with the slightest boisterous behaviour leading to a night in the cells.

'British soccer hooligans stir fear across Japan' ran a typically sensational large-point headline in a Japanese national newspaper. Numerous articles described the tactics and weapons to be used by the police in case of trouble including a pole-mounted noose designed to grab 'furrigan's' ankles. Said a police spokesman, 'The best way to defeat taller opponents is to trip them up and subdue them on the ground.'

Nets were another method. Shot from guns, they would cast an entangling web over a group of rampant supporters. This was Spiderman for real. And extra large handcuffs to fit Anglo-Saxon wrists were purchased.

Rabble-raising politicians had a field day. One was quoted, 'We must also brace ourselves against unwanted babies being conceived by foreigners who rape our women.'

Neighbourhoods surrounding stadium were warned to remove any items – such as flower pots from front gardens – that could be used as a missile, and shops were advised to close on match days. For the first time I saw armed policemen patrolling subway stations in Tokyo, and even schools had counter-hooligan plans.

How many times as I passed through customs at Narita – Japan's main international airport – was a hand held up – I stopped – my passport examined, asked where I flew from, what was I doing in Japan, did I carry a business card, anything to declare, and after I said no, could I open my suitcase? It didn't matter that I lived in Japan. Every time I was stopped and my belongings searched.

An irony of Japanese customs regulations is that no pornography can be brought into the country. Not unusual, as few countries allow hard-core porn to be imported but Japan also excludes what most/many/some/a few men would consider soft and innocuous like *Playboy*. Ironic as Japan has the most outrageous porn readily available on the high street, either in magazines or on videos. An ambiguous attitude exists towards porn. Despite strict laws that no pubic hair can be shown, everything and anything else exists – if sometimes masked by pixels. (If your bent is coprophilia, this is the place for you.) Up until 2000, when new laws were enacted, Japan ISPs were the gateway to paedophilia. Even today, Japanese web bulletin boards and newsgroups contain images of a dubious nature, and men's obsession with soiled schoolgirl knickers is a cliché but true.

Once when standing in line at customs, the American businessman in front of me was asked if he had anything to declare. 'No,' he replied. 'Open your suitcase,' he was told. He did so and lying on top of his clothes was a copy of *Penthouse*. The customs officer picked it up and waved it aloft so that most of us in the vast hall could have seen it.

'This is porn, not allowed, I have to confiscate it,' he said in a voice louder than was needed.

The businessman turned bright red and happily demurred. But the customs officer continued holding the magazine aloft, telling the traveller how importing porn was illegal and how he should have known this and didn't he listen to announcements or read what was permissible or not? The queue was growing. 'You must sign papers that agree I can throw it away,' the officer pronounced. The poor guy wished the earth had swallowed him up. 'Please just throw it away,' he whimpered.

Whatever route is taken to enter Tokyo: by rail, road or car, whether from within or outside the country the journey is akin to being swallowed and digested by a huge beast.

You need to experience first-hand the interminable forty-mile journey between Narita and Tokyo's centre to appreciate fully its tediousness. At best, it takes an hour and a half to reach Tokyo's centre. On a bad day, three hours or longer, and already an hour had passed walking through the airport – assuming that immigration control was fully manned and I hadn't arrived soon after a jumbo jet from Korea. (Whenever Koreans arrive, immigration officers take perverse delight in meticulously checking the minutiae of their passports and entry documentation.) If I touched down at nine in the morning, home wasn't reached until after midday.

At the end of every trip, I would leave the customs hall relieved I had made it through unscathed, but dog-tired and my back and legs aching. My mouth was desiccated, stomach bloated, scalp itched and my clothes creased, crumpled and faintly sweaty. As quickly as possible I wanted to undress, shower and lie out flat on a bed.

Three modes of transport were available: coach, taxi and train. None quicker than the other.

I always chose the coach: the Narita Limousine Bus. Taxis cost a small fortune, at least £150. The express train was a guaranteed hour's journey but departures infrequent, and inconvenient if burdened with heavy luggage, as the platform was several floors and many stairs below Arrivals. At least the Limousine Bus stopped immediately outside the Arrivals Hall, with a bus departing every ten minutes to TCAT (the Tokyo Central Air Terminal) and services directly – albeit less numerously – to many of the major hotels in Tokyo (in total, 1,200 departures daily, back and forth).

At the coach stop, baggage attendants would stow my luggage into the belly of the coach. Another attendant checked my ticket and, before the coach left, he or she would stand at the front, bow deeply and wish everyone a safe journey.

'Welcome to the Narita Limousine Bus,' said an emotionless pre-recorded voice – first in Japanese and then in English – once we were under way.

'We will be making stops at Tokyo City Air Terminal and Tokyo Station. For your comfort and safety we advice all passengers to remain in their seats and wear the seat belt.'

Advice ignored by everyone.

'Also for the comfort of your fellow passenger we ask all mobile phones be switched off as they can annoy your neighbour.'

To my relief, this rule was usually observed. In any case, those experienced of the journey were already fast asleep.

Having left the airport, the route to Tokyo passed through a narrow belt of farmland: mainly rice fields where a farmer, wearing a plaited straw hat, might be breaking the soil by hand, surrounded by attractive dense pine groves warmed by the sun. Pretty, like the glossy photographs in travel guides, until without warning the road hit the washed-up shoreline of industrialisation. Breakers' yards, corrugated iron warehousing and workshops; small dirty industry that encircled Tokyo like the muck deposited on a beach at high tide. This then merged with a belt of gaudy *pachinko* parlours and love hotels; the final twenty miles were uninterrupted suburb and commercial districts, densely built, bleak and dreary, further burdened by the impression that they were enveloped in a constant grey drizzle even on a sunny day. On this journey, there was no grand vista to admire nor distant city landmarks to see with mounting excitement – save for when Disneyland was passed and the Fairy Castle and Space Mountain came into view. For most, a first-time encounter with Japan was a disappointment. Where were the ancient temples, the wooden houses, the pretty countryside splashed with blossom, visitors would ask as the coach inched towards Tokyo, the first few miles of the journey now forgotten? We arrived as first-time visitors with eager anticipation, noses pressed against the cold coach window, expecting immediate fulfilment of our dreams. Instead, we might think we had entered Tokyo through its plumbing system.

For this reason I found it best to arrive at night, at least then experiencing the thrill of seeing miles of neon tube arcing and exploding in all directions, the millions of lit office windows hovering in the sky like enormous swarms of fireflies, the unremitting blandness of the shoddy architecture camouflaged by darkness and a neon façade.

But then darkness underlies Japan's approach to the aesthetic. In his book *In Praise of Shadows* the author Junichiro Tanizaki outlined how much of Japan's heritage – houses, a woman's make-up, food, laquerware, jade and crystal for example – had been created so best seen and appreciated in darkness or shadow. Darkness is an indispensable element of Japanese beauty, he wrote – a point of view I could now understand. Of course, he argued from a positive basis, that design and look are augmented when seen in shadow, not that darkness is a means of hiding ugliness, but then he was writing in 1933.

Narita Airport itself was dull, whether in light or shade, and wreaked of an institution that was impersonal and uncaring. Neither of the two terminals – even the newest – had architectural distinction – nor much thought for passenger convenience as both demand that passengers switch up and down levels as we walked to and from the plane. The variety of shops and facilities was inadequate, no better than a provincial town's high street, and expensive. Statistically, Narita ranked eighth in the world league table of passengers carried; cargo more important where it ranked second.

But behind this anonymous and admittedly innocuous façade, where cargo was more important than people, lies a turbulent and violent history.

'At 07:13 hours London time a suitcase being unloaded from Canadian Airlines Flight 003 in Narita exploded, killing two baggage handlers and injuring others,' ran the start of a news agency story. The year was 1985.

Fifteen years later, the Royal Canadian Mounted Police arrested two Indian Sikhs, subsequently issuing this press release:

'VANCOUVER, BC, October 27, 2000 — The RCMP has laid charges in connection with the Air India bombing off the coast of Ireland on June 23, 1985, which killed 329 people. Included in the Information are charges relating to the 1985 suitcase bomb which exploded at the New Tokyo International Airport in Narita Japan, killing two men and injuring four others.

At approximately 12:00 p.m. today, members of the Air India Task Force arrested 53-year-old Ripudaman Singh Malik of Vancouver and 51-year-old Ajaib Singh Bagri of Kamloops'.

Among the charges brought were: unlawfully conspiring to commit the murder of the passengers and the crew on board Air India Flight 301 from Narita, Japan to Bangkok, Thailand and the 329 passengers and crew on board Air India Flight 182 from Montreal to London England; First Degree murder of the 329 passengers and crew of Air India Flight 182 and First Degree murder in the deaths of Hideo Asano and Hideharu Koda.

The plan was to bomb simultaneously both Air India flights out of the sky. They succeeded with the flight from Montreal to London but were thwarted when the bomb destined for the Air India flight to Bangkok exploded on the ground at Narita.

Two years later in 1987, an earthquake seriously damaged the airport but the airport's most turbulent period started when it was first constructed.

Until Narita opened, the international airport was located at Haneda, a coastal town to the south of Tokyo, some way out but still convenient to reach Tokyo's central district. For unknown reasons, when Haneda became overcrowded and could no longer cope with the rise of air traffic, the government decided against extending its runways. Rather, it was felt better to choose the farthest distance possible for the site of a new Tokyo international airport. Maybe pork barrel politics was involved. Maybe they thought, as this was farming land, they would face less resistance from a rural rather than an urban community. If so, they were wrong.

When selection of the new site was announced in 1966, it came without warning. The government had taken the decision not to consult local residents over the project – although after the decision had been made, a sham of a public hearing was held. Not surprisingly, there was significant opposition primarily from the farming community who would lose their land and livelihood. Their protests were ignored. (It was also true that few international airlines were in favour because of the distance from Tokyo and the lack of direct, swift and easy transport.)

To rally and focus their dissent, the farmers formed the 'League of Sanrizuka and Shibayama Farmers Against Narita Airport', announcing they would literally fight any attempt to start work on the project. This threat wasn't ignored. The 1960s were a time of violent student clashes in Japan, and virulent left- and right-wing political parties were itching for further conflict. In October 1967, as initial work began, the government mobilized two thousand riot police to restrain the belligerent farmers. For the next few years, constant on-and-off battles were fought. Another crescendo of violence was reached in 1971 when the authorities confiscated the last tracts of land inside the site. To resist, the farmers (their ranks swollen with supporters from left-wing student movements – an uneasy alliance) dug defences around their land, chained themselves to trees, and fought and defended themselves with agricultural tools, bamboo lances and stones.

One ex-student said this of his period as a protestor.

'I'm now over fifty and when I look back there have been only two times when I felt that living was an exhilaration. One of those was when I battled at Narita.

As we fought all I could hear were sounds only: the sound of something hitting human bodies and helmets; the cries of the leader of our combat unit "don't draw back" and "don't spread out. Huddle up." It was a truly eerie sensation that the enemy were audible but invisible. Such was almost a daily, and nightly, routine of my life during that period.

We threw fire squibs to blind the police and brandished wooden staves at the signal of a whistle blown by their leader. When the whistle was blown – in a noticeably long note – we knew it was a signal for the start of a full-scale offensive. The police were extremely well officered, just like a well-disciplined combat unit but for us it was little different from Yakuza duels that we were familiar with in cheap movies.

Japan's Vietnam. That's how it became known. The people against the establishment. Four riot police were killed and one farmer committed suicide.'

The conflict at Narita was an example of how once consent is broken in Japan, convention rapidly unravels, society adopts extreme positions and constructive dialogue becomes impossible. Imagine society as a wound coil that needs to be gripped tight to stop it springing open.

The government originally set completion of the first 4000-metre runway for April 1971 but not until 1978 was the first phase ready and even then, in March 1978, just days before the airport was scheduled to open, supporters of the farmers occupied the control tower, causing damage that resulted in a further two-month delay. Finally, a single runway was inaugurated on 20th May, 1978. By now the airport's perimeter was ring-fenced with barbed and razor-topped wire. It was more prison than airport.

Ever since that time, the airport has remained securely guarded. To enter even the outer perimeter I had to produce my passport for examination. Narita will exist as a fortress forever. Yet, few arrivals probably know of the airport's history but no doubt if they did, and as they're stuck in a traffic-jam along the expressway to Tokyo, they would wish the farmers had been victorious.

How do you understand a city that had a man dressed as a polar bear participating in a civil emergency exercise at Tokyo Zoo? Undertaken with complete seriousness, the purpose was to practise capturing escaped animals. The man wore a white fur suit – with a smiley-face bear head – and large flat pads on his hands. The media watched. In our morning newspaper the following day, a story ran with three pictures: the first of the 'bear' climbing out of an enclosure, the second of it being chased by keepers and the third of the captured bear lying prone on the ground.

Sugoi, people would say on learning we lived in Shirogane. (This is Japanese for 'cor, that's good'.) Admittedly, in Tokyo it was an impressive address like Mayfair in London, the 16th in Paris or the Upper East Side in New York. But whilst no dreary suburb, neither was it immediately opulent. Obvious signs of wealth or fame were few: big silent detached houses could be found, obscured behind old pine trees and high walls but around the corner might stand a concrete company dormitory block, with washing hanging from hundreds of small balconies and bicycles scattered near the front entrance. But then that was Tokyo: a chaotic series of small villages and towns that over time had melded into one another, no longer well-defined, disfigured and losing most of their individual and distinctive character. Tokyo resisted being subdivided into rich or poor areas, trendy or conservative, up and coming or been and gone. Ninety-nine per cent of Tokyo was the same. Or to put it another way ninety-nine percent was bland, monotonous and thoroughly middle-class.

Whatever made Tokyo a great city – and it was – it certainly wasn't the buildings. Ever since my first visit, I found Tokyo architecturally, one of the most brutal places in the world. Buildings squeezed me in. Concrete slapped my face. I was blinded by steel and glass. But that's what made it edgy, rebellious and distinctive: people were secondary to buildings. There was no equal and one-to-one relationship. Buildings had the upper hand, and the population had to fight the tyranny of construction.

Tokyo's layout was unplanned anarchy. Zoning? This was supposed to exist but applied haphazardly and dictated by conspiratorial commercial interests. Neither immediate beauty, nor grand ceremonial statements of public works or monuments exist. Most buildings were not designed but assembled from components. Their average life span was twenty-six years compared to seventy-five in the UK. This meant the value of property started high and then deteriorated quickly. Indeed, the buildings themselves became worthless. When property was bought, the value was in the land, and often the old building torn down and replaced. No wonder they held little respect for man.

Latest figures show that the average temperature in Tokyo had increased over the last hundred years more than any other capital city. Meanwhile, the Tokyo Municipal Government revealed it was relaxing the already ignored rules on environmental impact assessments for property development. In short, developers can build how they like and where they like with scant regard for the environment.

Nor was Tokyo a green city despite the Emperor's practice of frequently planting a tree. Only five per cent of Tokyo's land area was given over to parks compared with thirty per cent of London. Most were small so it was hard to find a place where I felt I'd escaped, where I could relax and feel not hemmed in by buildings or distracted by the groan of antagonised traffic caught in a gridlock. Nonetheless, any park discovered was treasured.

That said, Shirogane was greener and less densely packed than most of Tokyo. This was part of the attraction of moving there even if it did boast all the usual vices: narrow streets with no pavements forcing pedestrians to battle with cyclists, cars and delivery vans; an unfathomable address scheme; and the frequent demolition of houses to be swapped by ones more ugly than the original. But when walking round the narrow lanes I could, at a push, forget the noise and acrid fumes of the main thoroughfare with its thick stream of twenty-four-hour traffic. Like clambering through the back of Lewis' wardrobe, to escape into a different world, into a peacefulness of sorts, I could hear in Shirogane the mellow call of birds or pause in the dappled shade of trees. Many houses, but by no means all, had small well tended gardens and, even if they didn't, the occupiers would neatly display flowers and small shrubs planted in white plastic containers (unfortunately the horticultural equivalent of white socks) outside their front door.

Shirogane was once described in a book as 'having a rich variety of natural charms, from the Furukawa Valley in the north, to the Meguro River in the South and the view across the sea to the East. It was once a popular site for hunting and fishing, and has been praised as a place of great natural beauty. The peaceful environment of Shirogane lingers on as a precious Tokyo oasis.'

Such an idyllic rural view vanished decades ago but the sense of oasis still existed, partly because Shirogane lacked a subway when we first moved in, creating a sense of isolation and exclusivity. Whilst bisected by bus routes, the nearest train and subway stations were a twenty-minute walk away. By Tokyo standards an inconveniently long distance, and made the area less popular with commuting office workers. But not long after moving in, the planned opening of a subway stimulated a flurry of building activity along Meguro dori, one of the two main thoroughfares crossing Shirogane. Suddenly slabs of ugliness, big piles of construction dung were deposited alongside the road. Twenty-storey apartment blocks – treated to fanciful names like Classy Shirogane Mansion – rose up obliterating the distant view and blocking out the sky. Some were monolithic, plain and would not have looked out of place in the old Soviet Bloc. Others grasped pretensions of grandeur, throwing together a hotchpotch of materials and design motives intended to symbolise taste, but looking more like Liberace's bedroom. And others, because they were faced with tiles, looked like giant urinals.

The local council was also slowly widening Meguro dori, buying up and demolishing old property, and then rebuilding twenty yards further in – a haphazard process that had been going on for years and would continue for years because small landowners were reluctant to sell. In the meantime, the half-completed road made the street unsightly. I never understood why residents put up with it. In places, the pavements were impossible to walk on; they hadn't been finished properly, their surface uneven, pitted and cracked. Parked cars, bollards, railings, diversions because of the construction, all contributed to making an uninterrupted walk of more than a few yards impossible.

Bangkok's pavements were better than this.

Perhaps the fame of Shirogane came from its royal connections: the Empress Michiko was born close by in Gotenyama and her parent's house still stood.

Shirogane itself had the Tien Palace; a magnificent art-deco house built by Prince Asaka, the eighth son of Prince Kuni, who lived there with his wife the Princess Nobuko, the eighth daughter of the Emperor Meiji in the 1930s. Long past were the days when any royals were in residence though; the Tien Palace was now an art museum and the Empress's house, a mock 1930s-built European villa, shuttered and barred, looked as if no one had lived there for decades. (Although when in November 2002, the government, who owned the house – it was handed to them in lieu of inheritance tax after the Empress's father died – decided to demolish it, local residents swarmed to the rescue. 'We desperately want to preserve the building, which is our heart and soul,' one of them said. 'We don't want the Finance Ministry to make the Empress cry.')

But preserving any building in Tokyo is a non-starter.

Most poignantly, one of the few old wood-built shops left in Shirogane, the one that sold cigarettes, packets of washing powder and a few household oddments was closing down. One day, I walked past the shop and the old woman who owned it was sitting hunched on the pavement, tears in her eyes as she watched two youngsters, maybe a son and daughter load a small van with her possessions. I too was close to crying when I saw what I assumed were her late husband's hat and clothes being packed in a box. Passing again the next day, the store was padlocked, and within two weeks it had been pulled down and a couple of months later it was a parking lot.

Sometimes minor film stars and other celebrities could be seen shopping in The Garden, our local supermarket, where beluga caviar and vintage Dom Perignon was sold alongside tofu and tomatoes. Always accompanying them were pampered dogs, adorned with colourful head bows and wearing smart jackets and collars. Not that there was any dog mess on the pavements. When out for a walk, it was expected that the owner (celebrated or otherwise) scooped up any mess made by their dog into a plastic bag. (It's easy: just turn the bag inside out, place your hand inside, pick up the stools and then turn the bag out again. The use of a scraper isn't necessary – although this method does demand something solid to grasp. Hence, feeding the pet with dry food is recommended as it firms the stools.)

In Tokyo during the eighteenth and nineteenth centuries, merchants and artisans lived in areas known as *Shitamachi* (downtown) whereas the elite lived on the surrounding hills (*Yamanote*) and Shirogane was one such hill. A number of *daimyos* (feudal lords) had their homes here. With the lords came wealth, followed by their samurai retainers and religion. Buddhist temples were built, and many still stand today – though selling much of their land to property developers. At the New Year, worshippers still undertook a tour around the seven most important temples, taking no more than half a day, as they were within easy walking distance of each other. Dedicated to a different god, each looked after a different aspect of life. So there was, for example, the Fukirokuju God for Happiness, the Foteisen God for Wisdom and the Bishamontean God for a Better Future.

One evening, Satoko and I were strolling along Meguro dori after dinner. Thick snow lay on the ground. Even in our heavy overcoats, we shivered. Coming from a side street, we heard the tinkle of a bell. We couldn't see from where. But the sound moved closer so we stopped. Four, saffron robed novice monks emerged from a narrow lane. They walked in single file wearing open sandals despite the snow. One rang a small bell. Without speaking – and unaffected by the cold – they marched in perfect step out on to Meguro dori, walked for a few yards before turning down another side street. For a few moments, we were transfixed.

Meeting Meguro dori at a T-Junction in the centre of Shirogane was Gaien Nishi dori, the second main thoroughfare. In contrast to the tardiness of Meguro dori, Gaien Nishi dori was a wide boulevard lined with trees, azalea bushes, and smart shops and restaurants with fast cars parked outside them – Ferrari, Porsche and Mercedes. The street was favoured as a film and photography location and had earned the nickname of Platinum Street, after the colour of the typical shopper's credit card – although the offices of the pipe valve company were out of sorts with the rest of the fashionable retailers: jewellers, patisseries and chocolate shops, numerous haute couture boutiques, perfumeries and handbag stores. Also on Gaien Nishi dori was one of the most architecturally distinctive but largely forgotten buildings in Tokyo with, at its top, one of Tokyo's most undistinguished bars (run by an actress). Designed by Philippe Stark, the six-floored, copper-clad building rose like a green rampant slug from street level. He christened the building *Unhex Nani Nani* and it was meant, according to Stark, to represent a monster rising from the Florida swamps. *Nani nani* in Japanese means 'what is it?' An appropriate description, I thought.

For about 500 yards of its length, Gaien Nishi dori had the whiff of Rodeo Drive and Bond Street. Consumerism is the dominant lifestyle in Japan. From the mid-1950s to the mid-1960s, washing machines, refrigerators and black and white televisions were called the 'three sacred treasures' that symbolized the new lifestyle; from the mid-1960s to the mid-1970s, they were automobiles, air conditioners and colour televisions. Now, at the time when some are claiming 'there is nothing we want', sales of products that befit the new age such as video mobile phones, plasma televisions and dishwashers are increasing. (Yes, Japan with its small kitchens has yet to catch on to dishwashers.)

Shopping is the number one pastime for Japanese women – this from both official statistics, and anecdotal evidence from my wife's own behaviour – and is the driving force behind the success of the advertising business I was in. (Government surveys showed men citing driving as their favourite pastime (thirty-seven per cent of men), followed by reading thirty per cent, watching movies on TV, rented or visiting the cinema twenty-seven per cent, fishing twenty-four per cent, karaoke twenty-four per cent, golf twenty-three per cent, music twenty-two per cent, domestic travel twenty-one per cent and, at number ten, walking at nineteen per cent tied with pachinko.)

The craving for brands among female consumers was stronger in Japan than anywhere else in the world. With an appetite verging on the voracious, they spent more money on luxury brands than achieved by any other market worldwide. So powerful was the obsession, that even branded paper and plastic shopping bags had become a coveted item.

I found it interesting to learn that women took longer to adopt a Western style of dress than men. In the 1930s, all women still wore Japanese clothes; the Royal Court, the government and civil servants and businessmen were wearing Western style clothes. John Morris wrote that 'the number of Japanese women who able to look well in Western costume was extremely limited'. He thought their physiology wasn't suited.

I wouldn't agree. Japanese women look elegant, whatever they wear.

Every year, Japanese women bought approximately forty per cent of the world's luxury goods. However, whilst sales had fallen since the heady days of the early 1990s, a small number of super-brands proved recession-proof: Louis Vuitton, Chanel, Gucci and the leading Japanese design houses such as Comme de Garcon.

The key consumer was the unmarried working woman, in her mid-twenties to -thirties, living at home and holding a large disposable income. A flood of information from magazines, the Internet, friends, and the street encouraged purchase. Manufacturers bought page after page of magazine advertorials, or paid to have their products featured in the supposedly independent editorial features. Entire magazines spelt out how to achieve the latest look – the right hair, make-up, clothes and accessories – using simple systematic picture guides. Their tone was didactic. Readers were told exactly what to buy, how to coordinate clothes, accessories, make-up and hair – to the tiniest detail.

In an essay on Japanese women's magazines, the sociologist Keiko Tanaka concluded that in part this prescriptive approach mimicked the rote-learning that the Japanese experienced in school. They were not expected to extrapolate or to think for themselves but to memorise only what was taught. In every aspect of life, clear and unambiguous instruction was needed. Living by a system of strict rules was fundamental to the Japanese – men or women – and this applied as much to fashion as anything else.

But what was fashionable today would be out-of-date within months, and consumers were fanatical in ensuring they stayed abreast of trends and were not left behind.

Kimiko Mizuno, a schoolgirl aged eighteen put it this way: 'Branded items are made from good materials and I'm happy to have some of these, like famous handbags, because then I can boast about it to my friends. I hope to have something before they do.'

It was common to see high-school girls wearing all manner of branded goods. Burberry scarves were a favoured item, worn with the school uniform and with the Burberry label always conspicuously turned outwards.

One afternoon, I watched a young girl waiting on a subway platform. School had finished. It was five p.m. She was slowly hitching up her skirt – as girls do once school's over – by rolling up the waistband. She wore 'loose socks' (thick white crumpled socks similar to leg-warmers) and had changed her shoes to a pair falling to bits. In places she had deliberately rubbed off the polish so they had a shabby and scuffed appearance, and she wore them so her heel had bent down the back of the shoe. They were wrecked but perfectly wrecked. To transform further her appearance to that of a street urchin, she had put on false eyelashes caked with black mascara. But she still wore a Burberry scarf, precisely folded and tied around her neck so that the label faced outwards.

I asked another young girl if she had worn loose socks, a salacious fashion that has endured among schoolgirls since the mid-1990s.

'I have never worn loose socks even though I wanted to wear them,' Hiromi said. 'When I was high-school student, it was so popular in my school. I felt embarrassed because I wore ordinary white socks even though everybody wore loose socks. I felt I should wear loose socks like other students. It felt strange feeling. I hadn't thought plain white ankle socks ugly but everybody said they were. I don't know why everybody wears loose socks. Some of my friends said, "It's good to hide our thick legs," or "In the winter, loose socks are so warm." In the summer, lots of students don't want to wear loose socks, because when we wear loose socks, our legs get musty but everybody still wears them. Maybe they want to do like other students.'

When our niece Rikako stayed one summer holiday, she arrived off the plane, proudly clutching a Louis Vuitton travel bag. She was barely a teenager. Angry that the child was being spoilt, Satoko phoned the father. He excused himself by claiming he'd wanted to give Rikako something that would last.

Luxury brands were an absolute guarantee of quality, an essential element of Japanese purchasing. Consumers in Japan are probably the world's most demanding. Men and women in Japan can be, once they progress beyond the urchin phase, the most elegant and well dressed in the world. They will not dress down for work. Daily wear was often what anywhere else would be considered for special occasions only. Personal grooming was high. Japan had more beauty salons per capita than any other country. The critical role of brands in the personal psyche was analysed by academics. Ohira Ken, a psychiatrist at St Luke's International Hospital in Tokyo wrote a book about the way his patients described their problems. He found they tended to talk incessantly about brands when discussing personal issues. From this, Ohira concluded that his patients 'try to fill their emptiness caused by flimsy human relationships with material goods'.

Hidehiko Sekizawa, director of the Hakuhodo Institute of Life and Living, a think tank affiliated with major ad agency Hakuhodo Inc, noted the driving force behind the brand boom was 'parasite singles', a phrase referring to women in their twenties and thirties still living with their parents and relying on them for food and lodging.

'Since a high percentage of such women's monthly income is freely disposable, they do not perceive the prices of those goods as overly expensive,' Sekizawa said. 'Japanese society is so free from the perception widely held in

Europe,' he continued, 'that luxury-brand goods are intended for high-class people that the boom has not fizzled out. Senior high-school girls also buy luxury-brand goods and they don't care that such goods don't necessarily go with their inexpensive clothes,' he noted.

Sociologist Masaharu Yamada, who first coined the phrase 'parasitic singles', concluded, 'Most of them willingly sacrifice marriage to economic freedom and unlimited consumption.'

'Yes, I am a parasitic single,' said one girl I knew in her early thirties, 'but my parents are happy for me to live at home until I find a husband with a steady job.'

Japan, as I found, was essentially a homogenous middle-class society. People's sense of identity was more associated with patterns of consumption rather than where they were born, their family background or their work roles – which tend to be levelling and conformist. Japanese – more generally than in the West – displayed prestige through personal luxury items. But then they had less opportunity to show prosperity though their house, garden or household goods. (In fact, considering the wealth of the nation, the daily living and working conditions of people were downright scruffy, tired and decrepit to say the least.)

Brands offered a sense of stability. They're always there and everyone could talk about them with knowledge and ease, a substitute, particularly for the young, for more cerebral conversation. Shopping was a central part, some might argue the essence, of the woman's way of life in Japan. Self-esteem and 'face' could be earned through shopping, in a society dominated by men, where women were viewed as second class. In no small part, brands satisfied that quest for identity. Flaunting good taste and possessions was not seen as recherché.

Even the lowly shopping bag had become a vital accessory. Where else in the world had the branded shopping bag become a status symbol? Not used just to carry goods back home, but becoming thereafter an essential accessory.

At Isetan (one of Tokyo's major department stores) it was possible to emerge with over 400 hundred different bags. Even though just paper or plastic they looked expensive, distinctive and well made.

'The bag is part of the total co-ordination of the day – for shopping, dinner even the train ride. It's image can't be lacking,' said Tanaka Sangyo, a bag manufacturer.

'Shopping bags are ways to reinforce that you buy the brand – particularly when the brand is less obvious with make-up for example.'

'Small nice shopping bags catch the eye,' said Yamada-san, aged nineteen. 'When the label is prestigious I want to show it off.'

There was even a website that sold used shopping bags. Egoiste bags for example sold for seven dollars.

'Even if they can't afford the prestigious brands, they can appear to do so,' commented Hirai-san, twenty-seven, a seller of second-hand bags.

But there were opposite forces at work as well. The purchase of cheaper clothes was booming. Among the retailers, Uniqlo was by a large margin, the most successful of the cheaper branded stores. One girl explained what the attraction for her was when she wrote on the web:

'UNIQLO and I come from the same prefecture and our relationship dates back from my high school days. From abt 9 years ago I used to shop there a lot, and at that time, UNIQLO, or the Unique Clothing Warehouse was just another wholesaler shop...kinda like K-mart or Daei or any other supermarket-department type of shop. I liked them for two reasons; one that they offered basic and simple style clothes, that they were cheap. u cud get a plain navy sweater or monotone sweat shirt for 1900 yen. I used to receive their ads in newspaper and stuff, but I stopped going there after some time... I mean, they were then a no-name. there was no reason for me to shop at that place only. I guess it was abt 1999 that they started to receive the light. by that time, many similar shops sprouted, taking advantage of the economy & consumers' passive minds i.e. shoppers were going for anything that was cheap. BOOK-OFF (bookstore which sells used books) is a good example. Stores which sells quality goods for low price were in boom. But what really encouraged UNIQLO's high sales was that (to my understanding) their schematic PR method. they started shooting commercials which emphasized sleek image of their product. I mean, if they were just another get-ur-clothes-cheap kind of shop, they wud not have bee so accepted by the young generation (who r the main money thrower in clothing industry) as they r now. they r well liked and well accepted by the young ppl by the image they have created that "its cool to shop at UNIQLO". its quite similar to what GAP has done. the clothes are cheap, and you would be ashamed to wear the same clothes if they came from any other store (I'm being extreme but…) I mean, the quality is not so high. but ppl, especially the young keep going back there bcoz they want that shopping bag with UNIQLO label on it. So to summarize, UNIQLO is now at is full bloom bcoz: they r cheap its the boom! Well we shudnt neglect their effort in promoting good image and providing customers with good plain simple clothes, but I say u can get similar item for more competitive price if u look more careful. So this I guess is a case of successful PR of a company, which wisely and luckily was supported by Japanese's easily-influenced characteristic.'

What struck me as particularly sad when reflecting on the rampant consumerism was how it flew in the face of Japan's unique Zen heritage. Zen teachings had not been the only significant influence within Japan but nonetheless they had been profound. Their rejection of the ego, of the self-focus of man on I, of the notion of self-gratification had been lost in daily life. Zen honoured the minimal, the subtle. The tea ceremony, *haiku* and *sumi-e* ink paintings were the result of Zen's impact and inspiration, where in Japan the theories of Zen were taken to a new level above that practised in India and China. But this eye and desire for simplicity had been lost from everyday life.

Kenzaburo Oe, the Japanese author should have the last word when he said that Japan's consumerism reflected the nature of society living 'in a state of outright spiritual poverty'.

Chapter Nine

Human Relationships

Since the early 'nineties, longer than any other developed country, Japan has been slipping deeper into recession. I witnessed the decline of a once pulsating, economically invincible nation. A precipitous fall in the stock market in 1992 stopped in its tracks the economic post-war miracle that had emerged in Japan. The bubble, it was often repeated, had burst. Since then, Japan's politicians had been incapable of leading the country out of the financial mess, and years of economic turmoil had had a profound and pessimistic affect on society. The days of secure lifetime employment were over and unemployment was rising month by month. (In the first few years of the twenty-first century it was at its highest level since the end of the Second World War; over five per cent of the population were unemployed and more than a million heads of Japanese households were jobless.) Property values plummeted. Businesses were going bankrupt at an alarming rate: more than 19,000 companies in one year alone. The Japanese had become an unhappy race. In global media surveys, they were persistently the gloomiest and most despondent in Asia. Within Japan, a national survey conducted by the newspaper *The Asahi Shimbun* showed that over seventy per cent had feelings of misgiving about their future; the word that was used to best describe the times was *konmei* or confusion. This description – along with selfishness, unfairness, change and collapse – made up seventy-four per cent of responses. The word *ense* means a tiredness with life, and this sense of futility was becoming common once again.

A loss of confidence started to pervade through society, a sense of self-doubt and mistrust that undermined the interpersonal cohesiveness that is so important within Japan. Men, who had sacrificed themselves to their job – a virtue expected by their family and society – now had to cope with the prospect of at best stagnant careers or, at worst, unemployment and the awful stigma attached to this. Their hard work, unquestioning loyalty and dedicated commitment meant nothing, and yet they hadn't the mental flexibility to retrain or hop from company to company or in some cases even to admit to being unemployed. It wasn't uncommon to hear of men who left home in the morning clutching a briefcase, dressed as if they were off to the office even though they had no position to go to. They couldn't face the embarrassment of being known by their neighbours to be jobless.

Some young people were not even taking the first jump on to the corporate ladder, behaviour that a few years previously had been unknown. They were termed *freeters* (a bizarre combination of the word 'free' with the German word for worker, 'arbeiter'), and increasing in number. Official estimates counted two million of them, eschewing full-time employment and opting for a succession of unskilled part-time jobs interspersed with free time. These weren't just poorly qualified school leavers. Their numbers included many graduates.

This unfortunately wasn't helping Prime Minister Koizumi reform the economy. In 2003 he said in a speech: 'It is said that the work *Self-Help* by the British writer Samuel Smiles and published in 1859, caught the imagination of many young Japanese in the Meiji era. The aspired youth of Japan applied themselves seriously to their studies, made diligent efforts and took the central role in developing the foundation for Japan as a modern nation. In any age it is always the young people with the spirit of self-help and self-discipline, concern for others, and high aspiration who pioneer to a new era. People are the engine for reform.'

What Smiles had written was that patience, ordering of the mind, and absorption in the task, are the key elements to achieve great advances. Tenacity, endurance and unremitting work are the personal qualities needed to succeed – for men that is. *Self-Help* is thoroughly sexist to the core and never cites one example of female success. And women certainly didn't have the opportunity to contribute to the success of Japan in the Meiji era.

Japan was now in the midst of a massive schism that was polarising the young from the old. It was obvious that change was happening. There was even a name for those under the age of thirty: *shinjinrui* (the new race). And when the Japanese passed that age, they thought they were old.

'Most of all Japanese men and women think that more younger is the best,' said one girl. 'Youth is the flower of life. Japanese culture is still a culture for child. There is no good, amazing place to which an adult goes. A situation that should be lamented. My friend is also afraid of adding her to her age, but she is still thirty! She always said, "But I am now *obasan* (I can't do it)". That is a waste. I think she has money, power and beauty but she always think she pales in comparison to the young. She will give up keeping her beauty, and she will become real *obasan*. I'd like to continue to watch many beauty. I think it's the most good thing to keep beautiful. I hope the young generation will transform into beautiful *obachan* in twenty to thirty years' time too.'

Setting this generation apart is a refusal to follow the myopic paths their parents took from school to career. They don't buy into Koizumi's vision of their role to define a new era in Japan. Some say they are the lost generation but I might argue that they are the enlightened ones who have seen for real the folly that underpins Japan's society.

Not only were there those who turned their backs on being the good salaryman but also others who had withdrawn entirely from society and lived as hermits holed up in a bedroom.

Tamaki Saito is the psychiatrist who has studied this condition and introduced the concept. He defines withdrawal (*hikikomori*) as a condition in which a young person – usually male – refuses to live and participate in society. Such youngsters refuse to go to school, to work or to socialise. They disappear and their number is thought to be as many as one million.

Others withdraw by becoming obsessively interested in some cult activity, forming groups who only communicate and socialise with each other.

The artist Murakami is drawn to the *otaku* who are a group – a large group – obsessed with science fiction and comics. They are seen as mysterious and strange, almost frightening. He says young people are attracted to these cults because only sub-cultures provide any sense of salvation. He says sub-culture is the Japanese culture of today and that increasingly the young want to live a life of fantasy, as this is their only way to be individualistic.

'There is no room for variation in our society,' said Matsuo, a young girl who worked in the same building as our office. She followed a 'seventies' style of fashion and had permed her hair in an Afro.

'But my bosses tell me I have to pin it down when I'm here as they are disturbed by it.'

'They see it as unsettling?' I asked. She used to join our group in the canteen at lunchtime.

'Yes, it upset some of the older men here and they feel uncomfortable dealing with me. But I want to do what I want for myself. And I hate others who follow everyone else.'

'Why's that?'

'Because being different is a freedom – it makes me escape from the drudgery of office life.'

'Why are you working in the office?'

'To earn money so I can go to a fashion college.'

She wasn't working full-time but alternated between the office and college.

We became her friends, her escape from her office routine by giving her a chance, if only for half-an hour over lunch to be herself. She was an attractive girl. Tall, slender and she had dyed her hair ginger – which sounds odd but looked perfect. She had a faultless grasp of 'seventies' style and yet she had updated it so that flairs and tank-tops looked attractive and alluring rather than ugly.

I asked her to show me where she would hang out with friends. She agreed without question and the first place she took me was Shibuya. We had to go on a Sunday, as this was her only free day.

Like a whirlpool, Shibuya sucks in the young. They tumble out of the station, disgorged into the pedestrianised square in front of the station (Japanese stations often have squares or *ekimae hiroba* at their front) and then are tossed like leaves into the surrounding streets. It doesn't matter what day or time of day you come here, the area heaves with humanity.

When we first emerged into the open air, we saw Hachiko Crossing: an enormous and complex intersection where as the lights switch from red to green, an army of bodies surged forward. Above us were stacks of massive billboards and video screens that hung from almost every available space on the sides and the tops of buildings. Music and advertising jingles blared out. Something was said or sung but all sound merged into an incomprehensible mush.

We sat down by the famous statue of the dog. She opened a packet of cigarettes and lit one, her bright lipstick immediately making a red band on the white filter.

'Do you believe in celebrity endorsement?' I asked.

'In advertising?'

'Yes.' I hadn't come out to chat about the weather.

'I used to but less now. But young people are in a stage of self-discovery and they use what celebrities wear or how they cut their hair as one way of finding their true selves.'

'Isn't it just mimicking?'

'No, self-realisation. It's a status, not copying. We never copy.'

'But look around. So many of the girls are dressing alike.'

'No, on the surface that may seem the case but everyone adds their own flourish. And it's a deliberate touch.'

People waiting for a friend to arrive surrounded us. I could see that every item of clothing, every fashion accessory had been chosen with meticulous care. Close by, three girls were chatting to each other. They were aged thirteen or fourteen at most. One girl wore a bright pink duffle coat, pink trainers, and white bobby socks. One of her friends wore suede desert boots, a tartan skirt and a fawn fluffy jacket. The third wore a baseball jacket, a brown suede skirt and big black leather boots with heels three inches high. Each was dressed differently, expensively and perfectly co-ordinated. They alternated between talking to each other and then talking on their *katai* (mobile phone).

'Those girls there. You see. Each one is different. Each one has designed her own look.'

'Did they design it?'

'Okay, no. They've been instructed how to do it in a magazine.'

We had talked about this before – the large number of magazines devoted to instructing girls how to dress.

Ganguro (dark) girls were still evident, though reduced in number. (I thought of writing 'fading away' but that would be such an awful pun.) They style themselves (inadvertently) as alien monsters with deep orange suntans, bleached hair – so that no original colour would be ever found – pale white lipstick and eye shadow, and blue contact lenses Their look is based on an extreme form of the 'holiday in Hawaii'. Their clothes are garishly colourful – and awful; they drape themselves with plastic bangles and sometimes wear plastic flowers in their hair. Most famously, they wear the highest platform boots that can allow a modicum of forward movement.

'I don't understand it. Do you find that look attractive? They look roasted.'

'Me personally, no. But for them it's a way of escaping the hopelessness many women feel. The Japanese world is one that closes down on us. Most of these girls have dropped out of school. Sorry to say but often they're single mums who are sex workers. It's no different to your punks.'

'Punks did rebel. They were genuinely anti-social – at least for a while. There are punks here but they're still polite.'

'Rebellion doesn't need to be spitting. This is our way to say no and gradually more and more youth are drifting away. I told you how even my look scares older people in the office. Just by us dressing up, the older people are scared. We don't need to do anything more. They know we are building our own world that excludes them. This is our truth.'

'But won't you have to conform eventually?'

'We have a word here called *seinen*. We use it to describe a sort of intermediary age between childhood and actual adulthood. Historically, it was a time when there was leeway given by society to our behaviour. We had a certain freedom of action but then we were expected to conform. The problem is that now many people don't make the switch into conformity.'

She stood up, walked over to a bin, and threw her cigarette into it. When she came back, she said she wanted to show me the streets but first we had to eat.

There is a good *soba* place not far, she told me. We found it: an old low-roofed wooden building. A queue formed outside and she told me this was always the case, no matter whether raining or a howling wind blew. As was typical for all these old *soba* places, reservations weren't taken and so we had to wait patiently in line. Once inside, we squeezed in at a long wooden table that had a rich sheen that only comes from years of being wiped down. It smelt homely, of polish and cooking, and felt cosy and intimate.

The room bustled. Six waitresses wrote down orders and food quickly arrived. *Soba* restaurants were the original fast food joint. Once finished, everyone was expected to leave promptly. Sitting around chatting was frowned on. But the *soba* was delicious, best washed down with ice-cold beer or sake. We ordered small fish cake, *tamago-yaki* or omelette, tempura hot *soba*, a handful of small shrimps fried in crisp batter, and a sticky sweet pudding to end the meal. Everything was shared between us.

The kitchen was part open to the dining area. Here, buckwheat flour was ground, the noodles rolled and cut, and then cooked to unique recipes. Every *soba* restaurant would use only its own recipes.

No doubt, he had told his wife he was playing golf but opposite us sat a middle-aged man taking out his Ginza hostess girlfriend. I knew that *soba* restaurants were popular places for such liaisons. These couples were easily recognised: other than the obvious age gap, and the complete contrast of styles, it was the fact that the hostesses always wore a hat pulled tightly over their head, their complexions quite pasty and they were the only women I knew who dressed down when they went out for an informal meal.

'Do they speak English, you think?' I said in a whisper.

'No chance.'

'What would you do if your boyfriend had an affair?'

'It's a necessity of life for Japanese men. Anyway, I don't care. We women have affairs too at least when we're young.'

'All women?'

'If I believe what my friends tell me.'

'Have you?'

'Not yet but then I don't have a steady boyfriend. But if you wanted to have an affair...' She stopped.

'I'm married.'

'I know. I didn't mean that. Not literally. But if you did want an affair, it wouldn't stop me.'

'But what about my wife?'

'You know that it is still often the case that men have to move away for their work and leave their family behind. Then a woman might have an affair. But it will be with a husband who isn't living with his wife. And love hotels make affairs very difficult to discover. The unseen hurts no one.'

We finished our *soba*.

Back on the streets, we were thrown into the mêlée. For so many people crowded together, there was no distinctive smell on the street other than no smell. No cooking odours lingered in the air; there were no trails of perfume or clouds of body odour.

People didn't bump into one another. With almost radar-like precision, we moved around each other like sliding droplets of mercury.

But neither did people stop and talk to one another. Or smile at each other. There was no laughter.

Tokyo was not a neighbourly place. Neighbours didn't pop round for cups of sugar. Families kept themselves to themselves. Salarymen didn't have friends, I was told. They kept drinking company with their work colleagues. Outside of work, many of their favourite activities were solitary: driving, reading, pachinko and fishing. Some lived in dormitory blocks provided by their company, surrounded only by colleagues twenty-four hours a day.

'After moving to Tokyo I found it isn't safe and it's hard to trust your neighbours. Most people have no connection with their neighbours and I think the media discourages relationships. We say hello but no more than that. I don't know who lives next door to me. I don't want to be bothered by them. I don't want to be friends with them. I exchange bows when I see my neighbours but we're not friendly to one another. Have you ever been to a Love Hotel?'

The question was once again unexpected. No, I told her.

'Not that far away there are many,' she said.

And then I thought I ought to get home. I looked at my watch.

'Do you have something to do?' she asked.

'I must get back soon as I'm expecting an overseas phone call.'

'I have kept you out too long. I'm sorry.'

'No, it's been an interesting time. You've told me a lot.'

'I should have been more thoughtful about the time.'

'I can take a taxi from here. Can I give you a lift?'

'That's very kind but I just need to walk to the station, that's all.'

I shook her hand and said thank you again. She moved forward as if she wanted to kiss me. I put out my hand and a taxi pulled up immediately. I waved as we pulled away and she waved back.

Opposite our apartment lived a typical Japanese family; watching them provided hours of interest and speculation for us. We could look directly into their home from the window of our 'family' room, and we became social voyeurs.

Their house wasn't a single entity. Facing the street was the oldest part, made of narrow planks of wood darkened with age, and roofed with black ceramic tiles. Behind, an early extension had once been a single storey. Later an upper floor had been added. Finally behind this was the newest two-storey addition. No effort had been made to harmonise the design of each, to use the same building materials or to make them individually attractive. The overall affect was an unsightly muddle.

Six family members lived in the house. The two eldest were a grandmother and a retired man. His relationship with the grandmother was unclear. Initially assuming he was her husband, we then decided he might be a brother or some other relative, and eventually wondered whether he was a lodger.

On the upper floors lived the grandmother's son and daughter-in-law. We were more certain of that relationship as such an arrangement is common: the daughter-in-law charged with taking care of her husband's parents. In their mid- to late-thirties, they had two young children, a boy and a girl.

The grandma lived somewhere in the old house. The old man lived on the ground floor in the middle extension. This was his living room and bedroom. At night, no later than nine, he would take out a *futon* and lay it on the floor, sleeping under it, with no mattress just the carpeted floor. By the time the sun had risen the next morning, he was awake and up.

The young family lived on the upper floors of the extensions, spending most of the day in a single large 'family' room that combined kitchen, dining and living room. Off to one side were the toilet, a separate bathroom and two small bedrooms: one shared by the kids and one by the parents. The 'family' room had large floor-to-ceiling windows with metal shutters and mesh mosquito screens that could be pulled across. Most of the time these were kept wide open, which was why we could see so much of what was going on.

They owned two televisions. A monster forty-inch-plus screen filled one corner of the family room, switched on most hours of the day. In fact, there were times when it was on for twenty-four hours, whether anyone was watching or not. In the parents' bedroom, a smaller TV was kept, as well as a PC. Dad also owned a laptop, which he used on the dining table. One long sofa sat in the main room. This and the chairs round the dining table were the only places to sit – unless the family sat on the floor.

The total size of the plot – house and land – measured about fifty yards square, valuing it upwards of several million pounds. In other words, the family were asset-rich. A small two-storey apartment block had been built on one side of the garden – two flats upstairs and two down. All were rented out. We estimated the rents totalled at least £3,000 a month, if not more, and were a key source of income.

The garden was lovingly tended by the grandma and old man. It centred round a small rectangular lawn. Some days we would see grandma, bent double from the waist, clip the lawn with a pair of kitchen scissors. In the dry season, the grass was allowed to brown, it was never watered but it would always green up when the rain came. Around three sides of the lawn was a single bed, planted with trees and evergreen shrubs. A mature plum tree was the largest of the trees. Every year in March it blossomed, signalling that spring was on its way. One year, a flock of sparrows adopted the plum as home. They grew more numerous as the months passed so that eventually there were about fifty of them. Slowly, they turned the branches white with their droppings. They ate grubs from the containers on our balconies but only ever flew a small distance from the tree's vicinity. Sparrows are lazy like that.

Few plants were planted in the garden itself but the ubiquitous potted red geraniums stood in a row alongside the house.

At one time, a dog lived in a kennel kept in the garden; the old boy's pride and joy. The dog was a garrulous rascal, weak on his hind legs. He would bark at the sparrows but was too infirm to chase them, and he glared at us with distain if we annoyed him by barking from our balcony. Only the old boy fed, brushed and walked the dog. Then the dog became ill and was taken indoors. A few times, we saw the old boy cycle off, with the dog carried on the back of the bike, sitting in a box. One day we noticed we hadn't seen the dog for a few days. A week or so later, the kennel was removed and thrown on a heap of rubbish. We realised he had died. At the same time, the old boy disappeared but, some weeks later, returned.

On a roofed balcony, the young family kept a washing machine. Laundry was a daily chore, and always hung on hangers to dry in the open air; the ubiquitous habit of drying washing in the sun was thought to purify laundry as well as creating a pleasing sun-dried smell. Also on the balcony were three air-conditioning units, a satellite TV dish and a plastic table large enough for the family to eat round but only used twice – so far as we'd seen – in five years. Neither did the kids play much outside – occasionally in the garden but this was rare; more often, if they weren't at kindergarten, they played in the house.

It was rare too that friends came round. Or they went out and played with friends. Play was more often the brother and sister chasing each other around the room, bouncing and scrapping on their parents' bed or just watching TV. A wooden rocking horse in the main room provided sporadic amusement. They were too young for video games even though the TV had a console connected to it.

Neither in the house nor on the balcony were any plants kept. The parents were clearly uninterested in gardening and neither of them help tend the garden.

And the only time I saw them altogether as a family group, with grandma and the old boy present, was when they celebrated Boys' Day in May. This is the official birthday for all boys in Japan and is a hangover of when Japanese society truly was a community. Parents rarely celebrate a child's actual birthday. Individuals were not to be sanctified. All had to celebrate their birthdays at the same time.

On Boys' Day (*Tango no sekku*) the centuries-old tradition is to hang out giant paper carp (*koi-nobori*) that swell and float colourfully in the breeze. The carp is the symbol of energy and strength – the attributes that the father aspires for his son.

Every year this tradition was celebrated in the garden below us. Not by the father but the old man. He strung up two long poles and hung one carp some ten feet long.

Inside, the house was frugal and purely functional, not even a single picture on the wall. It amazed me, that for a family that were clearly not poor, no attempt was made to create an interesting living space, to use the space efficiently, or indeed to encourage the kids to spend more time outdoors and less time watching TV.

Visitors, as well, were rare. I thought they lived a monotonous claustrophobic existence.

If it was typical, no wonder violent acts among schoolchildren were on the increase. Parents said things like:

'The kids are too self-centred.'

'They can't stand up to the system. They have no endurance or mental stamina.'

'It's also the family. Kids are given too much money and life is too lax for them.'

'They're too impatient.'

'It's too easy to get knives here.'

Even if the extent of a cohesive society had been exaggerated, it was no longer a pretence that could be easily maintained. If the cracks had been hidden in the past, they were now as clear as the cracks in mud under a scorching sun. At every level of society, I saw upheaval and a turning away from the old way of *wa*, the harmony – imagined or otherwise – that produced servitude within the social group. The rules that had been created for an inert and obedient populace ('the nail that sticks up will be beaten down' was an oft heard maxim) were being ignored but without being replaced by a new set of rules or values. A psychiatrist told me that every year she was seeing more patients.

'Is it because of lifestyle?' I asked and she said yes, people find only solitude in Tokyo.

In a book on Japanese contemporary art, called *Sex and Consumerism*, a number of artists put forward their views on Japan and Tokyo. The late Teiji Furuhashi said, 'Japanese society now, especially Tokyo, is like limbo. People think it's heaven but it's not. It's really destructive.'

Another, Hiroko Okada commented, 'Life in Tokyo doesn't have any thickness or gravity.'

I had no idea whether the husband was an orthodox salaryman or had his own business. I thought most likely the latter as there were days when he worked from home.

More often, he was out all day and late in to the evening. How late was of no consequence. His wife was expected to accept this behaviour.

On the surface, she was a typical wife who recognised her duty was to look after the family: her mother-in-law, husband and children. In Japan, wives were expected to create a harmonious home so that the husband didn't worry over domestic matters and he could concentrate without distraction on work. He wasn't expected to help around the house in any way.

(I saw this too in the men's changing room of the gym I attended: towels were left lying on the changing-room floor and not thrown in the bins provided; golf clubs were left blocking the doorway with no thought about the inconvenience to others; upstairs in the gym, the men wouldn't wipe the sweat off the equipment. The women did.)

One woman told me, 'Everything that my father says are orders which we have to obey absolutely. Furthermore, he can't do any housework and never has done and never will expect to until the day he dies.'

As women got older, they enjoyed hobbies or would go out during the day as a twosome or group, shopping together, having lunch, and maybe visiting a museum. In short, they escaped the four walls that had become their prison. But our mum found that difficult because the kids were still young, spent more time at home and her mother-in-law was still alive. Once the laundry had been done, she would often sit around all day, reading *manga*, a newspaper, watching TV, occasionally smoking a cigarette.

But although she stayed in for most of the day, the house was really quite messy. The dining table was never cleared of the laptop, a can of beer, food dishes, soy bottles, scraps of paper, a pitcher of cold *oolong* tea and a variety of household items. The two single beds, squashed together in the parents' room were rarely made up; the *futon* was left crumpled on the mattress. The kids' toys were left scattered on the floor or kicked into a corner. There was simply no pride in the look of the home.

Taking a bath with children was common in Japan. Fathers weren't prudish about being naked in front of their kids, and this home was no exception – though I never saw the mother naked. The Japanese approach the bath in a completely different way to the West. In the West it is functional, a mechanical exercise to remove dirt. The bathroom is bolted. Here, the bath is a ritual pleasure and an essential punctuation that separated work from home. It is to be enjoyed and taken at leisure. To rush a bath just isn't understood. Satoko could take hours and this time was sacred. I would interrupt or ask her to hurry along at my peril.

I once read in *The Economist* that the Japanese were tactile as a group, that they enjoyed touching one another. This bemused me. Like the Chinese, there seemed very little touching or hugging. It was rare to see couples holding hands and, when you did, it was more often school kids not adults. Nor did couples kiss in public. Our neighbours certainly didn't. Of course, as they had two children, they must have had sex in the past. Once, I saw the husband trying to arouse his wife when she was sitting on the sofa but she kept moving away and in the end he gave up.

In a survey conducted in 2002, thirty per cent of women said that they didn't have any form of intimacy such as holding hands or kissing; fifty per cent of both men and women said they had not had sex for a year.

One evening, I saw she had cleared the table, the first time in five years. She sat at it, facing away from the kids who as usual were playing on the sofa taking off and putting on their clothes. Her husband wasn't at home. She had lit a cigarette. She smoked without anything to drink. When the kids went to bed, she lit another, and this time poured a beer. The TV was off. She never put the cigarette down. Just dragged heavily on it, flicked the ash, drank a sip of beer and dragged again. She rolled the end of the cigarette against the edge of the ashtray. Her legs were crossed under the table. She chain smoked, save for a moment when she disappeared into the bedroom to change into a pair of pink silk pyjamas. She was still smoking, two hours later, when I went to bed.

I found she represented the void that seems to exist among too many people living in Tokyo. As part of an art project, I met a young twenty-one year-old girl, a college student, and had lengthy discussions with her about her life. She was studying psychology at university. I asked her first some general questions to oil the conversation. What was her favourite drink?

'The drink I love most is Dita. Why, why, why? I don't know. I am very surprised. I don't drink very much, and I only drink when I go out with a friend at night but these last few weeks I haven't been out at all. But then I'm not very good with alcohol. Sake makes me crazy or sends me to sleep. I don't like losing myself to alcohol because my father drank and he became crazy and got violent.'

And food?

'I like healthy food. I don't like oily food but I do like seafood. But I hate eel. It's the only thing I hate. It makes me ill because my throat is very slim and eel bones get trapped.'

I told her I liked *udon*.

'Aha, you like *udon*. *Shikoku Udon* is very nice but *Osaka Udon* is better. At the moment, I'm eating too many sweets because of stress. I know it's weak behaviour and I need to be strong and try to cut out sugar.'

'What do you think about living in Tokyo?'

'Tokyo is very a confusing city. It's also unique and very special in Japan. The sad fact is that all things happen from Tokyo. Tokyo has created a scary and very messy society. Tokyo has forgotten its soul and how to allow people to live as humans. It is just a work city, and people have no real spirit to live or for love. That's what I think anyway. I believe people want to enjoy life and want to find someone but unfortunately Tokyo doesn't allow people to rest and it makes people increasingly selfish. They forget the most important things of life and of being human. So, there are many sad people. They suffer and they inadvertently make other people suffer. They cheat each other, they betray each other. They are cold.

'So you think Tokyo people are inhuman?'

'I think anywhere in this world doesn't have a perfect person. Everyone has problems whether they are big or small. I find that everyone has a dark side like me. But Tokyo brings out this darkness. Now people should think more about world issues like Iraq and the Middle East. But here in Tokyo, people, almost all people are still thinking about themselves. They never think about the problems in Iraq or North Korea. They are only interested in fashion and their body. Very stupid. Well, almost all people are very selfish and it's very difficult to find genuine friends.'

'What about your friends?'

'Before I had very good friends but once I came to Tokyo I found people always cheated on me. Sometimes I feel it is better to stay at alone. I have tried to have normal relationships. At first, everyone is very nice, and they say, "Our relationship is very nice." But everyone is looking for a boyfriend and as soon as they find one they forget about me. And they only see their guys.'

'Do you have a boyfriend?'

'Unfortunately guys in Tokyo only see a girl for her body and for sex. That's my experience anyway. My past guys wanted to see me for sex. But I could feel it, so I never had sex with him. I couldn't do sex with just everybody. Only when I feel love from them. I want someone who can link both heart and mind. Of course, sex is a natural human emotion, and I don't blame anyone for thinking of it but I hate to see a relationship built around only physical attraction. It worries me to get old if guys only see me for my looks. What happens when my looks fade? I know. Husbands go off to hostess bars. So, I always rejected guys like that. But if someone is looking at my inside, I will not feel scared about my old age.

'I am not stupid. I understand how people behave. I have wisdom for life.

'My dream was to marry my destiny man and to have warm family. It is my biggest dream and if I succeed, I will be able to feel most happy. But "Don't fly into another cage," a friend of mine told me. And then I realised how stupid my dream is. If I can get married to someone, I can run away, believing I will live in a better situation than now. But it was a mistake, all my ex-boyfriends cheated on me. Their character was very bad, and now I have a stalker from it. He is my last boyfriend and maybe he is mentally ill. I think…or I want to think. But if you talk to the college authorities, they just laugh. They don't want anything to do with it.'

She then started talking about her father.

'I try not to think about him. He doesn't see my pain because he thinks he is the nicest father in the world. It is so sick it makes me scared. But now I can't do anything about it because I don't have the power.

'At the moment, my power is only just use about living. Now I am very weak…really. Now I just see my inside and see a very dark girl….haha scary about my self. Now I don't suffer violence from him, because I have learnt how to avoid it. I know what things make him angry and violent. So, I am always careful when he is around and try to not do the things that make him angry but sometimes he just gets angry for no reason.

'Then I will stop what I'm doing and freeze. My mother cries. My brother is only thirteen. The worst thing is he doesn't think that his behaviour is wrong. Rather he thinks that he is nicest father in the world. I can't laugh about it any more. I can't understand him. He is always shouting and crazy. Every single day I am a very unhappy girl by him. I can't laugh and I have forgotten how to smile.

'I should try to enjoy life because this is my life and I must go on to live. I must not run away from this life. I must fight with it. I think this world is fight world or suffer world. So, I believe in heaven. Maybe Heaven is a very nice country and only people can go to Heaven who live here with suffering bur try to fight it. So now I trying to fight with this situation and some day I can go to Heaven land live in my dream world. I try to think that if my life was perfect, I would be very bored about it.

'I don't feel bored any more. But I never express these feelings with my outside. If I do, people never understand me, so always I stop trying to explain and always I am alone.

'But I don't mind if I am alone because sometimes it is easy to stay with myself. Maybe my character is too sensitive. They thought that I am crazy or stupid and I stopped expressing my feelings. Sorry I'm talking too much and boring you. Anyway, I know that I have a limits time to live in this world.

Obliviously it is better to enjoy life, so I will try as much as possible but maybe it will take a long time. But my policy for life is to never regret everything.'

Read my journals, she told me. A few days later, they arrived by motorbike courier.

May 18

Self-portraits of myself.
A lot of times I wish I were a boy.
If I wasn't feminine, I would rather be boyish.
I don't like makeup, I don't like dressing in tight clothes, and I don't like being girly – wait, I CAN'T be girly. Because I'm like that.
If I were a boy, I would sleep with a lot of pretty girls. I know what girls like. But of course that's because I'm a girl.
My right side
My left side
Boys have all the fun. Go to a foreign land for holiday or work, screw a pretty girl, get her pregnant, and come back home. There is absolutely no worries that you'll get pregnant, if you're a boy.
Me... if I were a boy, I would wear baggy pants and be all comfortable. Guy photographers sound better, and gives me an image that they're tough, artistic, and sexual.
If I were a pretty girl —which I'm not – I would rather have photos taken by a guy rather than by a girl.
My infamous school uniform. No, that's not the complete outfit though, but it's nice. I had to fold the skirt three times to get it above my knees.
Me: "No guy's ever asked me for my email address."
Friend: "I'm exchanging emails with a guy from juku. He came up to me and talked and then yeah."
Me: "Dude, yesterday in juku there was a sweet-smelling guy next to me in the JISHUSHITSU."
Me: "But his girlfriend-like girl was coming up to him giving him notes all the time. Man, it ended so fast."
Friend: "Yesterday in juku, a guy gave me a piece of paper. His email address was on it."

Friend: "I don't even remember talking to him, but he said we did."
FEMALE HORMONES FOR ME PLEASE.

Pretty girls DO get love everywhere, anywhere, anytime. I'm complaining there is no DEAL for me, but there is. The thing is that I am not that kind of girl.

There are a billion guys in this world, someone MUST fall in love with me at first sight. I hope. Maybe one in every million people might think I'm hot. I hope that one guy would come up to me now and say to me, "you're beautiful."

But I know I won't be satisfied I know, I want compliments from every guy that walks down the street. Every girl wants that.

I didn't know that there were girls who ARE just alluring, and would turn everyone's head while walking down the street.

But I think it's by nature.

I need to smile.

Ultimate journey for orgasm

May 24

Yup, that's all what I've been thinking since last night. Actually, I watched this video (don't know the title in English, but it was in German. Japanese title was 'Kageki girls girls') about 3 girls being curious about orgasm. hehe! It's been a while since I rented videos (films = my passion) and I felt like porn so there. I only saw it halfway and had things to do, so I was imagining all these endings. I finished it after I slept for a while and everyone has slept. Sucks that there's only one tv and it's in the living room, someone's always in there. The ending was kinda sudden and the viewers are left to think that they HAVE experienced orgasm, but they didn't actually show it. It was like, "they found a perfect boyfriend." so maybe, no orgasm. eh. anyways.

I rented another video, QUILLS. I saw a lot of previews for it, and was interested in its SM play. lol. but the best scenes were all shown the preview. :/ shucks. the ending was well-thought, but it didn't leave me feeling nice. I finished it at 4AM. haha

Midterms were done yesterday. Went to canon shop in shinjuku to get 35mm camera fixed. It's going to be available in a week. :) yayyyy

I walked a lot, and by the end of the day my back hurt. sometimes this happens. Argh, and I had a horrible horrible headache. It's much better than stomach ache, but headache sucks too.

June 8

places I want to take photos at the very front of the inokashira line, where you can see the train rails. VERY pretty. it was especially so when it snowed.
starbucks 2nd floor in shibuya. take pics of people, of course.
a pretty love hotel. where the beds are waterbeds and tubs are glass, and the walls are mirrors.
roppongi hills. just cause it's hot.
the shopping mall in tokyo station. It's all made out of glass, and very like 21st century.
tokyo univ. NICE PLACE!! for a background though.
there's this futuristic building, and also very old rotten buildings.
people I want to take photos of friends doing archery, Ohta san doing painting, more yuu. reiko every day with her wonderful fashion sense.
at college random photos of people at collge baka yama.
GOTH CHICKS at harajuku.
people having sex. (<- I really want to do this)
hot naked hunks and chickas. karl!! I want to strip sexy girls too.
random people in the street.

June 11:

I don't like being with Ume but there is no one else to hang out with really, because me and her have ALL same class, and she always sticks with me and doesn't try to make friends with anyone. well yeah, she is always tired and half zonked away, her soul is somewhere else. she says that she is always sick, and complain of drowsiness, which I don't doubt—she is ALWAYS looking unhealthy. well, but she firmly states that she is fragile, and doesn't seem to realize that it's her mentality that's causing it. YAMAIWA KIKARA. she is absent from school like once or twice a week, and late 2 or 3 times a week. she's like, "oh I was sick…I had fever.." Yeah right, she always gets better in a day.

She was asking me in the beginning of the year, "so, even if I did not come to classes for like a month, do you think I can graduate??" if you didn't want to come, stop making lame excuses and say I SKIPPED CLASS (AND STUDIED ALL DAY AT HOME). just like natsu! she came to College on 3rd period for 4 classes of math, stating that she came to school for math. Ume should fucking do that as well. lame excuses are LAME. or like, come to College like Eri does. She says out loud she does not like classes but she's never missed a day. WHOSE MONEY DO YOU THINK YOU ARE USING TO ATTEND? She is too much into her "good old middle school days." well we are living a life RIGHT NOW.

June 20

My life is far from what I want it to be. I don't think it ever has the way I wanted it to be. It's all about the parents. From my observation, kids from broken families have it easy. they don't have strict curfews nor problem with getting a lot of allowances. broken family and a nice teenage life

=OR=

a tight knit family and a dull teenage life

hmm. latter is definitely better for now, because you can always have a nice life after you get out of the house. but man, I want to get out of the house. live somewhere small and nice, not having to tell my parents where I'm going when I'm coming home what I ate blah blah.

and living with a lover. because I can never live alone, nightmares are too scary. that's what all the girls dream about. but then again, thinking realistically, I don't want to do the housework. not yet. I will do them when I have to. but again, there are nobody who can live peacefully with me. will any gay guys want to share a house with me?

June 25

so today I woke up at noon. I dyed my hair with henna (250 yen!) but I don't think it dyed. my friends have been teasing me that I am a PURIN (japanese engrish for pudding, yellow custard with brown caramel on top— how a japanese's head will look after they breached their hair and new ones grew) hmm bah. maybe I should dye it black altogether. people are starting to stop dying their hair because NATURAL black hair is better for interviews. in other words, dyed hair will give bad impression. fuck this world.

ahh mann why do I feel so antisocial sometimes? this summer my friends have asked if I wanted to go disneyland, sea paradise, fireworks.. I said no to them all. I'd love to hang out, but I don't fucking want to go to disneyland. or into the crowds. but mom's making me go to fireworks. I hate the crowds though.

Mina also wanted to hang with me, she has souvenirs for us and all, but I casually declined.. err, I shouldn't decline, but I don't really want to see her now for some reason. she should first pay us back 50000 yen. I don't want to hang with Eri either, argh! I am a chickennnnnn, a whinnerrrrr where I want to go is a strip club! and a nice sleepover. that's all =/ I have no money. psht

June 26

Once I asked around where my friends' parents have met. Only one person's parents was an omiai. Omiai sucks in my opinion, I feel like it's something that losers do as a last resort.

For some reason having a gorgeous wedding and wearing a nice white dress wasn't my dream.. and the whole Christian chapel wedding is too cheesy. Same with wedding on boats and cake cutting all that bull. I hate being the center of attention and in the formal party is out of the question. Realistically thinking, though, the *kimono* cost like 200000 a n i g h t rental. Everything will be so expensive, so why not spend the money on something that can be useful? What I think would be nice is to have a nice restaurant to ourselves and party. I want to wear a pretty dress though. Too bad there is no prom in here. And another thing to look forward for is a honeymoon. And also buying interior goods! And a nice house! When I get old I will live in the countryside by a beach. Somewhere in Europe...maybe...or Okinawa.

We talk a lot about the future to come and the boy of our dreams. Who knows what will happen.

After 30, I am going to be fat. It's in the genes. I am also going to be blind :'(:'(Grease and meat is my life.. I don't want to give them up: '(:'(:'(

June 28

I am like, out of the group now. it's called being a habu. yes, a loner but the cause to this problem is Mami the girl I am always with. she doesn't want to socialize with them, and she hates College, and she hates everything at icu. so, well me being 24/7 with her didn't do much to make my friendship last with "the group." so instead I hanged out with Atsuko at Kichijoji. She introduced me to this guy, A JAPANESE GUY!! who goes to univ. what I hear is that he has awesome technique in bed. hmmn! <3 I have been exchanging emails with him since then, but I don't think it's gonna work out. hahah. I need more people to introduce me to guys!!! ah!

I have a huge bruise on my right ankle. I don't care if I get bruises but this one hurts... aw.
it's like, purple.

Chapter Ten

Sins in Roppongi

In daytime Roppongi slept, recovering from the excesses of the previous night. Some claimed it was the twenty-four-hour sector of the city but that's not true. In the morning, it was hung over and smelt of slopped beer, unemptied ashtrays and stale grease.

A pall of tiredness hung over the shabby ruffled buildings. Shreds of litter blew along Roppongi dori, the eight-lane wide main artery. Overhead ran the elevated Expressway; leaching rust down its columns and trusses like a dribbling drunk. Roppongi never looked its best by day, its pallid features best obscured behind darkness, disguised by the make-up and colour of neon light.

Unlike at night, during the day few people gathered outside Almond – one of Tokyo's famous meeting points and landmarks – a coffee shop with a shocking pink and white striped exterior. But this particular lunchtime I was waiting to meet a friend for lunch, watching a young guy sitting on a fake designer bag, eating peanuts and spitting the husks on the ground. When not chewing, he talked to himself. Then he stood, unzipped his fly and pissed into a small flowerbed separating the pavement from the road. I glanced round to see if anyone else noticed. No one did.

What was Roppongi? The most common answer was the ex-pat bar and nightlife zone. A handful (fewer than most thought) of throbbing lust-filled streets that sprung up when the occupying American forces encouraged the establishment of *gaijin* friendly bars. Why they first came here, nobody knew. The Japan joked it was where their tanks ran out of gas. My theory was that this was one of the few central districts left standing after the US firebombing. Immediately after the war, Japanese women migrated here seeking lipstick, chocolates, nylons, and foreign romance. The streets filled with jeeps and the buildings were turned over to brothels filled with young girls who had been left homeless by the bombings. Marriages between the GIs and Japanese girls were frequent – over 20,000 – but often came to a sad end.

The Japanese still thought of it as the only foreign enclave in Tokyo. One of my colleagues described it as a place where 'Westerners generally tend to prove their party prowess, by either being able to keep up with the best or by drinking themselves under the table, even if they just pretend to be drunk.' I replied that his comment was better directed towards his countrymen and that, whatever the nationality, Roppongi was a monument to intoxication.

Roppongi was home to a motley collection of American icons: The Hard Rock, Tony Roma's Ribs, Starbucks and a branch of Spago. At Roppongi Crossing, the Marlboro' Cowboy looked down benevolently like a guardian angel, and Citibank had installed a twenty-four hour cash point which often was the only angel an all-night drinker sought.

I rarely saw the military in town, not in a big way. Nowadays the revellers were a mix of bankers brandishing phones and making deals, English language teachers, tourists and business travellers packing bars with names like Gas Panic, La Rumba and Propaganda; or who casually slipped into lap-dancing bars: Seventh Heaven, Private Eyes and One Eyed Jacks. 'Sexy dance shows performed by beautiful ladies from around the world,' claimed Castel, another self-styled international cabaret.

Private Eyes boasted in a promotional message, 'When you step into Private Eyes you step into every man's fantasy. A luxurious décor showcases non-stop erotic dance shows performed by the finest dancers from around the world. Your evening will be one to remember! Private Eyes is the most exclusive gentlemen's club in Tokyo. You will find yourself surrounded by Sumo wrestlers, Hollywood stars, international sports heroes, and the most international business (sic) people in Asia.'

So exclusive they offered a discount on the usual entry price of Y7,000 yen if the right password was repeated. The fee then became Y5,500 including two drinks. Now that might attract a few more Hollywood stars. Nonetheless, it was a venue where I took visitors.

Recruitment adverts for dancers and hostesses could be found in *Metropolis* magazine. 'International and English speaking hostesses needed. Cheerful companions who are happy and who love entertaining people in an exclusive membership club. Excellent salary and bonus depending on your efforts.'

At seven o'clock, Roppongi yawned and woke up. Freelance hostesses gathered outside Almond. The girls liked to squat down on their haunches, applying the final touch of make-up. Their skirts were short, riding up their thighs. Guys would snatch glances, peering slyly, hoping for a quick flash of knickers.

Later, staff from the nightclubs, wearing their trademark long black coats, arrived to escort the girls to where they would be working that night. Most clubs employed short contract hostesses but with sick leave and days off, there was always a need for a nightly top up. The girls tottered off on high heels or platform boots giggling as they went, and lighting cigarettes.

Elsewhere on the streets, girls handed out flyers promoting hostess bars and massage parlours; well-dressed touts whispered a stream of well-rehearsed enticements.

'Please follow me, sir. I can offer you a very nice night. A very happy place. It's safe for you. Do you want a deal? I'll reduce the entrance fee. And you can have a free drink,' and so the patter continued as he walked by my side.

Most tried to snag Japanese. They spent more, caused less trouble and didn't argue about the final bill for, despite Roppongi's international reputation, it catered predominantly for the Japanese salaryman.

The salaryman first appeared during the 1920s as Japan caught up with the West's commercial and industrial might. Employers established a rigid work regime and ethic. Salarymen were paid according to the university they attended and not their ability. They discovered that it wasn't ability that led to promotion – it was how much they conformed and how loyal and unquestioning they were. Hours were long and, even then, there was a long commute to distant dormitory towns built on Tokyo's ever expanding margins. Drinking was one way to escape – momentarily – the compliant dullness of a day's work. Perhaps realising this, the company encouraged social drinking, and it became expected that salarymen joined company binges. No stigma was attached to getting drunk. If they were happier so were their employers. Over time, this became one of the few social activities enjoyed by salarymen and, over time, a particular orthodoxy came into play.

Drinking sessions provided a formal opportunity for salarymen to complain openly about work and their bosses, tell tales and have a good bitch about everyone. They would snigger at the office creep who always helped the boss and volunteered to work at weekends. Insults would be hurled and, for a few hours, the truth came stumbling out. The custom, though, was that what's said, 'in the glow of sake the night before, must be forgotten the following morning' (until, of course, repeated at the next drinking session). It became a ritualised letting off steam, and bosses were expected to take out their people just for this purpose – as I had to.

Drinking was the most important way that group bonds were built and maintained. Even lawmakers (as politicians were called in Japan) used alcohol to build bridges. A group of young politicians had formed a group with similar aged Korean politicians called *Bakudo-no-kai* or Bombshell Group, named after the cocktail drunk when meeting up. The purpose was to build stronger ties with Korea, Japan's closest neighbour, but still worlds apart politically and economically.

'I think this kind of way of building a friendship or relationship may help in the future and let us deal with more serious issues,' said one of them in a newspaper article I was reading over breakfast.

Beer was the most popular drink in Roppongi. Few young people drank *sake*, seen as being old-fashioned and drunk by buck-toothed *Oji-san* (men in their fifties and sixties) and neither were spirits fashionable.

Japanese preferred Japanese beer.

'Foreign brands like Heineken or Carlsberg are just too watery. I like Asahi Super Dry,' said one of my staff.

'Asahi is my favourite too. I like its fresh image,' added another. 'Foreign beer is too bitter.'

The bars were slow to fill – until after ten p.m. Before that, everyone ate dinner. Japanese don't drink on an empty stomach, a habit adopted by ex-pats as well. A Japanese/ex-pat divide existed, the latter denied access to the true Japanese bar and nightclub, and the Japanese salaryman tending to avoid through preference *gaijin* bars. But there were still plenty of choices for the ex-pat. Touts from Pakistan, Nigeria, Senegal or some obscure country in middle Asia, made seductive promises, guided them up lifts into small hostess bars where a complicated pricing system left everyone befuddled and paying more than they ever imagined for a drink with a girl and a quick grope in a tiny cubicle. Each session lasted ten minutes – the quickest ten minutes in the world. The clock ticked and an alarm clock rang when time was up. One more time, she would ask and, as quickly as she had slipped on her skirt, panties and bra, they'd slip off again.

Back in the bar, a waiter had brought over a bottle of cheap quality but expensive whiskey and a bucket of ice. 'Would you like a drink?' the girl asked with a coquettish smile as she poured two glasses. And another? And another? The girls drank heavily and I was not surprised to learn that alcoholism is a problem among them.

Not all joints were over-priced hostess bars. A typical run-of-the-mill bar was Motowns 1 or 2, favourite places for Japanese girls to meet Western men – and a bar that Satoko used before she met me.

'In the West, women are treated differently from here. There you are equals. It's the same in the bars in Roppongi,' said Ishikura, one of Satoko's friends who also enjoyed Motown: 'Speaking English allows me to get away.'

Motown 1 was the original, found at the top of some steep stairs where many a drunk had tumbled down. As the door opened, a sea of male faces turned, sizing up who had stepped in. Male or female? Competition or an opportunity? If a woman walked in, had she come on her own, with a boyfriend or other girlfriends? Were they easily approachable? Daft question, that. If a girl went to Motown, at least in the back of her mind was the thought that she might meet a guy. Not necessarily for sex but looking for the chance to chat and, maybe later, a date.

(Japanese men, picking up on American slang, called them 'srapper girls'.)

Where were they going to sit? Was there space to stand next to them? A room full of eyes followed as they walked across the bar.

Motown 1 had decoration typical of many *gaijin* bars: graffiti and messages written in felt-tip on the walls, ceiling and tables. All of it banal, unfunny and not worth illustrating.

A waiter or waitress would serve drinks at the table. The former were usually surly youths who took delight in pretending they didn't understand what was ordered even though they'd been employed to work in a *gaijin* bar. The waitresses were better. All sweet smiles and flared hands when they walked over. (I noticed that habit a lot: flaring out hands from their wrist.)

The music belied the name and wasn't predominantly Motown. But 'seventies and 'eighties classics abounded, perfectly matched to the average age of the drinkers. Memories of college discos stirred deep inside, a time when sagging bellies had yet to be held up by belts. Lyrics were mouthed, fingers strummed and air guitars made furtive appearances. Beer was swigged straight from the bottle.

For the businessman, the seriousness of yesterday's, today's and tomorrow's meeting could be put to one side. This was an exotic treat: little Japanese girls waiting to be plucked from trees.

The wife's back in Minneapolis, he thought (or was it Hong Kong, Toronto or a thousand other places?). I'm having fun. I'm sophisticated, a globetrotting, rich, interesting international traveller (whose armpits smelled and whose eyelids drooped lower and lower as drink took over).

Once I had a fight: a silly drunken bar brawl. How it started, I've forgotten now and I doubt I knew at the time. But I do recall an American guy sitting with a Japanese girl at one of the big round tables that ten people could squeeze around. It was a quiet night and they had the table to themselves. I came in with a group of visitors from the Saatchi agency in Hong Kong, and some colleagues from Tokyo, about ten of us. The only time I came to Roppongi was when entertaining visitors or clients. We stood close to the couple, swigging Asahi Dry straight from the bottle. We'd been out for a meal and had already drunk too much. At least I had. I must have started talking to the guy and his girlfriend. God knows what I said but in the end, he got really pissed off with me, stood up and flung a punch. It missed, I lunged at him and we locked in a punching, squirming mêlée. Takeda from the Agency jumped in and then John, our big surfing creative director emerged from the toilet, saw what was happening, and jumped in as well.

His worry, as he always pointed out afterwards when recounting and embellishing the story to anyone who would listen, was that the guy had a beer bottle in his hand. He might have used it at any moment. At this point, the fight broke up. John had dragged the guy away. We all stepped back. The guy realised the futility of carrying on. He seemed in okay shape. I could feel a black eye swelling up. We moved to another bar and left him in peace. But scraps and fights were rare, and virtually non-existent among the Japanese. No police were called. We weren't asked to leave the bar.

Most of the office ladies start to leave before midnight, to catch the last train home. They'd had their night of fun, a chance to live out their romantic notion of the West.

The men were left to hunt around a circuit, checking out favoured bars for the diminishing talent: Club Mogambo, Castillo, Acaraje and Geronimos might be a typical path – and one I favoured. Each within five minutes walk, so not too much of a problem if the pavement was by now a little fuzzy.

Someone fell in the street. Bang. Tripped flat on his face. His mates hauled him up and pushed him towards a bar. We were on the final leg of a night out with more visitors.

'Are you all right?'

'All right? Of course, I'm all right. Where we going?'

'Let's go to Climax,'

Up a lift to the fifth floor, the entrance fee paid for eighty minutes of time.

Ringed around the stage were long leatherette couches. Because of the gloom, it was difficult to see the rest of the décor but Climax had a trellised wall of dusty artificial plants at one end of the bar, and many of the other walls were mirrored.

On stage, a girl wearing a black bikini clung to a polished fireman's pole. Her shoes were made of a see-through plastic, pasted with silver decorations that glittered under the spotlights. The music thumbed with a heavy bass, and she slid up and down like a skilled acrobat, one second hanging upside down, the next splaying her legs as she slithered down. Never resting. Up and down. Legs apart. Legs together. Her pubic hair was shaved so no strand escaped from her bikini thong. A Brazilian wax was it called? A number of Japanese-Brazilian girls worked here, easily identifiable as they were usually taller than the locals (tall and handsome Russian girls as well).

As her dance continued, she removed her bikini top but kept her thong on. Climax was a topless, not strip bar. Despite the girl's attractiveness, the routine was mechanical and sexless, and little attention was paid to her. We ordered beer from a complex form, laid out on the table with different tabs of paper torn off as different items were consumed. It cost Y5,000 each for the entrance fee and, for the first eighty minutes, drinks were free. Thereafter we were charged for drinks and every thirty minutes 'over time'.

To drink with a girl she had to be asked over, otherwise they remained in their group, in a corner of the bar. It was relaxed like that, with no pressure to take a girl. If you asked for company, they would sit next to you and ask politely for a drink – the favourite drink was a strange-tasting coke and beer mix. If not, you could happily sit on your own.

The girl's ultimate motive was to entice the customer behind a set of curtains that separated the bar from a Rabelaisian encounter. This was how she earned most money. Behind the curtains were eight large armchairs, screened from each other on the side but not from the front. If you peeked into this area – as it wasn't very private – you could see a tangle of legs, the guys fully clothed, slouched on the armchairs, the girls sitting astride them, wearing only their thongs, grinding thigh against body and rubbing their breasts into the customers' faces. A session lasted the standard ten minutes but could be repeated without limit, racking up an expensive bill. In the end, one night's session could possibly cost upwards of Y100,000 per person if a group stayed for a few hours and joined girls behind the curtains. One girl told me she earned about Y40,000 a month, the more popular ones earned much more.

'Why do you do it?' I asked, repeating a question asked by every customer.

Yuki said because it was good money. She was bright as a spark but as a kid a few years ago, had stolen money from her parents, had stolen her friend's bike at school, and misused her credit cards. A loveable and very pretty rogue, she was tall, slim, and had dyed her hair blonde and put a wave in it. Tattooed on each arm was the same design of blue flames. She wore shoes with long straps that wound around her calves from ankles to knees. She was in love with a DJ, she told me.

'But he doesn't love me. Well he did. But not at the moment. Do you want to hear a poem?'

'Yes.'

'Have you heard of Ikkyu Soju?'

'No.'

'He was a Zen priest from six or seven hundred years ago. "It has the original mouth but remains wordless, a magnificent mound of hair surrounds it. Sentient beings can get completely lost in it. But it is also the birthplace of all the Buddha of the ten thousand worlds." You like it?' She started giggling, hiding her mouth behind her hand.

'Where did you learn your English?' I asked expecting her to say that she had lived abroad.

'At school.'

Why on earth a girl with such brains was working there, I couldn't fathom.

Afterwards I looked up Ikkyu. His was an unconventional priesthood. He loathed extremes of self-denial, openly went to brothels, even asked the wife of his closest friend if she would like to have sex, and wrote many poems that spoke of the satisfaction of sex, wine, and of frequenting brothels.

Brothels were now technically illegal in Japan. Instead, clubs, hostess bars, massage parlours and soap parlours had sprung up as a front.

One time we had trouble in one of the strip bars. We were leaving, waiting for the lift to arrive. We could have walked down the four flights of stairs but didn't and afterwards kicked ourselves wondering why.

We chatted to the bouncer, a rather large gentleman wearing a tight black T-shirt, square jawed, not an ounce fat hanging from his body. Just muscle. So large were they, I would not have been able to wrap both hands all the way round his biceps. Not that I would have attempted it.

'Where are you from?' I asked.

'Barcelona,' he replied.

'Nice place. Used to be one of my favourite cities in Europe.'

He smiled, I think, but he was a man who seemed reluctant to express emotions too openly.

The lift was taking its time to arrive, when three of the club's staff appeared.

One, who turned out to be the manager, said, 'You must come back inside. There seems to be a problem.'

'What problem?' we asked.

'With one of the girls.'

We asked again what the problem was.

'She's been cut. She's very upset.'

'What do you mean?' I asked.

'One of you cut her when you were out the back.'

I looked around at the others. They shook their heads.

'I don't think so.'

'I'm sorry but you can't go. We need to sort this out.'

'I'm sorry too but if there's a problem why wasn't it raised when we were inside? Isn't it strange that this has just been raised now? Which girl was it?'

'Let's go inside to talk about it. In my office.'

'Let's get out of here,' said someone.

'Look tell the girl we're sorry. Nothing to do with us though.'

'Let's go inside.'

As he said this, the man from Barcelona moved forward. His arms were folded.

'What do you think?' I asked one of the Japanese in the party. He spoke to the manager in Japanese; I couldn't catch what was said.

He turned to me, 'I think we should go inside. Just the two of us. The others can wait here.'

We sat in the manager's office, behind his desk. It was an untidy office full of files, folders and piles of paper. The light was orange and dim. The bouncer blocked the door.

'My advice is that we get this over and done with,' said my colleague.

I was angry though. I knew we were being ripped off. Nothing had happened, had it? Or if it had, purely by accident.

'Can the girl come here?' I asked.

'No she's too upset. She's crying.'

'I want to ask what happened.'

'She won't come.'

'Well what happened?'

'She was wearing a ring in her belly button. You know what I mean?'

I nodded.

'Out the back, one of your friends became too excited. He was told to quieten down by one of my boys. He didn't. The girl was upset. Your friend knocked off her ring. I know accidentally. But he was too excited. She's bleeding. You need to write an apology.'

My colleague nodded, 'We should do as we're told. Who knows? He might be right.'

'Your friend's right. And give her Y10,000. I will pass it on to her,' the manager said.

I wanted to fire back, 'Fuck you' but reluctantly knew the best thing was to get out as quick as possible. I did as asked: handed over an Y10,000 note, and scribbled an apology on a scrap of paper. I never took anyone there again.

Japan has one of the largest prostitution industries in the westernised world. Figures show that upwards of fourteen per cent Japanese men aged between eighteen and forty-eight use a prostitute – compared to rates in Europe of less than one per cent – and this rises to nineteen per cent of men between twenty-five and thirty-four.

But Roppongi was trying to improve its image. On its outer fringes, one of Japan's biggest development projects, a new Mori complex had opened in

2003; a Grand Hyatt hotel, a gallery atop a fifty-one-floor office building, luxury shops and expensive apartments, spread over thirty-two acres. It was claimed Roppongi would now change, the clubs and bars would go and the area be cleaned up. This I doubted. The complex was far-reaching but not central enough to have much effect. In any case, Tokyo everywhere has opposing elements co-existing alongside one another with neither winning over the other.

Mori was one of Tokyo's largest, most active property developers. They clung to a vision to turn Tokyo into the world's most daring high-rise city, tearing down houses, rebuilding with apartment blocks and substantially increasing population density by bringing in people from the suburbs. Their views on urban regeneration were based on old thinking. Back in the early 'seventies, it was Prime Minister Tanaka Kakuei who first said that high rise should be encouraged. 'We need to reverse our thinking. The only way we can solve the land problem in Tokyo is to build tall buildings but we are restricting the height of buildings. Land prices are high because the average structure in Tokyo is only 1.7 stories tall. What we should be restricting is the lowness of buildings.'

In 1974, he had to resign in disgrace, accused of accepting a $1.8m bribe from the Lockheed Corporation.

Mori believed that the labyrinth disorder of the old Edo street layout was outdated. They seemed to loathe the notion of people owning the streets, living in small houses of great individuality, and shopping at small neighbourhood stores, owned by people they knew.

But to whom were they going to sell? Mori didn't build low-cost affordable apartments. Conran had designed the apartment blocks; other famous architects had been responsible for further aspects of the complex. I found it an uninspired soulless design. Where were the flourishes, the intimacy that would give it personality and make it interesting and human? Once again, an outmoded Parthenon to money was built. And a Parthenon that had quickly become one of Tokyo's favourite destinations, despite the death of a young boy in a revolving door.

'Massage sir?' she asked. She was leaning against a fence, near to the Mori complex, one leg tucked behind the other.

'Where?' I asked.

'Follow me.' She stood up straight.

'Where?' I asked again.

'Close by.'

I followed her into the entrance lobby of an old shabby building that might have been a series of apartments. She pressed the button.

'How much?'

'Depends.'

'On what.'

'What you want, sir.'

'Only a massage.'

'It's late. I charge you 7,000 yen.'

'You're not Japanese.'

'I'm from Taiwan. We do very good massage. But I prefer foreign customers, they're friendlier. Japanese men are difficult to control.'

'Is that why you work round here?'

'Yes.'

'It's cold tonight.'

'When you stand still it's always cold.'

'Wear trousers instead of a mini-skirt.'

She didn't answer as the lift had stopped. We stepped into a corridor. She knocked on a door and it was opened from the inside.

Behind a makeshift desk sat another girl. She too looked Taiwanese. She smiled – it seemed an effort – and handed me a laminated card with a series of services and prices that rose to 30,000 yen.

'What do they mean?' I asked. They were Japanese terms but written in English.

'*Gokkun*, sir, that means swallowing after sucking, and *bukake* means facial or coming on girl's face.' Her fingers ran down the list.

'This *annaru fakka* means anal. You understand?'

'I just want a massage. But it's too expensive.'

Immediately she offered a discount of half-price. This is usually for regular customers, she told me, but it's late. Most men have caught the last train home.

Chapter Eleven

Low Culture

'Roppongi? It's nothing,' I would say to the wide-eyed and increasingly legless, leaving them to rub their reddened eyes as yet another girl brushed past in her highest heels. Roppongi is the most sanitised of the club districts, one deemed acceptable for the outside world to see and read about. Depravity knows few bounds in Japan. Which is strange when you think that every time an art gallery exhibits photographs or videos showing genitalia, the chances are the police will knock on the door and demand – ever so politely – that they be removed. Splattered across Japan are thousands of sex and BDSM clubs whose variety would make most people's eyes water (of course that's the intention of the latter).

Want to be rubbed by a girl's feet? (Not bare feet though, she must be wearing tights.) Or perhaps have a girl sit on your face? (But still wearing tights.) Or be sucked off whilst enjoying sushi and beer? (This time by a fully naked girl.) Or jeered at by a group of school-uniformed girls as you stand in the middle of a room with your trousers draped round your ankles? Or sit naked in a suspended rubber-ring and be tickled, prodded and poked? Scatological activities are but the everyday, as is a good whipping. Which is frustrating for the foreigner as their entry is barred to almost all of these establishments unless you have a Japanese take you – and most won't as they're too embarrassed; it's like being in a sweet factory with a diabetic teacher and all the sweets out of reach behind glass.

So what to do? Either trawl the web and then be content with dreaming pleasurably about these exotic delights or go to as many parties as possible in Tokyo when inevitably you'll meet a girl who works in one of these places.

Chapter Twelve

High Culture

There is high culture in Tokyo. If you look for it. I opened a contemporary art gallery in Tokyo. It was fun – mostly. We hosted great parties (better than any other gallery in Tokyo, I boast without shame), some lovely people became friends for a while, and a small impact reverberated on the Japanese contemporary art scene. And I discovered all the delicate sensitivities, deceits and hard-nosed political manoeuvring that could be found lurking in any creative business.

Japan was a tough environment for artists. Tokyo was no London, New York or Berlin. Finding affordable exhibition space was almost impossible – which did little to encourage talent. No matter their worth. There were a limited number of galleries (private or public), and public interest in contemporary art was less than elsewhere. What's more, too much work was hapless, obscure, and only on show because the artist had rented space. Our gallery was a non-profit space. Neither rental nor commission was charged. The primary purpose was to support young or emerging artists based in Japan although, as I didn't want to be bound by my own rules, I was flexible, so long as the work was distinctive, unconventional and good (and I made that decision, for wrong or right). Not necessarily Japanese – although predominantly our artists were Japanese – but any artist who I felt showed an invigorating spirit and was doing something new and challenging (although by this, I didn't mean just controversial).

Our opening parties quickly built a cracking reputation. At most gallery openings, a hushed and studious group of people drank warm wine and ate cheese and crackers. Our parties were always crowded with two or three hundred people. No one much studied the art of course. These were celebrated social gatherings and my Muse, a flamboyantly attractive girl, who was known to dress up with a condom in her hair, would act as hostess. Most guests remained upstairs – close to where the free drink was served – pulling up chairs and gossiping until we threw everyone out. If they wished, they could smoke on the large roof terrace. (Smoking was forbidden inside.) This was popular: sitting *al fresco*, sipping a beer or a glass of wine, looking at the Akasaka office blocks that towered over us. The scenery didn't matter, as it was so unusual to be able to sit in the open air anywhere in Tokyo.

At all our events, the same hardcore set found at every gallery opening in Tokyo would appear. I had never imagined it would be so small a group. No wonder artists were starving: too few collectors to sell work to – although at least we did sell work from time to time. At every party, one or two artists might be present but rarely many, even if the exhibiting artist had invited them. Artists don't seem to enjoy each other's shows or maybe it was too depressing to see so little work sold.

But then Japanese artists themselves tend to be very insular, reflecting the rigidity of society. Observed a friend, the English artist Sarah Waite who lived and worked in Japan: 'Painters in Japan tend to form societies that are closed to other Japanese artists, let alone a foreigner. I don't feel resentful; I just think it's rather sad. We have much to share and learn from one another.' She continued, 'It is very difficult for young artists to survive in Japan. In the UK, you can struggle but you will have studio space. In Japan, most young artists will work from their parents' home.'

In any group, there is always the party drunk. Ours was an American guy who had lived in Tokyo for many years: a well-practised slush, with beady eyes, hurriedly darting back and forth like a squirrel, prowling for alcohol. One of the first to arrive and last to leave he staggered away at the end, invariably clutching a bottle of beer or wine in one hand and a cigarette in the other. I had even caught him going to the fridge, snatching a bottle of wine for his journey home. Not even an amusing drunk – if such a type exists – just a wretched bore. He was never invited. He just turned up, even after being told he wasn't welcome for, like most drunks, he was thick skinned.

But the biggest single group at opening parties were women and, it should be noted that there is an important age bias: only women aged forty and above say they are interested in art and these were who we found always came, always dressed in black.

Indeed not just art but I found that the pre-dominant audience at the theatre, kabuki, anything with a high cultural aspect were middle-aged women. They don't go with their husbands.

Even younger girls prefer a girls' night out – which isn't surprising if men think driving is a pleasing hobby. (As they do – remember it's their No 1 hobby). In fact in one survey of married workers, forty-one per cent spent fifteen minutes or less per day talking to their spouse, including ten per cent who did not speak to their spouse at all.

Where can these women see art? There are 823 registered art museums nationwide. There are innumerable private art galleries in Tokyo although no official number is recorded. Many of the major department stores have their own galleries (which means that some of a woman's top ten pastimes can all be enjoyed in one place: shopping, book buying, eating and art).

As I said, our parties were better than most, at least the ones I have been to. Better than even the prestigious ones such as Sam Taylor Wood's opening at the Shiseido Gallery in the Ginza.

In a profile of Sam Taylor Wood in *The Times*, Richard Cook wrote: 'spanning modern decay and classical iconography, Sam Taylor Wood's art is still a sensation.'

In the previous few weeks you couldn't open a magazine or newspaper without coming across a proliferation of gushing reviews and profiles of her and her work, coinciding with the significant retrospective that was about to take place at the Hayward. Here was an artist that could do no wrong.

Just before the Hayward, she held a smaller and altogether more downbeat exhibition at Tokyo's Shiseido Gallery – owned by the cosmetic and skincare company.

In the centre of the gallery, a long table, covered with a white cloth, was set with food for the guests. If it wasn't that the food was limited to rapidly wilting cheese, it would have been a real-life rendition of Sam Wood's photograph *The Last Supper Wrecked* – her parody of Christ's Last Supper – where the table is full of fruits, meats and wine over which a topless woman presides as Christ. Was this a deliberate or unwitting parody of a parody? Off in a corner, bad wine was served but then the low-grade culinary experience was now to be expected at any opening in Tokyo. The bottom had fallen out of the contemporary art market, gallery attendances were declining and nobody was buying much work. Investing in expensive hospitality returned no value.

The exhibition was called 'To be or not to be'. The main body of work, five examples of Taylor Wood's Soliloquy series: big pieces that hung well in the space: a large white and high walled cube.

Sam Taylor Wood was there, with her husband Jay Jopling (the first couple of Brit Art) and young daughter, Angelica. Wearing a silver halo on her head (was this a deliberate continuation of the *Wrecked* parody?), Angelica sat on the floor, scribbling with green-coloured pens on sheets of paper. Jay Jopling reminded me of Bruce Kent: tall, clean cut and wearing a dark suit, white shirt and spectacles in heavy frames. He had a room-filling presence, an intelligent talker whilst Sam Taylor Wood would recede in a crowd. She looked like a harassed Mum, trying to get a belligerent daughter off to school and not at all like the stylish party woman whose pictures with the likes of Stella McCartney or Elton John graced the pages of *Tatler* or *Vogue*.

We were a more prosaic crowd, largely, the same bunch that came to our own opening parties: Johnnie Walker of course, who told me that the Shiseido Gallery didn't like him because he was a white nigger (his description of Jews). Like most Japanese galleries, he confided conspiratorially, they reluctantly tolerated the presence of *gaijin*. He hadn't been invited to the after-show dinner and when he asked where it was being held the staff refused to tell him. That response was typical, Johnnie said. When the gallery first opened, he sent an expensive congratulatory wreath but as he was *gaijin*, they didn't display it with the rest but by the toilet.

(Nonetheless, we both attended the dinner – at Kihachi, a pleasant but ordinary Italian restaurant in the Ginza.)

Benjamin Lee, a Chinese-born, Tokyo-based photographer was accompanied by an unusually tall young Japanese girl, some thirty years his junior. She wore an uplift bra, her breasts on the verge of exploding out of her low-cut top. After we were introduced, she demonstrated a trick involving a plastic figurine, lying prone on her hand, being induced to rise and stand upright. This provoked a series of comments from the other spellbound men watching about how they wished she could do the same thing to them. I learnt she once lived in Canada. Her spoken English was unusually good. This, she told me, had led people to believe she was a Chinese actress from

Hong Kong. The connection was lost on me so I asked her why. 'Because I can speak English,' she replied. Later she showed me a second trick, where she made a cigarette disappear. Impressed, I asked if she was a professional magician.

'No,' she laughed, 'I work in an S&M club. My parents don't like it,' she continued, 'I live at home with them and they object when I hang my leather G-string out to dry on the balcony. They worry what the neighbours are saying.'

As ever, very few artists are at the party and no A-list celebrities. (We wouldn't be featured in any gossip magazines.) Indeed, it was not a big party at all. Maybe a hundred showed up. Araki, the feted Japanese contemporary photographer made a brief and late appearance, accompanied by a young girl wearing a richly decorated *kimono*. She couldn't do tricks though. He had brought his camera and took pictures of Sam Taylor Wood's daughter, laughing and smiling as he did so. His hair was waxed and had been pinched into a series of devilish tufts that stuck out at odd angles – his trademark look.

In the *Japan Times*' review of the opening, Monty di Pietro wrote: 'She [Sam Wood] kept watching, growing more and more agitated. "What's wrong?" I finally asked. "It's my daughter," came the nervous reply. "Araki has got her cornered." '

Later, I took a photograph of Araki clasped tightly to an English girl with his tongue rammed down her throat. That's one way of greeting someone, I suppose. But then he claims not to like sex.

'I prefer photo to sex,' he said once. 'Recently I have declined offers to date because everyone wants to have sex. They are not satisfied only having dinner together.'

I should explain that Araki was the artist who photographed his own daughter naked and, at the Hayward, exhibited a photomontage that included explicit photographs of couples having sex, girls in bondage and close-ups of female genitals with plastic dinosaurs in the opening to the vagina. As he has said, 'When I became an adult a woman immediately meant her sex.'

Breadman – one of my favourite artists – was also present. Tatsumi Orimoto is famed for his performances, travelling the world, appearing in public with loaves of bread tied to his head. It sounds ridiculous, indeed certainly not to all critics' taste but it's wonderfully absurd and involving and has led to an appearance at the Venice Biennale. He also collaborates with his increasingly senile mother. Short, dumpy and with a permanent scowl, she is the subject of many photographs; 'Art Mama' he calls it. Sometimes she is photographed in oversize shoes, or with a tyre around her neck, or standing in a cardboard box. Whilst this might appear heartless – as if he is exploiting her illness and funny little presence – in fact he looks after her, cooks her dinner most nights and is devoted to her well-being.

He stood in the gallery clutching examples of his work packed in three plastic shopping bags. To anyone seeing him – dressed in a pair of scuffed black adidas training pants, three layers of threadbare T-shirts and a shabby coat – he would have looked like one of Tokyo's homeless instead of one of Japan's most gifted and original artists.

I was ignored by Nanjo-san – Japan's foremost curator. I had upset him when giving a lecture at the Tate where I had, without identifying him, criticised some of his curatorial behaviour.

As usual, the guests largely ignored the work on the walls. I saw Araki spend a few minutes studying it but he was in the minority. Mostly the guests talked among themselves, about anything but art, and the Japanese and *gaijin* kept largely in separate groups.

Waldemar Januszczak curated the show: an earnest fellow dressed in a loud Hawaiian shirt, a rather strange affectation for someone who was, to put it politely, rather portly. During dinner, he made a gushing speech which was in contrast to Sam Taylor Wood's rather terse, 'Thank you for coming, sorry, but my daughter is tired and needs to go to bed, and I hope I can persuade my husband to do the same.' However, I shouldn't be negative about Waldemar. His art column written for *The Sunday Times* is easily readable for an amateur like me and always razor-sharp and enjoyable. I take my hat off to you.

Over dinner, I told her that when I was last in London she was due to speak at the Tate on the day I flew out and I was disappointed to have missed it. She replied that she rarely did such speeches and was filled with terror beforehand, but she thought it had gone well. We had two things in common: we both attended Goldsmiths, and both knew the actor Ray Winston. (Well to clarify: I once had a drink with Ray, one long afternoon, twenty years ago in a West End drinking club. I was helping to develop a film in which eventually he agreed to star. By the time the film was shot, I had left the project; *Tank Malling* was made and was said by one reviewer to be 'a sleazy, lousy, nasty little film'.)

I asked her why she had used him in one of the Soliloquies. She replied blandly that he was an interesting character. In an essay on her work she said her intention was to present a figure that might be seen as either God or the Devil. It looked to me like Ray Winston, sitting in a steam room, smoking a cigarette with a towel wrapped round his middle. I was mystified. In fact, I was disillusioned by the work although I didn't tell her this (cowardly and dishonest of course). The photograph *Bound Ram* – what I had thought previously was an extremely poignant picture of a ram, with its feet bound, waiting to be slaughtered in a Marrakech market – now looked just a piece of opportunism. Many tourists had probably photographed it that day. Was it no more than a lucky snap, which was then given retrospective meaning? I say that because the Soliloquy series seemed totally without anything important to say. Each piece was one large single photograph, sitting on top of a narrow panel of three further photographs, which in some way connect to the main picture. It was a scheme derived from Renaissance altarpieces – a narrow frieze or predella with a series of paintings, which are both a continuation and a reflection upon the main image.

The point was, I thought her work, far from being 'psychologically charged, in which the thoughts of the sitters are tortuous, and almost audible' (to quote from the catalogue), lacked real emotion. To me, they were strained, clichéd and overly stage-managed compositions. My reaction was very much 'so what'? Every aspect of her work was laboured. I know she has battled bravely with cancer and her themes can reflect her life or death struggle. But why such obvious allusions? Even the title of the show, 'To be or not to be' seemed heavy-handed. If she was attempting to illuminate the Big Question – the meaning of life and death – this was done with little deftness.

The show was organised by the Shiseido Corporate Culture Department. Perhaps the whole affair was summed up by a request made of me by Nishimura-san the new Manager of the Gallery. He had recently been put in the job, having spent the last eighteen years or so, working as an in-house TV producer for Shiseido. 'I know nothing about culture or art,' he confided to me. 'Can we go out for a drink and will you help me learn?'

Shiseido is no better and no worse that any corporate gallery, of which there are a number in Tokyo. They support art to earn prestige – though to their credit they have done this for decades. They are buying a show. It will be good for PR and the company's annual report.

On the other hand, there was a delightful honesty about Nishimura's position. He didn't know a jot and really, what did that matter? It doesn't. Be ignorant and have confidence in your own judgment, I was thinking, and will tell him if I have that drink.

I said I would. Delighted with my response, he uncorked a special bottle of red wine. Special, he said, because there was cheap wine for some of the dinner guests, and more expensive ones for his table.

I should be so lucky.

Breadman sat next to me and I poured him a generous glass of the good wine. I wanted to take his picture holding a bread roll. I hadn't told him this as I took out my camera but then I realised it would be tacky and demeaning to his work and put the camera away. He talked and smiled a lot. His English was lucid but he really wanted to gossip with his Japanese friends.

'But you like my work, so please stay with me,' he said, pointing a finger and laughing at me. 'Excuse me but I need conversation,' he continued. 'With my mother, we don't talk a lot.'

At the end of dinner, I collected up the discarded corks in a paper bag, which I labelled 'Wine corks from a dinner with Sam Taylor Wood'. Look out for them at my next show.

Johnnie Walker had already slipped away, his departure unannounced. The next day he confided that the mood was wrong and he felt uncomfortable. 'I hate these corporate affairs,' he said, 'they have no heart.' Who is Johnnie Walker? Or Jani Waka, his legal Japanese name? That was a question posed in *Paletten*, a Swedish art magazine, by Magnus Bartas. He answered with twenty-four bullet points. But they were in Swedish, and I couldn't understand them so with thanks to Magnus for the idea I have come up with my own version.

1 Actually, I do understand the first point 'Han bor I Tokyo' or at least I think I do. 'He was born in Tokyo.' Maybe he was but I always thought he was born in Kobe.

2 His family were Jews who came to Japan, via China from India.

3   They were in the textile business.

4   'I think we have different sexual preferences,' he said once.

5   He's had a hernia operation and when he had the stitches out, the doctor asked him how he felt. 'It's tight,' he told the doctor. 'Well you haven't felt tight in your arse for years so enjoy the feeling,' the doctor replied.

6   He works in the finance business as a trader but is also a cat-killing sculptor in Haruki Murakami's novel, *Kafka on the Shore*.

7   He drinks red wine and is a vegetarian

8   Currently, he drives a black Mercedes G-Wagon. The central locking doesn't work.

9   He adored his dog Elton, a slobbering vegetarian bull terrier but who sadly died in 2003. Bacon, an Irish Wolfhound, has now taken Elton's place.

10   He was schooled in India.

11   He has a houseboy from Burma.

12   His houseboys stay with him for a year or so, before returning to Burma to marry.

13   In the past, his parties were famous but nowadays held less frequently.

14   If you are invited, he will tell you just to bring wine, cheese and French bread. (I think Magnus had this one as well).

15   He will always tell you that just a few people are coming and when you arrive, there are hundreds.

16   He is at almost every opening in Tokyo despite the fact that he is up early and trades all day.

17   He always attends the Turner Prize and Venice.

18   He set up and hosted the Tate Residency in Tokyo, and has now started his own art-project and gallery.

19   His clothes sense is eclectic.

20   He shaves his head.

21   He has a Turkish boyfriend. (Well, he did until recently.)

22   He knows everyone in the art world and will often arrange receptions for visitors. I'd call that natural generosity.

23   He tells the tale of how a scandal magazine in Japan, ran a story claiming that there was a photograph of Johnnie where his Mum

was holding his penis. Johnnie threatened to sue them. 'You're wrong,' he said. 'It wasn't my mother but my grandmother.'

24   Elton once starred in a film.

25   People either love him or hate him. I love him. No, no,no. Not quite like that.

Chapter Thirteen

The Full Circle

'But what is it that connects Japanese towns, after all?'

The Japanese artist On Kawara once asked this question rhetorically, *apropos* nothing, in the middle of a conversation about the differences between New York and Tokyo. 'Isn't it the railway?'

I told the artist Yoshie Keiko, a friend, about my plans to make a trip around the Yamanote line, a route that circles and defines inner Tokyo. Would she come with me, I asked? I knew she was fascinated by the experiences of commuters on trains and had extensively filmed them.

'On the train, I feel a sudden attention when I'm with foreign friend speaking in English. At the same time, I pay attention, checking who is speaking non-Japanese when I hear English. This sudden mild tension in public area interests me. I seem to go back and forth of different territory as I speak different language. Why do you want me to come? What can I do?'

'I want to be with someone else as I look at what's taking place around me. That's all.' We hadn't discussed my own fascination with people on trains.

'You're like me. I glance at people on the train when I am not reading a book or in deep thought. I judge people, categorise them and imagine their personalities. I think how beautiful she is, how nice her shirt is, what a beautiful neck she has, how tired he looks or how fat she is. These thoughts are all directed one way from me. On the other hand, when I feel someone stares me at, I think I must be pretty when I am in a good mood and I think I must be ugly when I am in a bad mood. Then, a person in front of me is probably doing the same thing. And they are not the only one. They must be thinking about something like I do. The person next to them, the next, next to them, the next, next, next to them and the next, next, next, next to them must be thinking something too. I am overwhelmed. In this situation, I literally remind of Simmel's observation. "We look at people all the time. But we never hear their words. The modern feeling, that is the lack of direction in the life of the mass, loneliness and the feeling of an individual surrounded by closed doors," especially in a rush hour when I am pushing against to someone's back who I don't know. At times, the train is so crowded the breath is squeezed out of you, as you stand wedged between the crowds.'

'Isn't this a bizarre?' I say. 'Our bodies are pressed against a total stranger in a way that is more intimate for longer than we might generally be with a girlfriend or wife.'

'Commuting is something which people do every day. They don't think about it in that way. People do it so many times and some may step same point every time and visualise every part. But it's not that exciting enough to tell the other about it. I like this mediocre experience.'

'Sometimes it's exciting.'

I told her of the morning I was pressed hard against a girl. We were facing each other, I explained, and she had her hands held in front of her.

'They were at the same height as my crotch. I knew she could feel me but she neither flinched nor tried to turn away. But neither did she show any acknowledgment. Her face was a complete blank.'

'Ha, she was terrified. I know that feeling,' Yoshie laughed. 'I don't know if it's funny. Groping is a big problem in Tokyo. Are you a *chikan?*"

There were twenty-nine stations on the loop, and I chose to start at Meguro. It was one of the earliest stations built, having been completed in 1885 when the first part of the line was opened. But whilst it looked dingy and unmodernised, no historic associations or references could be found, no matter how hard I looked.

In the station, for the benefit of blind people, a route of dimpled yellow tiles marked the way to the platform, but in the years I'd been here, I had yet to see one blind person use them. Neither had I seen a blind person on Tokyo's streets, even when I was once walking close to a blind school.

'Nor would I risk my life if those were my terrible circumstances,' commented Yoshie. 'We dislike disabled people.'

We ran down the stairs to the platform. The track was below ground level. Or at least I think so. In Tokyo, it's sometimes impossible to gauge where ground level begins.

Yoshie had brought a camera. She started to take pictures but I asked her to stop as I thought this would make us too conspicuous.

On the platform, a station master wore a blue uniform. It was pressed and spotless. He held a red flag with a tight grip. He glanced from right to left with deliberate and severe movements of his head. His mouth was turned down. With considered dignity, he checked his watch. He stood straight, legs slightly apart. I knew he knew he was in charge – the fat controller of all around him.

Without having to think about it, passengers lined up within a series of marks that showed where the carriage doors would open. As they waited, none were restless or impatient. Most stations had few seats as people were expected to flow from the street almost immediately on to the train – the gap between services was only two or three minutes. Every train stopped in the same precise position. Passengers would wait until everyone got off before filing on. No one ever pushed or elbowed on first. A short burst of melody then played, a warning that the doors were about to close.

The carriage was almost empty so we were able to find two seats adjacent to one another.

'I refuse to get off now,' said Yoshie, 'this is such a treat. I might stay on forever.'

As the train eased out of the station, the station master pointed, with both arms rigid and outstretched, to signal that all was clear and that the train could now go on its way. His head was held high and he nodded in severe acknowledgment as the train moved forward. Our adventure had begun.

Three schoolgirls from the local Sacred Heart School had jumped on the same carriage. I was reminded, by the way they dressed, of a prim school in the Scottish Highlands. No loose socks and scuffed shoes here. Just neatly pulled-up grey green socks, ironed blue skirts down to the middle of the knee and grey-green blazers. They were bored so they played a game, opening their mouths as wide as possible before one of the others poked a finger into the gaping hole.

'Did you play this at school?' I asked Yoshie.

'No.'

On the three-minute journey to Ebisu, we passed the Honsoman Driving School, an architectural oddity with a huge sphere jammed in the face of the building, looking as if a giant baseball had been hit and lodged in the façade. I couldn't understand its purpose or symbolism at all.

In Japan, driving is initially learnt off-road before graduating to the streets, and the school had a series of roads and typical street features marked out across a flat expanse of tarmac. The school's dark red cars, with a numbered cube on the roof, were a well-known sight around Shirogane and I had often wondered, as the general quality of Japanese driving was so poor, what learners were taught.

Ebisu: our carriage was half-empty and only a couple more people got on. One was a vagrant dragging three heavy bags: two were large striped carrier bags, the sort favoured by Filipino maids to store and carry their personal belongings, the third a ripped sports holdall. He sat opposite us and scratched slowly behind his ear. He smelt. Japan is a country where people don't smell. Nor does the country. I can't associate Japan with a smell, only with colours. His was the only smell of human perspiration in the carriage, and because of that it seemed more pungent than would be the case, for example, if this had been the tube in London.

His hands were calloused and black. He picked at something in his ear and through his dirty glasses – it looked as if vomit was smeared on them – he looked inquisitively our way.

I looked away, down at his bags. They were stuffed with used copies of *manga* he would later sell on the streets – a favoured way for vagrants to earn money.

After the vagrant, a girl had stepped on, looking as if she has walked off the page of *Vogue* or Elle. She carried a slim, tan coloured Louis Vuitton briefcase, and was wearing a Chanel black and white coat over red velvet flairs and the daintiest of black velvet court shoes. Her hair was immaculate, as black and smooth as the night sky; her skin was as flawless as a polished pearl. She didn't sit, but leant against a rail, taking out a book from the brief case.

'Who do you think she is?' I asked quietly.

'Maybe she's been visiting one of the boutiques in Ebisu. I think she may be a fashion rep or something like that. She's beautiful.'

'What's she reading?'

'I can't see from here.'

In Japan, books often have a plain paper dust jacket wrapped around them, not to disguise the title but to protect the cover.

If we had got off here, we could have taken the moving walk-way that goes from the station to Ebisu Garden Place: a large shopping precinct with a Mitsukoshi Department Store, a cinema, the Tokyo outlet of the famous French restaurant Le Taillevent and a wonderful wine cave where the Beniot, the most languorous Frenchman I had ever met, worked as a sommelier. But we didn't and carried on to Shibuya.

Shibuya: both the vagrant and we left the train at Shibuya. (I didn't say we would make one continuous journey.) Shibuya was a major hub where several subway and JR lines meet. Finding the right exit is always a chore as the signage is typically Japanese: incomplete and not helpful. So having Yoshie with me was an asset. I wanted to see the unveiling of the Japan National Team soccer jersey. A giant inflatable poster of the soccer player Shineske had been suspended on the side of the Tokyo department store building overlooking Hachiko Square. The poster was twenty metres tall, and Shineske had been photographed naked from the waist up. The idea was for him to be seen shirtless for a few days. Then a giant shirt would be pulled over his torso to announce the launch of new shirt technology from adidas. I was told that obtaining permission from the local government to erect such a large poster had been difficult. By making it an inflatable poster, it could be classified as a balloon, which allowed certain rules to be circumvented.

However, just before the shirtless torso was put up, officials said that it would be inflammatory for young girls to see such a huge expanse of naked flesh. You must black out the nipples they insisted. A black strip was pasted across his breast. But they still weren't satisfied as they thought this was just as provocative, and demanded that the poster be taken down until the day of the shirt unveiling.

'What they expected to happen on the streets I don't know,' I said.

'Maybe there would be instant orgasms,' replied Yoshie. 'It would be bad if it was seen that girls were having fun. After all, it's okay for men to read pornographic *manga* on the train but have you seen a girl?'

'No.'

'In fact they do read them but usually in privacy. Homosexual stories are popular.'

Now the poster was back. Eight men, suspended from ropes, hitched the giant shirt around the torso.

Whatever day or time of day, Hachiko Square was always crowded. It's one of world's great meeting places, like Piccadilly Circus, Carfax in Oxford and Times Square. A bemused crowd looked up, fascinated by what was going on. Even the vagrants gathered at the edge of the square were rapt. And a rare women itinerant, drunk and possessed, was shouting what I could only guess were obscenities at the men as they swung from the ropes. Yoshie confirmed that she was swearing heavily.

'I swear a lot in English too but never in Japanese,' she continued.

'Why?'

'I can be more talkative. I think I sound less stupid, even though I sound stupid now.'

Matchball Man was standing among the crowd. He was supposed to represent a man of mystery, turning up at events wearing a dark suit and the adidas Fevernova ball on his head, but he reminded me of the Smash alien. Because of a crucial design fault, two minders wearing adidas tracksuits always accompanied him. He couldn't see out of the ball, was effectively blind and the minders were responsible for guiding him around when out in public. What was funny, well for me at least, was to scare the living daylights out of him by suddenly jumping on him and screaming Matchball Man. Poor guy. No wonder he suffered from a severe case of dandruff.

Eventually the shirt was securely fixed, the media arrived to take pictures and interview some of the spectators. We returned to the Yamanote line and were lucky to find two seats again. 'This time I'm not getting off,' said Yoshie.

On the hop to the next station, we passed a semi-permanent encampment of blue tarpaulin homes in Miyashita Park where the homeless, and most likely our vagrant, lived. There was no squalid mess around the tents. They might have been pitched in a well-kept holiday campsite.

Harajuku: around Harajuku was an eerily deceptive feel of the countryside because of the surrounding park and temple. You don't expect to be surprised like this in Tokyo. Harajuku was a small station elevated above the ground and to the outsider it wouldn't be immediately obvious that this area was the centre of Tokyo's youth culture. A man had stood in front of us, wearing a black anorak with a motif printed on the front in gothic script: 'D.J. Free Jacket. The thing that darkness is controlled always controls the world.'

Yoyogi: a group of schoolboys swaggered on. A typical school uniform for senior high school pupils includes white socks. An unfortunate rule that had encouraged white socks to be worn as adults.

I asked Yoshie about this habit.

'I think they must take for granted that their significant others don't mind to wash their socks,' she replied.

'It's the colour, not the washing. It's not cool. We think it tasteless.'

'We might have learnt it from the Germans.'

'In England most women find white socks a real turn-off.'

'It's actually because priests wear white socks.'

Like schoolboys found anywhere in the world they lolled listlessly, eyes dulled and only half-seeing, hair a ruffled mess, bored by what they had learnt that day. They bumped into one another as the train swayed on the track, exaggerating the movement and moaning in mock pain.

Shinjuku: we were now in the metropolitan heart of Tokyo. Tower blocks soared ominously overhead; great man-made slabs of mountain blocking the sun, and the train snaked between them as if we were hurtling along a precipice. We had arrived at the busiest station in the world and all the platforms were rippling with commuters, a *Tatsumi* of people rolling into and out of the station. One and a half million people pass through everyday. People crowd on to our carriage, more than got off, they politely but firmly push each other along and we sit with bodies and bags hanging over us. Salarygirls had pushed on – they're usually known as OLs, Office Ladies. They wore their equivalent of the salaryman's business suit: a plain black or grey suit, a white blouse, light ivory, cream or off-white pantyhose, simple black sling-backs and a black handbag. They stood above us and bitched about a male colleague at work. I didn't catch all they said but it seemed his boorish attitude was grating with them.

'They don't care if people hear what they say,' says Yoshie, 'here they are out of work. The train is neutral. Just like a bar or restaurant.'

As the train left, tiers of apartment block windows were just a metre from the edge of the track. Were the residents immune to the deafening roar and the buffeting of passing trains? Did the noise seep along pipes, through vents, out of the showerhead?

Shin-okubo: in the past, Satoko and I had often used this station. Then, we crossed the road from the main exit, turned right down a narrow street and, five minutes later, arrived at Tokyo's own Globe Theatre. This district had been taken over by Koreans, the largest of the minority groups in Japan (the others being Chinese, the Ainu [from Hokkaido], the Okinawans from

Okinawa and the Burakumin; although the latter aren't an ethnic group but the lowest of the low in Japan's caste system which has the Imperial Family at the top, followed by politicians and bureaucrats, everyone else, aliens – that included me – and, at the bottom, the Burakumin).

The Burakumin number around six million or five per cent of the population.

Japan continued to promote the notion of ethnic purity and there were still whispered half-accusations when someone was thought to be of Korean descent. I witnessed this with a client. 'Oh yes, we think his family is Korean but we daren't ask him,' said one of the people who worked for me.

When we pulled away from the station, I saw an old man slumped on a street. I assumed he was drunk.

Takadanobaba: the atmosphere has changed again as we reach another unassuming station. This area is mostly residential and in one sense, although there are no fields, retains the spirit of its rural past. We pass over one of Tokyo's fetid rivers. Most people don't think of Tokyo being on a river. More than that, it's on a large delta, bisected by many rivers and tributaries all of which have been either filled in, or reconstructed as narrow concrete aqueducts. Most look more like sewage mains than rivers; indeed, when it rains heavily, raw sewage is dumped directly into them.

As we travelled away from *Takadanobaba*, blocks of apartments with large alphabet letters painted on their side now dominated the view. When you see these monotonous districts with not an ounce of life to them, you can imagine why Tokyo's workers spend either a long time at work or then go off drinking and eating. Whoever built these monstrous blocks did so with no sympathy for those who might live in them. They are not homes but a space to fill with a few necessities of life.

Meijiro: as the carriage doors opened a cacophony of sound flooded in. Schoolgirls jostled their way on to the carriage. They made a sound like hungry chickens in a battery. Lucky charm bracelets and chains hung from their satchels, *katai* and pens. One had a 'Fuck It' badge pasted on her satchel. As she was no older than fourteen and immaculately dressed, I guessed she was ignorant of its meaning. I asked Yoshie.

'All American dirty words give them a feeling as if they are taken to somewhere more liberal place I guess.'

The train pulled out. Apartment blocks now gave way to houses, and the streets were full of small stores. All new houses, no old ones; homes 'system built' by the manufacturer and chosen from a showroom catalogue. You could chose a base model and add options. Because everyone chooses a different model, there is no uniformity of style in any single area. There was no sensitivity to context or surroundings. Aesthetics are ignored.

'It's a shambles,' I say, stating the obvious.

'Unity was destroyed by nature. Everyone loves the little wooden houses with their black tiled roofs. But come the next earthquake I'd rather be in one of these homes. You know that most people in earthquakes are killed by burning alive or by being hit on the head with a tile.'

The only rule was to build whatever was liked, wherever it was liked. A comical pastiche of an English Tudor house would sit alongside a Swiss chalet, alongside a Middle American dream home, alongside some monstrosity that beggared any description. That Japan has some of the most innovative architects and designers is not apparent at all on any part of the journey.

Now, Japanese homes are designed like Western homes with locks, barred and punctured windows. They no longer commune with nature – as I saw so beautifully expressed at Satoko's ancestors' house on Hiroshima Island.

The journey was boring at this point so I told Yoshie about my visit, two days ago, to the British Council. Their offices had been refurbished and I had been invited to the opening reception. When I walked in – having noted that Johnnie Walker had sent a large bouquet of flowers that were prominently displayed in the entrance – the speeches had already begun. (Glad to see that British timekeeping was up to scratch.) On stage, one of the guests was making a speech, surrounded by an audience almost all dressed in black and grey suits, including the women.

'I have a speech that can last for one hour or you can all have a drink as soon as you like so long as those that can promise to vote for me,' droned Dr MacNeash, a junior government minister with responsibility for the British Council. He was followed by Sir Stephen Gommershall, the British Ambassador, who spoke in measured Japanese, his short speech punctuated by a little cough he made every paragraph or so.

Then came the Japanese junior minister from the Ministry of Education, Sport, Culture and Science Technology (quite a grouping) who made a valiant attempt to out-drone our own minister. He was under the impression that the UK and Japan had enjoyed long and deep relationships for 400 years. A slight bending of history that forgot the exclusion of all foreign contact in the Tokugawa era – lasting for 250 years – and the more recent spat we had in the Second World War.

'But many of us didn't learn about Britain and Japan being at war,' Yoshie said. 'We did learn it was only about the war with the US and the fighting in Japan.'

I said I thought the minister was probably more educated than that. 'Anyway, we were able to eat food based on Jamie Oliver's recipes,' I continued.

'Was it good?'

'Not really. I was told he was every girl's favourite in Japan.'

'Who is he? What kind of food does he cook? I rarely watch or read gourmet guide neither. I love eating but I just believe appetite is the best sauce.'

'Actually I don't know myself. He seems to have become a celebrity cook after I left England.'

Ikebukuro: 'bye bye' echoed around the carriage as many of the schoolgirls left. This was a common way to say 'bye' by Japanese girls, although they say it with a different intonation than we do. We say it mainly flat or with an upward lilt. Japanese girls say it with a downward lilt, rather in the same way as the Teletubbies speak. It can be heard all the time and often appears to be the only English they know.

'I've heard it said that you can tell what station you are in just by looking at the uniform of the schoolgirls who get on.'

'How do you mean?' I asked.

'Each school has a different uniform and many are well known.'

'So the girls who've now got on?'

'They're from Toshimagaoka School. You see a very dark blue blouse, with a long collar with three white stripes on it.'

'And those ones who got on at Meijiro?'

'From Kawamura School.'

Ikebukuro is one of Tokyo's main shopping areas. Huge department stores, Toyota's flagship showroom, Tower Records, Virgin, they're all here. Everything is jumbled and disordered. Chaos and a mess, I say to Yoshie.

'But it's a cultural void,' said Yoshie. 'There are no boundaries pushed here. It's like a sponge soaking up cultures from the rest of the world. I hate this place.'

Otsuka: for the first time I noticed a number of *pachinko* parlours with their gaudy flashing lights. I have never been into one but then have no intention. Nor had Yoshie.

'Have you heard of Sammy?' she asked.

'Sammy who? I know several.'

'Sammy the *pachinko* machine makers. Not a person.'

'No.'

'So you won't know their corporate slogan then?'

'No. Do you then?'

'We contribute to creation and development of culture with our creativity and foreseeing in entertainment while moving forward with people.'

'For real?'

'Yes. I once worked for them part-time to earn some money. I find pachinko obnoxious. It disturbs me. Yet the Governor of Tokyo who says he too hates this form of gambling wants to open casinos in Tokyo.'

Sugame: the apartment blocks had returned. I couldn't see a single soul walking on the streets, nor dog or cat.

'Sometimes, you might think that a giant vacuum cleaner has sucked everyone up.' said Yoshie. 'This is always a quiet area.'

'Do you know it?'

'My grandparents live nearby. I went to see them recently. They are in care house and did not look very happy. I felt very sad. They were losing their mind also but they can still be very straightforward…I am glad that I went to see them though.'

Komagome: on the banks either side of the station, privet bushes were cut into near-perfect semi-spheres. This was the first station where a hint of effort had been made to make it attractive. The station and tracks were in a series of deep cuttings, on the edge of which, houses sat precariously. An elderly gentleman had got on. He sat bolt up right in his seat, his back perfectly straight. From a thin briefcase he pulled out the morning paper, unfolded it, and then refolded it in to a narrow strip so he could read without intruding into his neighbour's space.

Tabata: home of track engineering trains, and freight carriages full of ballast. I had to get off, as I wanted to use the toilet. Not that I looked forward to this, as contrary to what might be thought, Tokyo's public toilets could be as dirty and smelly as anywhere else in the world. This proved to be the case.

The door to the toilet was broken and the floor wet. A mixture of vomit and faeces sat in the bowl. I had to go outside and take deep breaths, in the hope that I breathed as little as possible when inside.

'Women make groups when they do something,' said Yoshie when I had re-emerged. 'At junior high school, we had toilet-mates. It means, when somebody goes to the toilet, she always ask her toilet-mates to go together. At first I didn't like this habit. I wanted to go when I wanted to go, not when someone asked me. However, I noticed going to the toilet means chatting at the toilet. Toilet is an important place to communicate, and get trivial but important information. Then I started to accept friends' offer to go to the toilet.'

'And you haven't stopped since?'

'No.'

Nishi Nippori: the carriage – full when we got on again at Tabata – now almost empties. Running alongside the Yamanote line was the *Shinkansen* track that headed north. Why were there so many love hotels here? Paplon, Prestige, Palace. I asked Yoshie if she had ever used a love hotel. She didn't answer immediately but then said no. I didn't believe her.

So I asked if she had seen the work of Kyoichi Tsuzuki, his homage to the Love Hotel; an institution he claimed was fast disappearing due to new government regulations.

She hadn't.

I told her that I had recently seen it at a show in Tokyo where it was one of the more popular exhibits, particularly with girls. At times, it was impossible to find a space to sit inside. Yoshie didn't answer.

'Oh come on,' I said, 'tell me the truth. You're an artist, aren't you?'

'While I was college student I used it sometime. What I liked about it is that there were notebooks in those hotels and lovers had left some messages on the notes. Curiosity, anxiety, expectations. I could totally relate to girls who'd stay and written down their feeling on it.'

'Do you think there is a fixation about sex in Japan?'

'I think we have more of a thriving business than your own country. I would say we're healthier about it. Except for stupid censorship laws but for us its something to get on and do.'

Nippori: another large station, the few remaining passengers – bar us – get off. More love hotels. Tokyo has that public but secretive side to it. Love hotels are obvious but who knows how many people are inside them? I wondered if they would be a success in the UK.

Why did young people use them?

'Because having sex is such a big treat for couples, and they want make it something more special...no, the boring fact is that they live with their parents and love hotels are the only place they can have a fuck. Anyway, it's every teenage girl's dream to use one. If only once.'

I knew a guy who worked in one: a cleaner, who had compelling tips to pass on.

'Don't drink from the cups in the room,' he told me, 'all manner of couples come and, in particular, S&M couples use the cups to hold all sorts of bodily secretions. Before taking a shower, run it for a while as the shower might also have been used for some peculiar activities. Always check for hidden recorders under the bed, as well as hidden cameras nowadays; with wireless technology, it's easy for someone to wire the room and to stand in the street to pick up the signals.'

'Well, I don't like love hotels if I can be clear about this.'

Okay, Yoshi, I get the point.

Uguisudani: the Valley of Nightingales. The platform melody sounds like a nightingale's song. (Every station has a melody and I wasn't surprised to find that a fanatic had uploaded many of them on to a website.) Our local yakitori owner was born here. Scaramouch, the restaurant he owned, had quickly become our local *yakitori* in Shirogane. He cooked, his wife hid in the kitchen and did the washing up – but her head sometimes peered through a hatch – and their daughter acted as waitress. It could be found at the top end of Gaien Nishi dori on the ground floor of a two-storey narrow house. If full it would seat sixteen diners at three tables and one counter. The food couldn't be faulted or any simpler: grilled fish, meat and vegetables cooked over charcoal — the freshest ingredients with no embellishments. Not that all out-of-town visitors I took there could eat everything. American visitors in particular rejected the chicken's gizzard, heart and liver. Nor did they like the beef tongue much. They would choose white chicken breast meat, grilled mushrooms, peppers, asparagus, and bowls of salad.

We relished the grilled whole garlic bulb with a bright red chilli dipping sauce, and if salmon tail – its skin grilled crisp – was on the menu we were in heaven – except for our friend William, an Austrian living in Tokyo who disliked fish intensely. (But that's the problem of coming from a land-locked country.) Scaramouch stocked good *sake*; was filled with the fragrance of the cooking; the owner loved jazz and blues, and played this as background music. (His sixtieth birthday was held at Blues Alley in Meguro.)

If we didn't visit regularly, upset, he'd want to know where we'd been. They were a beautiful and elegant family. The wife was thin and delicate like a porcelain doll, haired tied neatly back in a bun, the most elegant washer-up I had come across; the husband, with his trimmed moustache and close cropped hair, might have been ten years younger than his age, and their daughter now in her early thirties looked like an innocent and very attractive teenager. As I felt guilty at finding her so adorable, I looked for something to undermine her attractiveness: usually her crooked smile. The father worried that his daughter had yet to marry but then I couldn't see how she'd be able to meet a potential husband if she worked every night. Scaramouch wasn't a place to meet young handsome men.

Always, at one end of the counter, stood a large arrangement of flowers and stems, and the toilet was a miniature Japanese garden, with a fountain and pebbles on the floor, and a bonsai tree on top of the cistern.

The more I ate there, the more I dreamt of running a *yakitori*: a simple romantic life grilling skewers of meat and vegetables over charcoal, working only in the evening and chatting to the people who ate at the counter.

'You'll get bored,' said Satoko, when I told her this.

'No, I won't.'

'And anyway, you can't hold a conversation in Japanese.'

Ueno: a man with a bad toupee sat down. His hairpiece looked as if it was made with an early experimental version of nylon.

More men are losing their hair. Now over twenty-five per cent of the adult male population suffers this problem. The major causes are down to first, the obvious – the increased average age of the general population; secondly the increased Westernisation of the Japanese diet, most noticeably the greater consumption of meat, high calorie and high fat foods. Third, increased physical stress due to irregular lifestyles in urban areas particularly going out drinking every night and finally increased psychological stress due to the prolonged recession in Japan. That's what I had read anyway.

Okachimachi: the streets had a different feel to them. More lively than the past few stations. There was a feeling of returning to Tokyo's heart, back to commercial sophistication. Colour, people and chaos had returned to the streets. Hanging in the air was the rustle of millions of consumer transactions, notes and coins being handed over, and goods neatly wrapped in tissue paper taken away. No nation wraps better than the Japanese.

Akihabara: gadget city. Contented shoppers clutched plastic bags stuffed full with merchandise from the computer and electrical shops. The streets were packed with shops that sold every conceivable type of electronic gadget from the very latest robotic rat, dog, cat or budgie to ancient vacuum tubes. Did any of these things make the purchaser's life any easier or more enjoyable? Hearn observed that in the late nineteenth century the Japanese lived without much of the Western impedia of life. They owned the least possible amount of clothing and furniture. He was forced to reflect on 'the useless multiplicity of our daily wants'. How disappointed he would now be.

Kanda: more people get on. The carriage had become crowded again. Kanda is famous for its tens if not hundreds of second-hand bookstores, where the complete knowledge of the world can be found if you stayed long enough. It is still very much a student quarter. The track runs by offices. By now, I am overwhelmed by the endless dizzy commercialisation of Tokyo.

Tokyo: the main station, in the centre of Tokyo's original office district. On the outside, it is a replica of Amsterdam Station although once inside just another vast maze of tracks and walkways, shops, restaurants and hotels. On 1st September 1923 at 11.58 a.m., this area and much of Tokyo was shaken to pieces by one of the worst earthquakes in world history. The dead and missing numbered over 70,000. The district around this station, Tokyo's prime business district was destroyed. But the station remained standing. When it came to rebuilding the area, what I could see today was the result of ensuring that Tokyo didn't again suffer such devastation: the streets were widened to broad boulevards to prevent the spread of fire and they widened parks so that people had somewhere to escape to if another severe earthquake struck.

And yet Tokyo was once again razed – when firebombed by the Americans in 1945 – and in a way it gives an explanation as to why Tokyo is such an unplanned city for twice in the space of less than thirty years it was almost completely destroyed and surely that would take the heart out of building something with any sense of permanence? For such a thing would be a deceit. In one form or another nature will come to destroy it.

Yarakucho: the carriage was still crowded. There were office blocks everywhere. An expressway ran alongside the rail track. In the distance, I glimpsed the outer walls of the Imperial Palace: high grey walls surrounded by a tremendous moat. It is one of the most lifeless palaces in the world. The Emperor and his family are hidden away as if they had done some huge evil. The palace and its garden are never seen by the public except for one day during the year when the Emperor appears, to wave to the crowd. Before the Second World War, it was forbidden for anyone to take a photograph even of the surrounding walls and moats. Such distance and remoteness serves no purpose; no wonder the Crown Princess is ill with depression.

Shinbashi: a dark foreboding station surrounded by a mass of construction sites. This was the first train station to be built in Tokyo and was a symbol of the start of Japan's Westernisation. Not long thereafter, the centre of Tokyo was already turning itself into a replica of New York or Chicago. The building has never stopped ever since. New office tower blocks were being erected, one of which houses Dentsu, the world's largest advertising agency. This is one of the most prized building plots in Tokyo and has transformed the area from one that was low rise to a high-rise mini-city crammed with offices, hotels, shopping areas and a park. The monorail runs from here, built as part of the Tokyo Bay redevelopment project.

Hamamatsucho: an area of cheap offices and apartments that are wilting at the edges.

'They look as if someone has thrown a bucket of dishwater over them,' said Yoshie.

'Could you work here?' I asked.

'If I had no choice, yes.'

'But how could you get up in the morning?'

'We ignore these things. We dream when we sit on the train. We have this natural ability to distance ourselves from the reality round us. Our world comes from inside our heads. That's one reason why *manga* is so popular. We slip into the *manga* world as we read them on the train.'

Tamachi: from here, I could see Tokyo Tower in the distance. Yesterday, a thirty-two-year-old man committed suicide when he jumped from the observation platform. Whilst this is glassed in, he had hidden somewhere until the building closed and then smashed through the window with a garbage bin. Every year, there are on average some 30,000 or more suicides: two-thirds men and one-third women. (The per-capita rate is twice that of the US.)

'As you fall, what happens if you change your mind?' asked Yoshie.

'Pray, I suppose.'

'When a family commits suicide together, we call it *ikka shinju*. When a parent kills the children before killing himself, we say *muri shinju*. We have this problem here, which is taboo to talk about. Now we have Internet suicides, and group suicides are becoming more popular.'

Shinagawa: home of Sony and where Sony was first established – in a garage. Shinagawa was at one time the limit for foreign vessels sailing into Tokyo but now, with years of landfill, it was impossible to have any sense that this used to be a port. Nonetheless, at night, the sound of a ship's hooter crying out mournfully could occasionally be heard from my bedroom.

A girl and her mother got on. They sat next to us with shopping bags piled on their laps and on the floor around their legs. The daughter had one of these Japanese singsong voices: high-pitched and staccato and she talked non-stop about shopping bargains she had found.

Between here and Osaki, there was a rash of construction, a mad rush to be ready for when the new *Shinkansen* station opens. Tall office and apartment blocks are sprouting skywards like a newly planted forest. We passed empty canals and run alongside subway, JR and *Shinkansen* lines. There were possibly more railway tracks here than anywhere else in the world.

Yoshie had fallen asleep. Her mouth had opened slightly and I wondered whether to stick my finger in it.

Osaki: an ugly dark station full of dampness, moss and dripping pillars. Back in the nineteenth century, Shinagawa and Osaki were the fag-end of town. Mitford, in his journals, called it 'that sinister and ill-famed quarter...we would come upon the bloody traces of the night's debauchery'. He saw headless bodies left on the ground outside teahouses, the result of some petty quarrel, and often passed by the execution site where criminals were crucified.

A schoolboy carried a bag bearing the slogan, 'I think that square is top of cool shape in the world.' He had taken his blazer off and pulled his shirttails from his trousers. His tie hung like a noose round his neck. He slumped down next to me, crossed his legs, opened a textbook and read English Lesson, Number 7.

'Today the world's problems are too complicated for individuals to feel they have the power to influence them. Our educational centres pay lip service to training our children to think for themselves and, in any case, once they leave school or college we force them into a society where independent thought is no longer an advantage. Our sense of responsibility for the outside world has left us.'

Gotanda: in the middle of a shopping centre surrounded by an almost incomprehensible variety of shops and restaurants. Why do many stations attract all this activity? Because of commuting. At least half of Tokyo's thirty-one million inhabitants go to a station at least twice a day. This was the final station before we returned to Meguro. Sitting opposite was a man in his late twenties, with a nervous tic. He kept running his fingers through his hair. Incessantly, never stopping. But otherwise, his appearance was perfectly normal: T-shirt, jeans and sneakers. His hair was tidy and his nails cleaned.

Meguro: I nudge and wake up Yoshie, just as the train drew into the station. We had passed through twenty-nine stations and had completed the loop, which had been finally constructed in 1925, forty years after it had first been started. We decide to have a coffee at the Starbucks, in the new over-track commercial and shopping tower that has just been completed. In fact, the Yamanote Line has never been finished. Not in truth. It is itself a monument to the impermanence that pervades this country. Always there but never there.

So, that was Tokyo in one trip. Journey over.

Chapter Fourteen

Reflections

In Hearn's book *Kokoro*, written in the 1890s, he attempted to predict what would happen to Japan during the course of, and by the end of the twentieth century. He foresaw a country that would continue to be immersed in war and offered the possibility that it might become a military dictatorship.

On a more prosaic level, he wrote that the Japanese would improve physically for reasons of the imposition of a systematic military and gymnastic training, the introduction of cheap 'Western Cooking', and thirdly by an increase in the average marriage age, which would reduce the number of children of 'feeble constitution'.

Hearn was a great believer in the moral uprightness of the Japanese, and here he thought a decline would take place: there would be increased crime and a decline in virtues.

Interestingly, he thought the Japanese would remain as a nation intellectually inferior to the West, particularly in the area of the sciences and mathematics.

But his most interesting point was that he felt that, despite the great influx of Western ideas, values, language people and goods, the Japanese would never truly respect the West.

Hiroshi Masuyama wrote, 'Japan is an unstable society that hasn't recovered from its own economic crash, as well as the strategy of a generation that uses young people purely as consumers to benefit their own lives.'

However, the public – and the media – seemed unable or unwilling to upset the political status quo. The inertia of the dominant government party, the Liberal Democratic Party (LDP) remains a stupefying presence. At every election the LDP should be kicked out for rank incompetence; instead, they keep their hold on power.

It could be argued that the citizens of Japan had decided to forfeit the benefits of democracy (after all, broad-scale democracy had been foisted upon them by the Americans in the immediate post-war period) and had no interest in what policies the political parties advocated. Perhaps they cynically reasoned that all politicians were as bad as one another, that not one of them could find a solution. But a Japanese politician put it another way to *The Economist* magazine. It was due, he said, to 'the Japanese people's amazing inability to be disappointed'.

Inoki Masamichi, a senior advisor to the Research Institute for Peace and Security, once wrote, 'In almost all sectors of life, leaders with strong decision-making power are shunned, and those who adapt themselves to majority views are favoured.' What this led to were lowest common denominator consensus policies, which if enacted at all, were implemented at a snail's pace.

The press remained reluctant to galvanise public opinion, lead debate and a charge against the deep-rooted mismanagement of the country. With the system of *kisha* – press clubs operated by the government, political parties and the civil service (as well as major corporations, the police among others) – journalism was bland, conformist and uniform. Through these clubs, news was spoon-fed to selected journalists and was often no more than a press release being handed or read out. There was little independent investigative reporting. On top of this, foreign reporters were banned from joining the *kisha*. In other words, a cosy, protected cartel existed in the media just as it did in many other areas of Japanese life.

Prime ministers used to have an average shelf life of eighteen months to two years before being ousted, mere pawns of powerful factions within the LDP. More often than not, even if they genuinely desired change – a moot point – prime ministers and their cabinet ministers demonstrated nothing but impotency against the bureaucracy of the civil servants and the core, unshakable, stagnating tenets of the LDP. Junichiro Koizumi was unique for having lasted so long.

Corruption and scandal were endemic; pork barrel politics existed at its murkiest. A succession of scandals among the country's leading corporations – fatal nuclear accidents, mass food poisonings and cover-ups about defective cars were three examples during recent years – smacked of an awful cynicism that managers and leaders had for the country at large. Snow Brand, a major food company was discovered selling contaminated dairy products due to management-sanctioned deficiencies in manufacturing hygiene. Shocking news in Japan – where locally produced food is promoted to be the best and safest in the world – leading to the resignations of senior Snow Brand management and much public hand-wringing, deep bowing and utterances of apology. Yet, only a few months later, the same company was caught falsifying records for the origin of beef so they could fraudulently claim government subsidies.

But how did consumers react to the scandal?

'They're stupid, but they didn't sell anything harmful. The beef was okay to eat. They'll be more honest in the future,' said Mayu-chan, a young girl in her twenties who worked with me.

'That's the problem, the milk scandal shocked everyone but people still bought Snow Brand products. Japanese people easily forget these things and once the excitement goes they will buy again,' commented Kawada-san, a fifty-year old salaryman.

'I think Snow Brand will learn from this so personally speaking I will keep buying them the same as before,' said one of Mayu's friends.

Perhaps the most shocking, for the only country to have suffered a nuclear attack, it was discovered in late 2002 that the nuclear power industry had, for several years, been falsifying records and had covered up safety problems, notably cracks in the reactors.

Starting from the mid-nineties and into the twenty-first century, Japan lost its way: morally, politically and economically.

When Etizione wrote about the moral decline in the UK, he could have been writing about Japan.

In *The Spirit of Community*, he writes with reference to the UK (1995 edition):

'True, the United Kingdom has not yet reached the levels of moral anarchy and the crumbling of social institutions that we witness in the United States, but the trends point Westward. Increases in rates of violent crime , illegitimacy, drug abuse, children who kill and show no remorse, and, yes, political corruption, are all indications. It matters little if these portents are old or new, or that other societies are more decayed; it only matters that by any measure the readings of social ill health are far too high for a civic society.'

First, the United States, then the UK, and now Japan – all following a convergent path of social and civic decay. During the 1980s, Japan could fairly claim the title Masters of the Universe. The economy and the people were the second richest in the world after the US. Personal and corporate wealth expanded at an exponential rate. Japanese businesses became the global economic conquerors, buying up companies, land, vineyards, golf courses, film studios; a seemingly relentless pillaging of famous assets around the globe. In their boardrooms, hung the world's greatest art. (In 1990, the equivalent of tens of billions of dollars of fine art is said to have entered Japan, including major works by Picasso, Van Gogh, Renoir, Chagall and Monet.) Countless business books analysed Japan's corporate methods, arguing the rest of the world should mimic the same winning approach. Hailed as the experts at perfecting processes and systems, the Japanese had a zealot-like belief in the principle of Total Quality – the ability to produce goods with zero defects, in the most efficient way and at the lowest cost. It suited their temperament: to make no mistakes.

Books extolling Japan's excellence are now rare. Japan's International Competitiveness Rating dropped from first to thirtieth between 1990 and 2002. International businessmen stopped studying Japanese methods. Instead, Europeans and Americans now steadily invest in moribund Japanese corporations, and, little by little, take up senior jobs, a phenomenon previously unknown.

When the economic bubble burst, the nation regressed to type, starting to look inwards once again, rejecting outside help and advice. Throughout its history, Japan has oscillated between cautiously welcoming the world from across its surrounding seas or erecting xenophobic barriers, resisting outside contact and exhibiting a nationalistic chauvinism that insensitively ignored what other countries might think. So, for example, in 1999 without any thought for the diplomatic consequences, Tokyo's right-wing, nationalist Governor, Shintaro Ishihara pronounced that illegal foreign residents such as *sangokujin* (a post-war term for Koreans and Taiwanese who remained in Japan after 1945) should be imprisoned if a major earthquake occurred, to stop them from rioting and thieving. It was the same Ishihara who wrote that the Nanjing

Massacre of the Chinese never happened and that it was a lie made up by the Chinese; who called Philippe Troussier, Japan's national soccer coach, a foreign bully, and who almost daily let fly with some barb about a foreign country. On the positive side, in 2004 he proposed a ban on the sale of used schoolgirl panties in sex shops.

He's not representative of the people, I was assured many times. But this didn't square with the fact that he was elected with a comfortable majority and was seen as a future prime minister.

There are strict limits on the numbers of foreigners who can enter the country to work and live, a policy driven by a profound belief that ethnic diversity creates destructive tensions within society; a belief that society will only run smoothly and reach its peak if it is as homogenous as possible. In 1986, the then Japanese Prime Minister, Yasuhiro Nakasone made the rather controversial statement: 'Japan is now a highly educated and intelligent society. Much more so than America, on average. In America, there are quite a few black people, Puerto Ricans and Mexicans. On the average, the level is still very low.'

Few Japanese would accept or understand the opposite: that tension, conflict and diversity could be beneficial qualities leading to creative thinking, innovation and the new ideas that might have lifted the economy out of the doldrums.

Racist remarks by politicians were common in Japan: in 1990, Justice Minister Kajiyama Seiroku had to resign after remarking on the presence of foreign prostitutes in Shinjuku.

'They drive out all the good people,' he said. 'It's just like in the US, where black people move into a neighbourhood and force all the white people out.'

He didn't leave politics but remained in the LDP. In 2001 he was still causing controversy: at a Japan-Korea summit the now Chief Cabinet Secretary said Korean women forced into sexual servitude by Japan during World War II were no different from Japanese prostitutes who worked in government brothels for pay. 'Many of the comfort women went for the money,' he was reported as saying in the press.

Over a dinner, the Japanese guest's conversation veered to the topic of purity of race. After several minutes of listening, I interrupted to say that in England, we would never even begin a conversation about whether we were pure or not, or whether it mattered. It was of no concern other than for a few misguided fanatics. (I was thinking of the BNP in England, only to find subsequently that they were gaining increasing popular support.) This led the conversation to the notion of *wa*: that a peculiar Japanese behaviour – neither shared nor understood by outsiders – creates harmony within society. This, they thought, was breaking down and today's youth weren't interested in conforming to this Japanese way. 'Why should they?' I asked. 'Haven't your leaders let them down?' The group agreed but too quickly so I guessed they were just being polite. When we continued talking about the Japanese way, they couldn't understand my view that this was a pernicious misguided obsession holding the Japanese back.

'But we have 2,000 years of history,' one person said and I realised how important history is to the sense of self because they all started talking about it, all holding a belief that because they had 2,000 years of history, based on the unbroken lineage of the emperor, they were a unique race.

'But in England I can see and touch 5,000 years of history within ten minutes walk from where I have a house,' I retorted, thinking of the Neolithic long barrows that can be found close by. 'The difference is I can see it on the ground and by seeing it I understand how history has changed. Our culture hasn't been rooted in one particular way. It has grown and evolved.'

They looked at me as if I was some sad case and when dinner finished the two husbands left without saying goodbye; an example of how the Japanese will not tolerate an open critical discussion about their problems.

(Not that my dinner was spoilt. Hosted by Cave de Taillevent – of the celebrated restaurant – the food and wine were outstanding and more than compensation for the tetchiness of my fellow diners.)

In Japan's history, there have been longer periods of national introversion than international engagement. Nonetheless, during the late 1990s there was a gradual realisation in the media that increasingly Japan was being viewed by the outside world as being ridiculously isolationist and is relevant within global power plays. Why was it that Japan was never requested to solve global issues, was one of the questions asked?

Japan possessed no statesmen of global stature bar one, and it played no role in global diplomacy

A view was held that, as the world changed at an inexorable pace around them, the men leading the country sat back, bewildered and unable to cope with the issues that threatened to overwhelm them. With increasing exasperation, the US told them to get their act together and implement the structural reforms particularly within the banking system, recognised as necessary for Japan to ease back in to fiscal growth. Nothing happened.

I watched a leading Japanese businessman interviewed on television. Will Japan restructure the banking system he was asked?

'Yes,' he replied.

'But when?'

'In Japan things take time. It is the Japanese way.'

'But it's already been ten years of decline. How much time do you need?'

'We have to reach consensus.' He sat there, arms folded, with a complacent smile on his face, clearly thinking what a stupid question to be asked. It was a discussion going nowhere.

What drove this stubborn resistance to change whilst, at the same time and whilst loathed and fearful to admit it openly, they acknowledged there will come a time when other Asian countries – most notably China – will overtake Japan as the economic and political powerhouse of Asia?

Why was there an inherent tendency for the Japanese to continue to believe that only what Japanese think counts and that change can only be done in a Japanese manner? That there is a real phenomenon of *yamato-damashi*, the Japanese way, defined by Japan's divine origins, a way diametrically opposite to and better than the Western way. And that only Japanese can understand and do things Japanese, and that the outside shouldn't interfere.

One day Konuma-san, a senior executive from our Japanese partner, strode in to my office. He was livid, his cheeks scarlet, his mouth scrunched in rage.

'What's this ad?' he asked, brandishing a copy of a daily newspaper. I explained to him it was for Jubilee 2000, a charity organisation formed to persuade governments to eliminate Third World debt. The key visual showed a child nailed to a yen crucifix, signifying the fact that every minute a dozen or more children die in these countries because of the debt burden. Provocative, yes. Untruthful, no.

'What's your name doing on it?' he said, his voice getting louder. He meant that we had printed the Saatchi & Saatchi name, one of 13,000 in the advertisement, which asked the Japanese government to support this initiative.

'We don't want foreigners telling us what to do. Keep your views to yourself.'

'But the Japanese in this office support this view,' I told him; 'they're responsible for the ad.'

'You're lying, you're lying,' he screamed, incapable of coherent thought.

'Are you talking on behalf of Yomiko?' I asked.

'No, I am here in a private capacity.'

'Well, in the same capacity I'm telling you fuck off and get out of my office.'

The subject of Third World debt was a sensitive issue. In March 2000, Jubilee 2000 met with Keizo Obuchi, the then Japanese Prime Minister, to discuss the opportunity for Japan to cooperate with other leading nations to eliminate debt. Discussion time was limited to ten minutes. Yoko Kitazawa of Jubilee 2000 recorded minutes for the meeting:

He hardly listened to what they had to say. She noted that once their presentation was finished, 'Mr Obuchi took up a paper which he had been holding tightly in his hand since the beginning and started to read like a school child reads his text book in class.'

He read aloud a civil-servant prepared statement that said that whilst Japan would work with other governments he could not even start to cancel their own Third World debt unless the public and parliament demanded it. And they weren't doing that. He said that at the end of WWII, Japan borrowed money from the US and worked very hard to pay it back.

'And he suddenly started to shout,' the minutes recorded, 'that he was accused that he made a huge deficit in the nation's budget. However, this is not his personal borrowing, he screamed. It is the nation that is borrowing. He refused to be accused of this.' Obuchi then stood up and stormed out of the room.

A few weeks later, he died of a heart attack.

What made Japan such an introverted and myopic race? Only around twelve per cent of Japanese have travelled abroad (compared to over eighty per cent of British people), and most of these are women. Hence the Japanese knew little of foreign ways; that we humans could be remarkably similar. (A naïveté sometimes encountered at an absurd level, such as being amazed that foreigners could master chopsticks. I had lost count of the number of times my ability to use chopsticks has been praised. Is it so difficult to hold two sticks of wood?) It was even admitted, albeit with surprise, that I ate more correctly than most Japanese. (This was a compliment from two strangers, a husband and wife, sitting adjacent to us in a restaurant in Kyoto. My manners became their talking point for much of the evening. After they made the remark, I went to ridiculous lengths to be even more proper in the way I ate, sitting with a rod-straight back, hands held on my lap when not eating and eating the smallest pieces of food possible.)

One day, I stepped off the pavement to allow an old man to walk by unhindered. He stopped and asked me, 'Are you American?'

'No,' I told him, 'English.'

'But you are so polite. Thank you, thank you.'

'Thank you?' I was surprised.

'But I have never seen such politeness from foreigners before.'

In his long life, could foreigners have been so consistently rude to him? And didn't he realise that what he said was actually insulting to me? Not that I cared.

The Japanese were obsessed by their cultural uniqueness.

In a book by Dr Jon Carter Covell, *Korean Impact on Japanese Culture* he and his co-writer, Alan Covell, write about the deliberate cover-up of Korea's role in Japan's development and that in fact much of the culture of Japan came from the Korean peninsular. 'Both in the East and the West, scholars have customarily ignored the pivotal role played by the Koreans in the early centuries of Japan's cultural development.' Not surprisingly, the book was unobtainable in Japan, and my wife bought it on a visit to Korea.

Even more surprising therefore, was the admission by the Emperor that he had Korean ancestry. In a typical act of media self-censorship, this sensational revelation didn't make front-page news but was quietly hidden away. No one wanted that debate opened up yet, at the same time, the media felt duty-bound to report it.

There exist many examples of religious sects and orders of learning devoted to the study and proof of the purity of Japanese culture, that the notion of *yamato-damashi* (the Japanese divine spirit) is true and not a myth. Regular revelations are made to the public of more conclusive proof: a new text or an archaeological artefact for example. Once I read a pamphlet issued by the Jinja-Honchu (the Association of Japanese Shinto Shrines) celebrating the ten years of Emperor Akihoto's enthronement that, to all intents and purposes, insisted that the story of the Emperor being the 125th divine descendant of the sun-goddess Amaterasu-omikami was true.

Is there a deep-seated belief that Japan is not as great as it seems? That it needs to prove itself constantly. Does an inferiority complex loom large in the collective psyche? In one sense, I believe it does. A sporting perspective gives an insight. Sport helps bind a nation, providing a rallying cry and a point of national and collective focus. Sport allows all of us to have a sense of belonging to the global village. Sport can unleash and define a country's national pride with glorious moments to galvanise a nation's heart to beat as one. Japan rarely has that opportunity for, more often than not, Japan fails at global sporting events. For example, with a population of over 126 million, twice hosting the Winter Olympic Games, and with more snow more accessible than for most other countries, you might think it would excel at winter sports. No, it came twenty-first in the 2002 Salt Lake City Olympics, even behind its smaller neighbour Korea.

Thank goodness, that for two weeks, the nation had something to get excited over, with the nation's heroic performance in the 2002 World Cup. Pity that Korea did better.

Golf? Rugby? Soccer? Baseball? The four most popular sports in Japan: limited, short-lived or no international success at all (although coming from an Englishman this sounds a bit rich).

For whilst Japan falls flat as a sporting conqueror, suspicion of Japan's long-term national defence strategy remains high among her neighbouring countries, driven by acute memories of Japanese occupational and wartime atrocities. Seemingly, not a month went by when there wasn't a flare-up between Japan, China and Korea over an issue with Japan's militaristic past. Unlike Germany, which accepted that its actions in the 1930s and 1940s were wrong, Japan has never been able to offer an unequivocal apology. Atonement is a word that doesn't exist in Japanese. Hence, unbelievable as it seems in the twenty-first century, there were lingering suspicions of Japan's motives and long-term territorial goals.

Why does Japan write school textbooks, these countries repeatedly ask, that gloss over their behaviour in China and Korea during the 'thirties and 'forties? Why do high-ranking politicians visit the Yasukuni Shrine, where Japan's war criminals are commemorated, to pray for the war dead?

'I think the Japanese should apologize until historical issues are resolved in the hearts of the South Korean people,' said Won Hee Ryong, who, in his late thirties, is one of Korea's younger, more progressive politicians and hence you would expect him to be more conciliatory and open-minded. To counter this, Japan is adept at manipulating the emotions of the nuclear bombing of Hiroshima and Nagasaki, to remind the world and its own people that in truth it is the victim. But it won't admit to its own victimisation of the 'Comfort Women', the women in Korea, Taiwan, China and elsewhere who were forced to work in wartime brothels and whose plight has only recently come to light. The artist Yoshiko Shimada has written, 'These atrocities committed by Japanese soldiers were accompanied by the "quiet" support of Japanese women. Japanese women were in fact "not silent", many of them were eager fascists and happy to sacrifice themselves and to victimise others in the name of the Emperor.'

Would it once again attempt to become a military super-power in the East?

The warmongering was fuelled by the nationalist organisations. It was said that as the police supply them with their vans and coaches, the nationalists agree they won't travel the streets or parade outside the Chinese and Russian Embassy after seven o'clock, meaning the police can go home without having to worry about disrupting influences at play.

Whether this is a true story or not there was an underlying paradox: these noisy demonstrators were allowed to parade the streets in their black coaches, swathed in banners and the old-style Japanese flag, holding up the traffic and being bloody annoying with their blaring slogans and music. Not an acceptable level of proclamation but intrusively loud.

So, they could go about their business, denouncing the communists, the West and anybody who they disagreed with, taking advantage of Japan's freedom of speech. But when it came to criticism, they tried to stifle it. When a DJ criticised their methods on radio, when he suggested that the Rape of Nanking was a historical fact, they threatened to park their coaches outside the radio station, play their deafening music and slogans so that broadcasts would be impossible unless the DJ was dismissed. In the end, the radio station was able to get away with a half-apology.

Nationalism was bubbling under the surface. Not deeply buried. That's why her near neighbours go apoplectic. Japan cannot be trusted, is what they think.

It was a kind of nationalism that could easily move from the fringe to the centre of politics, and it was a nationalism of a pernicious kind. More than pride, it bordered on an arrogance that forgot past crimes; it was an arrogance that allowed big corporations to steamroller over rules and regulations to the detriment of their employees and customers, and it was an arrogance that belittled all outside influence. None of her neighbours would be surprised if, again, Japan slipped into being a military nation. It seemed to be in her blood.

Or did it more reflect the uniqueness of Japan's reliance on conformity, inaction and conservatism to sustain society? A belief that only hard work, determination and endurance would lead to group success, in this instance the Group Japan. Just as the school and the company developed strong camaraderie through learning history, inspiring stories, memorising company songs, speeches by management and even enduring gruelling physical tasks, so the role of everyone was to reflect only what was to Japan's advantage.

Since the terrorist attack against the World Trade Centres, and the subsequent Global War on Terrorism (GWOT was the American acronym), the UN and the US had put pressure on Japan to be an active participant. (And this came to a head at the time of Japan's post-conflict presence in Iraq.) In the past, Japan argued that the Constitution severely limits what activities can be undertaken in any conflict and even UN peace missions: limited to a behind-the-lines support role, her soldiers not allowed on the front-line and not allowed, for example, to carrying munitions.

Fundamental to this is Chapter II, Article 9 of the Constitution that states: 'The Japanese people forever renounce war as a sovereign right of the nation and the threat or use of force as a means of settling international disputes... . In order to accomplish the aim of the preceding paragraph, land, sea and air forces will never be maintained. The right of belligerency of the state will not be recognised.'

Since it was written, Japan has indeed built a military capability but under the guise of a civil defence force.

The increasing pressure to loosen the grip of the Constitution had given the nationalists both inside and outside the government the opportunity to amend or at least reinterpret the Constitution, giving Japan a greater role.

Was this the thin edge of the wedge?

Inadvertently, were the UN and US lighting a fuse?

For the UN, whose resources are limited by what its members are prepared to offer, the inability of Japan to make a contribution that matches its resources both economically and militarily has been a long-running issue.

Neither could the US continue forever to have a vast and expensive military presence in Japan – or Korea either, for that matter. This has been a costly economic burden and one that has been borne with little thanks from either the Japanese or Koreans. Both would prefer that America's armed forces weren't billeted on their soil, a practice that comes too close to occupation. Wouldn't it be so much cheaper and easier if Japan could remilitarise and pick up the responsibility? Yes is the answer. In 2000, the neo-conservative US Armitage Report said as such: 'Japan's prohibition against collective defence is a constraint on alliance cooperation.'

For Japan's neighbours this is nothing short of tantamount to giving Japan the right to become an aggressor again.

Up until the Meiji Era, Japan had been a non-aggressive country locked largely in its own internal conflicts. With the Meiji Era, Japan opened itself to the world, moved from a feudal to a nation state (albeit one centred on the supposed absolute authority of the Emperor but in fact controlled by politicians and civil servants) and began the process of modernisation and Westernisation. Coincidentally it was not many decades before the supposedly peaceful Japan was waging war on Russia, China, invading Korea and subsequently half of Asia.

What were the real intentions when a leading politician, Chief Cabinet Secretary Yasuo Fukuda's remarked that Japan should review its three principles of not possessing, not producing and not permitting nuclear weapons in the country? This remark, made in mid-2002, provoked a furore of press comment, anti-Japanese vitriol from China and disquiet among ordinary Japanese. Subsequently Fukuda attempted to blame the press for misquoting him and taking the remark out of context. He claimed that all he said was that there was always room for discussion on any existing policy as circumstances changed. In fact he was just in the long line of senior politicians who have called for Japan to rearm: in 1993 Japan's Foreign Minister told an Association of Southeast Nations meeting that, should the US withdraw its protective shield from Japan, then it was important that Japan should possess nuclear weapons. In 1994, Prime Minster Tsutomu said that Japan had the capability to produce nuclear arms: true. As it moved in to the twenty-first century, it possessed more than fifty tons of separated plutonium, sufficient to make 10,000 nuclear warheads.

Was Japan losing its moral backbone? A country with a huge indigenous sex industry, where students convicted of serial gang rapes were sentenced to two years' jail, whose men were said by global organisations to encourage paedophilia prostitution when abroad, and where the only religious icon seemed to be the Brand. Japan's one unique and most laudable moral tenant, that of renouncing war and believing in the sanctity of mankind, was under threat. The only country that had suffered the horror of nuclear war and had suffered when it went on an aggressor's rampage, was beginning, if only in the smallest way, to turn its back on history. This was the one area where Japan could stand far above the world and claim moral superiority and it was in danger of throwing it away.

Ultimately I am left with the impression that Japan and the Japanese live under the burden of a never-ending mental siege. The country is battered by the economy; there was a realisation that as a nation it is neither loved nor admired.

Neighbours openly distrust it. Whom could the Japanese trust? Politicians, bureaucrats, police, industry managers? In a recent survey in the Yomiuri Shimbun, seventy-four per cent of voters said they distrusted bureaucrats citing reasons such as 'corrupt ties with politicians and businesses' and 'irresponsibility'. (Such a figure might not be surprising in other countries but in Japan the voters were expected to respect their leaders.) No wonder the sole role models for most were celebrities, no matter whether talented or not. The mere fact that they were tagged a celebrity was sufficient. Viewed as neutral and unthreatening, more often than not they were – as most were the vacuous artificial product of the entertainment industry. They were individuals who themselves entertained no natural talent and little personality of their own. But such was the hold of celebrities that over ninety per cent of advertising used them to endorse products but demanding no more than they shout, 'Here is a good product,' in frenetic, formulaic fifteen-second commercials. And in between the advertising, the majority of TV programming relied on empty-headed celebrity chat and variety shows.

But this cerebral vacuum may have been another defence mechanism for I could understand that spending a lifetime living in Tokyo's metropolis of thirty-one million people, burdened and constrained by society's rules, was mental and physical torture. If there was ever a role for *wa*, it was here, as a sense of harmony was crucial for everyone to live together without ripping at one another's throats, like rats in an overcrowded cage. I was amazed at the self-control, that there weren't flare-ups every minute of the day. But these conventions stifled what I also saw were the inherent flamboyant emotions that the Japanese have and which they were forced to wrap tightly within themselves.

The world was moving on whilst Japan was trapped by convention and history, unable – at least now – to create a robust, sustainable future dismembered from the past. In some ways, Japan lived within its own shadow – cast so long when the country was booming. This was a country that up until recently had an existence based on the permanence and security of religion and tradition, defined by the repetitive cycle of the rice crop and the recurrent rhythms of the season. Now with that framework torn apart by relentless economic progress, society had become transitory and thoughtless. I was reminded of an addict looking for the quicker and higher fix. Here was a society driven by the drug of consumerism, a 'spend, spend, spend' society where brands had durations of months, where there was a maniacal search for the new, and obsolescence was a sin, and rampant excessive consumerism was a distraction from the underlying troubles. For all its World Heritage sites and national treasures, Japan was the world's most disposable society: packaging, cars, clothes, houses, prime ministers, ad infinitum. Everything had a shorter life span than anywhere else in the world. Save the people themselves, the world's longest lived.

Looking at the swirling crowds of people shopping every day in Shibuya or along Omotesando, the expensive clothes they wore, the glitz of the window displays: who would think that Japan was in recession? Sheer escapism; all part of a collective avoidance mentality that preferred to ignore rather than tackle the issues they faced. At least shopping was an enjoyable distraction, another outlet for a society seeking the least mental effort, where a blur of cartoon characters, anime, manga, video games, I-mode, video phones and mindless chat and variety TV shows were the means of averting eyes from the fundamental problems that stared everyone in the face.

If there ever was a society that illustrated the thoughts of the American historian, Daniel J Boorston, it was here. 'Nearly everything we do to enlarge our lives,' he wrote, 'to make life more interesting, more varied, more exciting, more "fabulous", more promising, in the long run, has an opposite effect.' A cursory glance at Japan created the impression that here was one of the most vibrant countries in the world. The colour and pace of Japan was astounding: like running twenty-four hours a day on a kaleidoscopic hamster wheel.

Outsiders were hypnotised by the overwhelming density of life. Beware: nothing was as it seems on the surface. That's why foreign writers, who make short visits to Japan, often get it wrong.

Japan is a nation of immense contradictions and extremes. Most first-time visitors, fumbling along Roppongi's pavements, cried out with conviction, 'We love Japan.' With all-night drinking, sex and shopping this seemed the most unencumbered and liberated country in the world. Only by living here, would someone recognise that in play were rigid rules governing every aspect of life. This was a society as tightly bound as the bandages on a Chinese child's foot. Freedom of expression, spontaneity and the vitality of choice hardly existed. Life's progress was rigidly mapped out from birth. Rules even existed in the trivial area of gift-giving – and I think the Japanese are the most generous of people. A gift was given; the receiver obligated to give one in return of the same or slightly higher value, the cycle continuing until, I assume, one of the recipients passed away or went bankrupt.

A lot of nonsense is written about Japan either by the happily misinformed or those who like to see everything though cherry-tinted spectacles. Polite, reserved and obedient were the sort of descriptions often applied to the Japanese. If any of the writers had ever attended a *Matsuri* summer festival – or any number of religious festivals – they would have seen the same intense, delirious, drunken, naked, disorderly behaviour. In a company's social event that I attended, with five hundred or more employees present, four men ran round naked, pinning down girls in chairs and rubbing their bare bums against them. Nothing was done to stop them. The Japanese possess an amazing ability to go wild. It's just that, most of the time, they live suppressed lives. It could be argued that Japan is the world's biggest example of a government-sanctioned social experiment where absolute control of the masses is paramount and persistent.

From the time of the Meiji Restoration in 1868, Japan's leaders had reached and stuck to a profoundly influential conclusion. If Japan was to rise from an agricultural-based culture, it needed to have imposed a strict regime that focussed on work and the necessity for everyone to subjugate their individuality to the greater good of society. After defeat in the Second World War, the same principle was just as valid.

On the eve of our wedding, I stayed at Tokyo's Four Seasons Hotel (the older one at Chinzan-so) and watched a TV interview with the pianist Mitsuko

Uchida, a woman of great intensity and passion, and an inspired speaker, thinker and artist.

'Japan functions very well as a country,' she said, 'because people's individuality is suppressed for the good of the whole. You belong to society…you must be part of the majority…I am not.'

I should have marked those words.

But then Japan was the only place where I met a girl, violinmaker by day, who owned her own shop selling her exquisitely crafted instruments but by night an S&M dominatrix owning a club called Nemesis where she practised.

In that same hotel, several years later, someone who I knew well, invited me to their room, dropped their trousers, pulled down their underpants and invited me to spank their bottom – I declined but the full story is for another book.

And this was the only country where a tattoo artist gave me a shrunken head, thankfully a fake one.

(But it still frightened Satoko when tucked under her pillow.)

Selected Bibliography

Frommer's Tokyo, 4th Edition. Beth Reiber with Janie Spencer. Macmillan 1996

Japan Times, on-line editions and the pre-eminent English language newspaper in Japan.

Japan Today, on line English language newspaper.

Tokyo Q. 2001-2002 Annual Guide to the City, Stone Bridge Press, 2001

Little Adventures in Tokyo, Rick Kennedy, Stone Bridge Press, 1998

The Worlds of Japanese Popular Culture, Edited by D.P Martinez, Cambridge University Press, 1998.

Classic Japanese Inns and Country Getaways, Margaret Price, Kodansha International, 1999.

I Love Art II, Published by the Watari-um Museum, 1992.

Japan, the Ambiguous, and Myself, Kenzaburo Oe.

Percival Lowell, *Atlantic Monthly*, Vol 67 1891.

The Inland Sea, Donald Richie, Stone Bridge Press 2002. Undoubtedly one of the best books on Japan.

Ryokan, A Japanese Tradition, Gabriele Fahr-Becker, Koneman 2001

Japanese Culture, A Short History, H Paul Varley, Faber & Faber 1973

The Mountain is Moving, Japanese Women's Lives, Patricia Morley, Pandora, 1999

Order by Accident, Alan S Miller & Satoshi Kanazawa, Westview Press, 2000

In Praise of Shadows, Junichiro Tanizaki, Vintage 2001

Some Prefer Nettles, Junichiro Tanizaki, Vintage 2001

Japan: Cities and Social Bonds, Augustin Berque, Pilkington Press 1997

Traveller From Tokyo, John Morris, The Cresset Press, 1943

Lafcadio Hearn His Life, Work and Irish Background, Sean G Rowan and Toki Koizumi, Ireland Japan Association, 1991

Meeting with Japan, Fosco Maraini, Hutchinson 1960

Consuming Bodies, Sex and Contemporary Japanese Art, edited by Fran Lloyd, Reaktion Books, 2002

My Reality – contemporary art and the culture of Japanese animation, edited by David Frankel, Faith Brabenec, and Sheila Schwatz, Des Moines Art Centre, 2001

From Sea to Sea, Rudyard Kipling, 1889

Japan: An Attempt at Interpretation, Lafcadio Hearn, The Macmillan Company 1905

Kokoro: Hints and Echoes of Japanese Inner Life, Lafcadio Hearn, Gay and Bird, 1895

Unbeaten Tracks in Japan, Isabella L Bird, G P Putman's Sons 1881

Collected Works of Basil Hall Chamberlain, University of Cambridge 2000

Mitford's Japan, edited and Introduced by Hugh Cortazzi, Japan Library 2002

Blogging: the world of on-line web-logs (hence blogging) is a relatively recent phenomenon. There are over a hundred English language-blogs written (mainly) by foreigners living in Japan. They can be turgid. Others offer a readable insight into life, society and culture from a variety of perspectives. The better ones currently include:

www.easterwood.org (where you can also find links to many other blogs)
www.kindofcrap.com
www.sasori-gal.diaryland.com
www.no-sword.sieve.net
www.consumptive.org
www.harmful.org/homedespot/ADIARY.htm
www.sushicam.com
www.souzouzone.jp/japanbloggers/index.html (the Japan bloggers club.)
www.antipixel.com
www.myprivatetokyo.com
www.hunkabutta.com
www.kissui.net

www.grahamthomas.com/Extremes.html
to read more about the book, Japan,
and to find up-to-date web links.